The Writings of Antonio Vol. V



# The US Judicial Branch of Government; Supreme Court Justices and Their Decisions

Antonio A. Sweeney

iLearn Research and Consulting Firm

ISBN: (paperback) 978-1-7355925-1-0

ISBN: (eBook) 978-1-7355925-2-7

Library of Congress Control Number: 2020907506

This book is a work of non-fiction.

Front Cover image by Artist: iStock by Getty Images: bbourdages

Book design by Designer: KDP and Antonio A. Sweeney.

Printed by Amazon Kindle Direct Publishing

First printing edition 2021.

iLearn Research and Consulting Firm Phoenix,

Arizona 85013

authorsweeney2020@gmail.com

https://www.facebook.com/antonio.sweeney.982

## Other Books by Antonio

The Writings of Antonio Vol. I

(Witty, Philosophical, Political and Sometimes Controversial Commentary on Scripture)

The Writings of Antonio Vol. II

(Philosophical and Political Commentary)

How Scott Walker Became A Spy

(Ghost Writer Spy Novel Series Vol. I)

The Writings of Antonio Vol. III

(US Presidents, Their Generals and Their Wars)

The Writings of Antonio Vol. IV

The Parables of Christ; His Dark Sayings Concerning the Kingdom of God and of Heaven

To Follow and see other Books by Antonio go to: amazon.com,

then search:

(iLearn Research and Consulting firm).

## Dedicated To:

My Fellow American Citizens,

To All People,

To Those that Sit and Stand in the Courts

And Conduct the Business of Life, Livelihood, and Government.

And

To My kids:

*Imani, Nathan, Ophelia, Sonia, and Neshia*

And To My

Wife

## Contents:

Introduction

Chapter 1: The Structure and Powers of the US Supreme Court and the Federal Judicial System

Chapter 2: Justice John Jay (1745–1829)

Chapter 3: Justice John Rutledge (1739–1800)

Chapter 4: Justice William Cushing (1732–1810)

Chapter 5: Justice James Wilson (1742–1798)

Chapter 6: Justice John Blair (1732–1800)

Chapter 7: Justice James Iredell (1751–1799)

Chapter 8: Justice Thomas Johnson (1732–1819)

Chapter 9: Justice William Paterson (1745–1806)

Chapter 10: Justice John Rutledge (1739–1800)

Chapter 11: Justice Samuel Chase (1741–1811)

Chapter 12: Justice Oliver Ellsworth (1745–1807)

Chapter 13: Justice Bushrod Washington (1762–1829)

Chapter 14: Justice Alfred Moore (1755–1810)

Chapter 15: Justice John Marshall (1755–1835)

Chapter 16: Justice William Johnson (1771–1834)

Chapter 17: Justice Henry Brockholst Livingston (1757–1823)

Chapter 18: Justice Thomas Todd (1765–1826)

Chapter 19: Justice Gabriel Duvall (1752–1844)

Chapter 20: Justice Joseph Story (1779–1845)

Chapter 21: Justice Smith Thompson (1768–1843)

Chapter 22: Justice RobertTrimble(1776–1828)

Chapter 23: Justice John McLean (1785–1861)

Chapter 24: Justice Henry Baldwin (1780–1844)

Chapter 25: Justice James Moore Wayne (1790–1867)

Chapter 26: Justice Roger B. Taney (1777–1864)

Chapter 27: Justice Philip Pendleton Barbour (1783–1841)

Chapter 28: Justice John Catron (1786–1865)

Chapter 29: Justice John McKinley (1780–1852)

Chapter 30: Justice Peter Vivian Daniel (1784–1860)

Chapter 31: Justice Samuel Nelson (1792–1873)

Chapter 32: Justice Levi Woodbury (1789–1851)

Chapter 33: Justice Robert Cooper Grier (1794–1870)

Chapter 34: Justice Benjamin RobbinsCurtis (1809–1874)

Chapter 35: Justice John Archibald Campbell (1811–1889)

Chapter 36: Justice Nathan Clifford (1803–1881)

Chapter 37: Justice Noah Haynes Swayne (1804–1884)

Chapter 38: Justice Samuel Freeman Miller (1816–1890)

Chapter 39: Justice David Davis (1815–1886)

Chapter 40: Justice Stephen Johnson Field (1816-1899)

Chapter 41: Justice Salmon Portland Chase (1808-1873)

Chapter 42: Justice William Strong (1808-1895)

Chapter 43: Justice Joseph Philo Bradley (1813-1892)

Chapter 44: Justice Ward Hunt (1810-1886)

Chapter 45: Justice Morrison Waite (1816-1888)

Chapter 46: Justice John Marshall Harlan (1833-1911)

Chapter 47: Justice William Burnham Woods (1824-1887)

Chapter 48: Justice Stanley Mathews (1824-1889)

Chapter 49: Justice Horace Gray (1828-1902)

Chapter 50: Justice Samuel Blatchford (1820-1893)

Chapter 51: Justice Lucius Quintus Cincinnatus Lamar (1825–1893)

Chapter 52: Justice Melville Fuller (1833-1910)

Chapter 53: Justice David Josiah Brewer (1837 – 1913)

Chapter 54: Justice Henry Billings Brown (1836-1913)

Chapter 55: Justice George Shiras Jr. (1832-1903)

Chapter 56: Justice Edward Douglass White (1845-1921)

Chapter 57: Justice Rufus W. Peckham (1838-1909)

Chapter 58: Justice Joseph McKennna (1843-1926)

Chapter 59: Justice Oliver Wendell Holmes Jr. (1841-1935)

Chapter 60: Justice William R. Day (1849-1923)

Chapter 61: Justice William Henry Moody (1853-1917)

Chapter 62: Justice Horace Harmon Lurton (1844-1914)

Chapter 63: Justice Charles Evans Hughes (1862-1948)

Chapter 64: Justice Edward Douglass White (1798-1847)

Chapter 65: Justice Willis Van Devanter (1859-1937)

Chapter 66: Justice Joseph Rucker Lamar (1857-1916)

Chapter 67: Justice Mahlon Pitney (1858-1924)

Chapter 68: Justice James Clark McReynolds (1862-1946)

Chapter 69: Justice Louis Brandeis (1856-1941)

Chapter 70: Justice John Hessin Clarke (1857-1945)

Chapter 71: Justice William Howard Taft (1857-1930)

Chapter 72: Justice George Alexander Sutherland (1862-1942)

Chapter 73: Justice Pierce Butler (1866-1939)

Chapter 74: Justice Edward Terry Sanford (1865-1930)

Chapter 75: Justice Harlan Fiske Stone (1862-1946)

Chapter 76: Justice Charles Evans Hughes (1862-1948)

Chapter 77: Justice Owen Roberts (1875-1955)

Chapter 78: Justice Benjamin Nathan Cardozo (1870-1938)

Chapter 79: Justice Hugo Lafayette Black (1886-1971)

Chapter 80: Justice Stanley Forman Reed (1884-1980)

Chapter 81: Justice William O. Douglass (1890-1949)

Chapter 82: Justice Frank Murphy (1890-1949)

Chapter 83: Justice Harlan Fiske Stone (1872-1946)

Chapter 84: Justice James Francis Byrenes (1882-1972)

Chapter 85: Justice Robert Houghwout Jackson (1892-1954)

Chapter 86: Justice Wiley Blount Rudledge (1894-1949)

Chapter 87: Justice Harold Hitz Burton (1888- 1964)

Chapter 88: Justice Fred M. Vinson (1890-1953)

Chapter 89: Justice Tom Campbell Clark (1899-1977)

Chapter 90: Justice Sherman Minton (1890-1965)

Chapter 91: Justice Earl Warren (1891-1074)

Chapter 92: Justice John Marshall Harlan II (1899-1971)

Chapter 93: Justice William J. Brennan Jr. (1906-1997)

Chapter 94: Justice Charles Evans Whittaker (1901-1973)

Chapter 95: Justice Potter Stewart (1915-1985)

Chapter 96: Justice Byron Raymond White (1917-2002)

Chapter 97: Justice Arthur Joseph Goldberg (1908-1990)

Chapter 98: Justice Abraham Fortas (1910-1982)

Chapter 99: Justice Thurgood Marshall (1908-1993)

Chapter 100: Justice Warren E. Burger (1969-1986)

Chapter 101: Justice Harry Andrew Blackmun (1908-1999)

Chapter 102: Justice Lewis Franklin Powell Jr. (1907-1998)

Chapter 103: Justice William Hubbs Rehnquist (1924-2005)

Chapter 104: Justice John Paul Stevens (1920-2019)

Chapter 105: Justice Sandra Day O'Connor (born 1930)

Chapter 106: Justice Antonin Gregory Scalia (1936-2016)

Chapter 107: Justice Anthony McLeod Kennedy (born 1936)

Chapter 108: Justice David Hackett Souter (born 1939)

Chapter 109: Justice Clearence Thomas (born 1948)

Chapter 110: Justice Ruth Bader Ginsburg (1933-2020)

Chapter 111: Justice Stephen Breyer (born 1938)

Chapter 112: Justice John Glover Roberts Jr. (born 1955)

Chapter 113: Justice Samuel Anthony Alito Jr. (born 1950)

Chapter 114: Justice Sonia Maria Sotomayor (born 1954)

Chapter 115: Justice Elena Kegan (born 1960)

Chapter 116: Justice Neil McGill Gorsuch (born 1967)

Chapter 117: Justice Brett Michael Kavanaugh (born 1965)

Chapter 118: Justice Amy Vivian Coney Barrett (born 1972)

Note from the Author

## Introduction

Well, here we are, another *Writings of Antonio Volume.* I am astounded at how quickly I have been able to get through writing them. It makes me want to kind of kick myself for not forcing myself to start writing earlier in life, with the goal of publishing in mind. Yet and still, I needed time to read, develop, and mature, and I know I'm not done reading. This leads me to our next discussion topic; The US Judicial Branch of Government. Let me just immediately premise this book by saying I know I'm in way over my head and I'm not even sure how I'm going to manage to talk about many of the Supreme Court Decisions since the inception of the US Supreme Court was founded, not to mention give a brief bio on all of the Justices like I did with the Presidents and Secretaries of State in Vol. III. I mean, you need a certain knowledge and language skill set to even approach writing this type of book; albeit, my Dad went to Law School and practiced for a number of years; and that was his career, not mine, and further I'm not even sure why I am writing it, besides teaching myself some US litigation. Who is going to buy a law book from someone without a law degree? LOL.

Anyway, beside the point, it gives me something to do; challenges my mind in areas where I am weak, and hopefully gives me some more insight into how things work in life and country. I think Jurisprudence is a special and chosen career. I mean, you really have to be called to a career where you have to interpret the Laws that govern country and man, handle disputes, and without equivocation execute judgments, some benevolent, and some that may seem harsh, even the sentencing of death in some cases. Notwithstanding, such is the responsibility of those in position of Judge. And I wonder and imagine, given this divine responsibility, do those Justices who rule well; pray to their Father and also consider the scriptures, considering our Constitution mentions a

Creator, and in those Scriptures, the Holy Bible of course, upon which they swear an Oath, that do they also consider the 12 Judges who ruled in Israel, and some of the great men of God, like Abraham, Isaac, Jacob, Moses, Samuel, David, Solomon, Daniel, Christ, and even the Devil for arguments sake. Such a record of human history, human behavior, and the judgments of God, who is said to be Self-Existent, Judge, and Ruler of Heaven and Earth, should be a mandatory study, in my personal opinion anyway.

And so, as I proceed with caution; I seek to even peer into the future of the Justice System, and see what our New World will see from our Courts; District, Appellate, and Supreme. Will laws change, be amended, or our constitution modified? Will technology and globalization change US? Moreover, will Justice and Mercy reign, over cruelty, negligence, and disorder--fighting to take the center?

All these things, I cannot possibly know; notwithstanding, we can all know the One who does. And such is our clearance with God, and this is no religious book, but a scholarly one and one for the Mind. And yet, does not our Spirit gain strength, from the strengthening of our Mind. Fore even Christ said, that the children of this world where in their way "Wiser than the children of Light (Luke 16:8)." I need not interpret this proverb here, but that He also said to his disciples to be, "Wise as Serpents and harmless as Doves" (Mat 10:16). And yet, we know that the office of Judgeship indeed, at times must do harm.

Antonio A. Sweeney MS

August 19, 2020

# Chapter 1:

# The Structure and Powers of the US Supreme Court And

# The Federal Judicial System

So, herein we have and find that the Framers of the Constitution had the idea of a hierarchy of courts in mind. Not only that, one Superior Court to take precedent in the Inferior Courts. Nevertheless, let us not get ahead of ourselves and first begin by stating that US Supreme Court Justices are appointed by the Executive Branch and confirmed by the Legislative;--Namely appointed by the President and confirmed by the Senate, respectively. So far so good, I think this is general knowledge and not anything that a High School student wouldn't learn in their Civics or Government class.

Now on to Judicial powers; the US Constitution gives "Judicial powers to one Supreme Court," giving Congress authority to ordain and establish Inferior courts. In so many words, Congress has the jurisdiction to establish this hierarchy, so to speak, or courts under the Superior Court. And, it has been so ordered, that there be 13 Courts of Appeals which hear Federal Cases from District Court; that is the 94 Federal Districts, including the District of Columbia and Puerto Rico, as Congress has so divided.

Under normal circumstances, Congress determines the jurisdiction of Federal Courts with the exception of the dispute between two or more states. At this point, the responsibility falls to the Supreme Court without any authority to usurp by Congress.

Federal Courts possess the sole power to interpret and determine the Constitutionality of the law and apply it to individual cases. They can compel the production of evidence and testimony by way of issuing Subpoena. Inferior Courts are held by the decisions of the Supreme Court. District and Appellate Courts must implement Supreme Court interpretation of the law to the facts of the particular case.

The Constitution does not specify how many Justices are to sit upon the Supreme Court. Presently, there are nine Justices since 1869. Due to the fact that Justices do not have to run or campaign for re-election, they are considered secure from political pressure when deciding cases. Federal Judges serve for the term of their whole Life, until retirement, resignation, or impeachment. Something I learned, The term Federal Judge applies not only to the Supreme Court Justices, but also Court of Appeals Judges, and District Court Judges as well. These Judges make up the US Federal Judicial System which litigates matters, all federal matters contained within The Constitution.

## Chapter 2

## Justice John Jay (1745-1829)

Justice John Jay was the first Chief Justice to sit upon the US Supreme Court from October 19, 1789 to June 29, 1795. He was also a diplomat, abolitionist, one of the Founding Fathers of the United States, and at one time, also the governor of New York. Before Mr. John Jay was Justice Jay, he served in the capacity as a lawyer, essentially writing policies contrary to British rule before the War of Independence. He held a number of official positions, that is he was elected to Congress, he held an Ambassadorship to Spain, and also on an executive level served as Secretary of Foreign Affairs as well as Secretary of State, after which point in his career he was appointed by President Washington to Chief Justice of the US Supreme Court.

Due to the number of Justices to serve on the Supreme Court, I will try to be brief in the biographies and move unto their Decisions on selected major Court cases. There are a total of 114 Justices that sat on the Supreme Court bench in some capacity during the history of the Judicial Branch of Government; so in light of these facts and in the idea of being concise and holding on the brevity, I will try to cut strait to the point, including only those facts pertinent to this work, and I'm sure omitting others.

Out of the many cases that Justice John Jay made judgments or decisions on, I will only touch on a few as well with other Justices, as I will briefly touch on their opinion. Let the Reader remember that I speak from a laymen's perspective, and not as one with a Juris Doctorate. Nevertheless, the first case that comes up is that of *West v. Barnes (1791).* In this particular case that dealt with a man who paid his mortgage on his farm for twenty years and held a lottery to raise the funds for the last payments. Well, this being one of the first Supreme Court Cases all the technicalities weren't ironed out yet. And, as the story goes, the issue with the payment is that it was with paper tender or notes instead of gold and silver and this was unacceptable for the Note holder. Thus the case went to court and West was unable to make it to court as well as some paper was not filed with the correct clerk, so Chief Justice Jay ruled, Motion Refused on the technicality that the writ was not brought to the court from the right channel or right Appellate court. I think I understand that correctly—Clear as Mud. So, the moral to this story is, protocol, procedure, rule of law; one must follow the rule of the court in order to be properly heard, and be sure they are in the right court for that matter. Finally, it seems that West was eventually forced to relinquish his farm and may have sold it to his son. There was controversy over the matter even after his death.

The next interesting case that comes up is the Hayburn's Case (1792). I'm sure there is more to it, but it seems that this case was about petitioning veterans of the American Revolution seeking a pension. Apparently, the Supreme Court ruled to continue the case given the fact that it was not one of judicial matters and laws changed in Congress that the next term relieving Circuit courts of deciding the matter. It was the legislative branch in the first place who wrote up the Pensions Act; that directed disabled American Revolution Veterans to apply directly to their Circuit Courts for Pension. Moral to the story: Seems that Supreme Court felt that it was a matter for a Veteran's Affairs office or maybe a Social Security Office instead of the US Supreme Court. Not sure if either of those offices existed in 1792, but probably not; notwithstanding, the matter was continued by the courts, judgment never given by the Jay Court, and eventually handled in some other way, because Congress changed the Act. On another side note, and maybe I'm meddling, but the matter seemed political as some sources say Attorney General Randolf did not bring the matter to the Supreme Court on behalf of US or Mr. Hayburn but wanted the High Court of the land to rule on an inferior court decision, in which maybe this was a reason why the Supreme Court refused to do so. Who Knows?

Another significant case reviewed by the Jay Court was that of, *Chisholm v. Georgia (1793)*. In this case the Court decided by majority opinion (even though that wasn't a thing just yet), that two Loyalist from the state of South Carolina, could not have their land taken by the State of Geogia. The controversy behind this ruling was that it appeared that a party from another state or foreign could demand repayment of debts from a sovereign state. This ruling was eventually reconsidered and overruled when the Eleventh Amendment of the Constitution was ratified which essentially said that no state could be brought to Supreme Court by a citizen another state of foreign country without it's given consent. Future developments confirmed these decisions but added that also Congress could abrogate States sovereignty if Fourteenth Amendment rights were being exercised. Moral to the Story: Well, I would think that Georgia personally had right to seize property from two who were still loyal two the crown even after the Revolutionary War; but then again, I'm not a judge. Secondly, if I understand things correctly, $11^{th}$ Amendment makes sense that citizens of other states and foreign countries can't bring other States to court without their consent, and yet one must consider Congress's check of the $14^{th}$ Amendment.

## Chapter 3:

## Justice John Rutledge (1739–1800)

Justice John Rutledge served as an Associate Justice as well as a Chief Justice. His tenure as Associate Justice was only for one year, that is from February 15, 1790 to March 4, 1791; we will talk herein about some of the cases that fell to him as he was Chief Justice. He held a number of official positions before he was a Judge. He worked on the constitution, he was the first President of the State of South Carolina, as well as served as governor after the Declaration of Independents was put forward. His time as governor was primarily during the American Revolution.

Mr. John Rutledge attended college in England at Middle Temple. The first out of the two cases heard during his short time as Chief justice dealt with a matter of Jurisdiction in light of the limited powers of Federal District Courts to rule when dealing with foreign powers, ships, or individuals causing harm or capturing American Ships on International waters. The Supreme Court ruled in the case of, *United States v. Peters, (1795)*; that District courts had no power to rule when damages from foreign parties upon American interest occurred on International Waters. Basically, injuries or damages occurring on the International Seas must have a writ to the Federal Supreme Court and be considered there.

Before we briefly discuss the second case heard by the Rutledge court, it must be noted that there was a great tension between Chief Justice Rutledge and his predecessor's work, that is, the work of Justice John Jay, as Justice Rutledge highly criticized Justice Jay's, "Jay Treaty" which essentially was a treaty that communicated peace, matters of trade, taxes, territories, and averted matters of war, between America and Great Britain. Justice Rutledge, as he inherited the office after the resignation of Justice Jay, both being appointed by President Washington, advocated more notions of War before the notion of Peace with Britain. And in one particular source is quoted saying that he, "rather the President die, than to adopt that document." Such details give us the Reader a peak into the mind of Chief Justice Rutledge as he would also later resign, having the shortest term of Chief Justice of the Supreme Court as it was rumored that he was a struggling alcoholic as well as one who suffered from mantle illness. He is recorded among many other Great things as attempting Suicide by jumping off some embankment into a body of water and being rescued by two slaves after his own resignation.

On to the matter of the second case in the Rutledge Court, which dealt with the matter of multiple citizenship and set a precedence for future rulings. In the case of the *Talbot v. Janson, (1795)* it was so ruled that jurisdiction was given to the Federal court when American Citizens travelled on international seas, and so, under whatever circumstance, if an American Citizen shall acquire another citizenship from another country, they shall not have to relinquish their American citizenship, therefore making them a possessor of multiple citizenships, which was thereby allowed.

## Chapter 4:

## Justice William Cushing (1732–1810)

Young Justice Cushing was born in Massachusetts Bay. He came from a family of

Justices, his father and grandfather also serving as Judges. He attended and graduated from Harvard, and practiced law in Massachusetts. He was a pioneer Attorney in the Eastern region of Maine, and continued to hone in on his craft until he was appointed by the Governor to relieve His father and sit as magistrate upon the Superior Court.

The Massachusetts Provincial Congress, this is before the Union was established of course, came in and made drastic changes to do away with the entrapping of British rule, parliament, and Justice system in America. Justice Cushing aggressively held on to his position of American Independence by refusing to be paid in British Pound and sat as chief Justice of the Court of Massachusetts until slavery was legally abolished.

Justice Cushing served as one of the Associate Justices on the US Supreme court besides being appointed as Chief Justice after John Rutledge. In light of the fact that his Associate tenure was in the Jay Court; we will consider one his cases while he served on the Massachusetts bench. A major decision that ultimately lead to the state of Massachusetts being the first state to abolish slavery, that is there were no slaves in the state by 1790. In the case of Mr. Quock Walker, that is *Commonwealth v. Jennison* which was one of three cases, considered the Walker Cases. The story goes, according to Jennison that Walker was a runaway slave, and for this he was beaten by Jennison. Apparently there were some other matters in a prior case as to Walker being free because his previous owner had deceased. Nevertheless, Walker's counsel countered Jenison's assault on humanity by stating that slavery was in fact Unconstitutional and won the decision Chief Justice Cushing on these grounds. As foretasted, this precedence led to the all out abolishing of slavery in the State of Massachusetts, although rumor had it that some slave owners found the loop hole by legally registering their persons as "indentured servants" thus bypassing the law. Nevertheless, a first for the New World and the colonies. Moral to the Story: One must know to fight legally for their rights, even in the midst of great pressure and even oppression. The Law of the land should prevail. Even though, parts of the constitution have yet and still been not amended such as the "3/5 all other persons" clause, if I read correctly.

## Chapter 5:

## Justice James Wilson (1742-1798)

Justice James Williams was born in Scotland and although he attended college, he left before attaining his degree and later petitioned the college for his Master of Arts degree. He was one of the original writers of the Constitution and signers of both the Declaration of Independence and the Constitution. After much reading, he eventually became a Professor of Law at Pennsylvania University and at the climax of his life, suffered from being thrown in debtors prison, and was the first US Supreme Court Justice to die while serving on the court.

Justice James Williams was appointed by President George Washington as an Associate Judge to the US Supreme Court. There were nine cases that were heard during his tenure as an Associate Justice serving on the court from 1789-1798. We will only briefly focus on one case herein in this section on Justice Williams as to save some cases for when we cover the other Justices who sat on the first Supreme Court.

This Case is, *Calder v. Bull (1798)* in which a matter of a will where a first decision was overruled, and it was so ordered to be reviewed by a higher court as said by the state legislature. That sate being Connecticut, and the Supreme Court deciding whether it possessed the powers to rule in a case that was decided by a state legislature. And so, the Supreme Court upheld that the State legislature of Connecticut was not out of line with Article I, Section 10 of the Constitution; the ex post facto law referring to criminal charges or that can be levied against a defendant after the fact. In other words, new laws that can affect "crimes" that were committed before the law was written. If I am understanding things correctly. This law is still in effect today. Moral to the Story: Although I did not look up any instances where this ex post facto law was applied, it seems a bit harsh and seems that citizens must be circumspect as to not be charged or punished with an criminal offence retroactively.

## Chapter 6:

## Justice John Blair (1732–1800)

Justice John Blair was born in Virginia and did his undergraduate work in the States and his and his professional Law degree in London at Middle Temple. After this it was on to start practicing Law, delving into the richness and technicality and Virginian Constitution and Declaration of Independence which he helped to interpret and draft after being appointed to a number of government level positions once the American Revolution was underway. More thatn a few cases heard his decision as he was appointed to the Virginian Court of Appeals and then to Chief Justice, and ultimately to the Supreme Court Justice. It is recorded that Justice John Blair was a Freemason.

One case that it was decided while Justice Blair sat on the Court but did not necessarily make a decision on was the case of, *The Commonwealth of Virginia v. Caton et al. (1782)*. This cases final decision is a bit ambiguous to me, even after reviewing a few different sites, notwithstanding, I'll give my understanding. Apparently there were those who supported Britain during the Revolution who were charged with treason after the War. Canton and two other individuals applied for pardon which was granted by the House of Representatives in Virginia but didn't fly in the Senate. The issue was sent to the Virginia Court of Appeals, and in this case; court of appeals stayed the position. What is unclear to me is if the men were executed as their sentence was death, but the language in the documents seems that they were just not permitted freedom. Moral to the Story: Don't commit Treason. Also, a later case clarified that Federal Courts did have power to check the legislative branch of any decision that was deemed unconstitutional.

It was in the case of, *Marbury v. Madison,(1803)* that judicial review was set as precedence. That is that Federal Courts could invoke their judicial authority and overturn any congressional decision that was in fact unconstitutional. Furthermore, the Constitution and Declaration of Independence was deemed as Law, and not simply a document. There were many complexities behind this case as the nature of it was political as one Presidential candidate, James Adams, a Federalist left office he appointed a number of Federalist officials to have influence in the incoming President Thomas Jefferson's administration, a DemocraticRepublican. And the story goes, some of Adams officers were not fully commissioned when President Jefferson took office and Jefferson ordered a halt to this. Marbury, one who's commission was delayed and halted, filed a writ of mandamus, ordering his commission released to him, which was later denied by the Supreme Court. This case is more involved then I state here, but the Moral to the Story is: The US Supreme Court has ultimate say so, in all matters constitutional.

## Chapter 7:

## Justice James Iredell (1751-1799)

Justice James Iredell was born in England and came to the Americas around the age of 17. Young Master James worked on the port of North Carolina in Customs. After a few years of paying his dues daily acquiring knowledge through reading law books was admitted to the bar in 1790. Sources report that Justice James began to practice law under the late governor of North Carolina Samuel Johnston and had proclivities toward the Anglican Faith, Spirituality, and Metaphysics.

During the Revolution, Mr. James wrote a few essays and political theory papers that were before the Constitution and the Declaration of Independence. Also, he began to take initiative and organize the courts of North Carolina and was subsequently elected to the Superior Court. Thereafter, he served in a number of legal and political positions; not the mention the Attorney General. Avid Federalist and leader of the party, and advocate for the Constitution and it's ratification, even though he was not present during the Philadelphia convention.

Justice James Iredell sat on one of the first Supreme Courts as he was ultimately appointed Associate Justice by President George Washington. They had a reasonalbly small case load that first session, as they only covered nine cases, and we have herein so far covered the major ones. In this vein, there will be no cases covered under Justice James Iredell for his tenure on the Supreme Court.

## Chapter 8:

## Justice Thomas Johnson (1732-1819)

Justice Thomas Johnson was born in Maryland to a large family, being one of ten children and was primarily self-taught as a youth, participating in home schooling until he landed an opportunity to study with a local firm that allowed and aided him in his study of the Law. He was soon admitted to the bar; passing convincingly, he was eventually elected to the assembly, and hence began his political and legal career. Mr. Thomas Johnson was sent off as a delegate to the Continental Convention and got to rub shoulders with some of the other framers, such as, Benjamin Franklin and that of Benjamin Harrison V.

During the actual war, Mr. Thomas Johnson and his biological brother made ammunitions for the artillery. He also served in the capacity of the Maryland Militia's Brigadier General. Finally, he was elected as governor and held a good number of judicial posts throughout the state before he was appointed to the Supreme Court as Associate Justice. He also was appointed by President George Washington. Those cases he sat on were the same as these mentioned herein beforehand. One of them being *Georgia v. Brailsford (1792).*

In this case, Justice Thomas Johnson's opinion followed the majority, deeming states the right to sue the state in Supreme Court on account of federal debts collected, until it be determined whose moneys it is. This rhetoric slightly different from the actual law that was enacted and said that individuals can only bring States to Supreme Court with the consent of that state being persecuted, unless federally mandated. Moral to the Story: Again, don't commit treason. And secondly, It takes some Cajunas to sue a whole State in the Supreme Court.

## Chapter 9:

## Justice William Paterson (1745-1806)

Justice William Paterson was a native of Ireland and came to the New World and settled in the North. He did his undergraduate studies at what is now known as Princeton University, and ultimately studied Law and was admitted to the bar with time to practice for some years and become one of the signers of the United States Constitution in 1776. He attended and contributed to the Philadelphia Convention and held a number of government positions until his appointment as Associate Judge to the US Supreme Court. Attorney General, Senator and Governor were some of his positions; not to mention he resisted the appointment to the office of Secretary of State in 1795.

Justice Patterson was serving as a Senator and completed his term before accepting his Supreme Court appointment in compliance with the Judiciary Act of 1789. One of the issues that we will consider while Justice Patterson was sitting upon the circuit court was that of the trials for those charged with treason during the Wiskey Rebellion. In this case, there was basically an insurrection that took place fueled by those who opposed the Whiskey tax, and in their minds even though themselves patriotic extracting a phrase from the Constitution "no taxation without representation."

Well, the story goes, an angry mob of over 500 armed men surrounded the house of the wiskey tax Inspector General. Meanwhile, President George Washington heard word and sent peacekeeping officers to deescalate and manage the crisis while at the same time ordering militias to be sent out by the Governors. Fortunately, there was no bloodshed according to records, many from the mob left peacefully; others were arrested and had their day in court, with charges dropped, released upon their own recognizance.

## Chapter 10:

## Justice John Rutledge (1739-1800)

Justice John Rutledge traveled to England to study Law and in fact won more than a few English cases. Headed back the to the American Colonies found him prosperous in his new legal career, as his services were in great demand and he contributed to building his family's wealth. Setting an example for future American leaders, he was a Delegate, Governor as well as appointed Associate Judge to the Supreme Court fulfilling the position of Chief Justice John Jay. Ironically He stands as the only "recess appointment" Justice, as his taking the position of Chief Justice was during the time when the Senate was on break from meeting Justice Rutledge was the second Chief Justice to sit on the Supreme Court. In fact, Justice Rutledge sort of had three judicial positions. He was first appointed to the Supreme Court under the Chief Justice Jay Court as an Associate Judge, and after about one year in 1791 resigned his position to take on a Chief Justice position in the State of South Carolina Court. He eventually also resigned from this position as he was, as aforesaid, appointed by President Washington as Chief Justice of the US Supreme Court in 1795.

One of the first matters that Justice Rutledge spoke out against was the Jay Treaty. This was a treaty that would strengthen economic and trade ties between Great Britain and American economies. This Jay Treaty or Britain treaty carried support in the Senate and President George Washington as it eased tensions and was sort of the solution after American Revolution. It also precipitated the great division between Federalist and Jeffersonian Republicans in America's early party system stages; the Federalist being Pro-Treaty. Those opposed to the stronger foreign relation ties with Great Britain feared the treaty would strengthen British influence in the States, usher in aristocracy, and undermine the rising republic, and therefore most dissenters preferred a French type governing system, while Federalist preferred a British form.

One of the cases that Justice Rutledge sat on as Supreme Court Chief Justice was that of *Talbot v. Jansen, (1795).* This case dealt with the matters of US Supreme Court jurisdiction in cases dealing in International Waters, and the right for American citizens to poses duel or multiple citizenships from being citizens in other countries.

## Chapter 11:

## Justice Samuel Chase (1741-1811)

Justice Samuel Chase was born in Maryland, eventually studied law and brought controversy to the Judicial Political Scene, as we will see herein, he was accused of allegedly allowing his political bias to influence his jurisprudence. Before his Supreme Court appointment, he was a representative of Maryland as well as a signer of the Declaration of Independence. Justice Chase was actually impeached by the House of Representatives on 8 counts and it was the Senate that acquitted him of all charges.

In the matters leading to the impeachment of Justice Chase, it seems that Justice chase as well as other political officials were using their office as a means of power and the events that took place as various factions, ie. Federalist and Republican- Democrats feuded amongst each other, the scene setting could remind one of the politics that took place in a Roman Senate or the infighting of Greek City States. Apparently what started the whole matte was Allies of Thomas Jefferson in Congress shortly after he was sworn into office attack or repeal of the Judiciary Act of 1801. This was a piece of legislation that President Jefferson and those that subscribed to his party felt was incendiary gave the Judicial branch of government more power or power over the Executive branch, thus the balance of power thrown off. The repeal of this act also was thought to be political as it abolished many Federalist Judges, lower courts, including those with lifetime appointments. These actions precipitated a comment by Justice Chase as he said to these events, that it would "take away all security for property and personal liberty, and our Republican constitution will sink into a mobocracy"( https://en.wikipedia.org/wiki/Samuel_Chase).

Further things that led to the impeachment of Justice Chase, although he was acquitted, was his alleged political attack on Thomas Cooper who was being indicted under the Aliens and Seditions Act; an act that made it easier for Presidents to jail and deport immigrants and noncitizens thus making it harder for them to neutralize. Thomas Cooper was an Academic and in his writings and philosophy leaned more toward Republic-Democratic ideas and praised President Jefferson, thus the attack from Justice Chase, he being Federalist appeared politically motivated. A second instance was in the case where a Grand Jury went easy on a printer company, and Justice Chase refused to discharge them recommending a printer company for them to indict thus sparking the attention of President Jefferson as another attack by the Federalist agenda and he in turn recommending an impeachment of Justice Chase which was eventually resolved as an acquittal in the Senate. Moral to the Story: Playing Politics can cost you your Job. And secondly, playing politics might forward your agenda.

# Chapter 12:

## Justice Oliver Ellsworth (1745-1807)

Justice Oliver Ellsworth held a number of positions before his ascension or appointment to the Chief Justice of the US Supreme Court. He was born in Connecticut, and completed his undergraduate degree in New Jersey. It was during America's War of Independence that Mr.

Ellsworth served in the Continental Congress aiding with the framing of the Constitution. Assisting with Framing, and Ratifying the Constitution; Justice Oliver also served as a Senator before his ultimate appointment by President George Washington as the third Chief Justice of the Supreme Court.

Unfortunately, no cases where heard during Justice Oliver Ellsworth time as Chief Justice on the Supreme Court. Nevertheless, there were four cases that were heard and that the court made decisions on between the years (1796-1799), that were of Major importance to America's civil, criminal, economic judicial systems. The first of those issues being the case of *Hylton v. United States* (1796) on keeping the federal carriage tax. Although this decision would be eventually overruled by the *Pollick decision* years later; one Justice commenting that taxes on purchases and consumption are considered indirect taxes, and that taxes on the said carriage are not considered a direct tax. An example of a direct tax would be that of the tax on land. Moral to the Story: Pay taxes and don't gripe. LOL.

Another Case heard on the Court was, *Hollingsworth v. Virginia*, (1798). This very involved case primarily dealt with the 11$^{th}$ amendment which was ratified and overturned the issue of US citizens being able to try States in Court. Ultimately, Hollingsworth's lawyers tried to get the President involved in amending the Constitution to help with their case with Indiana Company and Virginia, but US Supreme court ruled that the President has no official role in amending the constitution especially to decide civil cases. The ratifying of this amendment was also applied retroactively to prior cases; hence the overturning of *Chisholm v. Georgia* (1793) was in effect. Moral to the Story: Don't bring the Chief Executive Officer of a country in to settle trivial affairs.

In another case, *Calder v. Bull* (1798) the Judicial Branch decided upon four main points of Constitutional law. The ex post facto clause or retroactive law was considered applied only to criminal cases and not in civil matters. Thus, the ex post facto clause had four major points; 1) in any event that an act that was committed that was considered innocent by the law, before the new law was created and now considered a punishable act. 2) Any law that heightens the level of severity of a crime. 3) Any law that heightens the level of severity of the punishment for a crime. 4) Every law that changes the legality and protocol of the way evidence is entered and considered. These were the four major points considered by the Supreme Court in the case of *Calder v. Bull* (1798). Moral to the story: Don't commit a crime, even if you don't yet know it's a crime?

A fourth case that was of importance during this time was the first case where the US Supreme Court held jurisdiction between two states. The case was a complicated land dispute between New York and Connecticut with injunctions and ejections filed, as well as, Court held with one party in absentia. This case was *New York v. Connecticut*, (1799). Moral to the Story: Changes in administrations over the passage of time or new election, business, of fiscal cycles can be problematic and cause conflict in pending cases or business.

## Chapter 13:

## Justice Bushrod Washington (1762-1829)

Justice Bushrod Washington was appointed the US Supreme Court and served for around 32 years. Before his appointment he was an attorney, politician, and social architect, as he helped organized programs that advanced Blacks who were free going back to Africa. I am assuming this was considered a progressive movement considering it was before the emancipation proclamation; nevertheless, he was co-founder of the American Colonization Society. His last name tells on him, as America's first president George Washington was his uncle.

Justice Bushrod's appointment came around the year 1798 and he was fully in his judicial office before the age of 40. He served on the Marshall court and usually his opinions did not dissent from the Chief Justice, except on three occasions. One of those cases being the matter in *Ogden v. Saunders* (1827). This was a typical case where Saunders from Kentucky demanded payment from Ogden of New York who filed bankruptcy. The conflict arose over whether or not State Court judgements applied to past and future cases. Which struck me as odd, it seems obvious that a ruling would apply to future cases as being established as precedent. But, what do I know. Moral to the Story: Don't try to skip out on your debts by filing bankruptcy from another state; you might get away with it. This moral is not a typo and intended to be ambiguous and funny; reason being, after reading the ruling as well as the dissent, I was still a bit unclear as to if Ogden had to pay.

Another case considered by Justice Washington was that of *Corefield v. Coryell* (1823), a case in which Corefield a resident of Delaware loaned out his boat to someone who desired to persue their life, liberty and happiness by diving for Oysters. The boat was confiscated under New Jersey Law, and later in the trying of the case, this law was penned as unconstitutional in Corefield's prosecution. Moral to the Story: Let people pursue their constitutional right to fish or catch oysters; as long as there is no environmental or ecosystem threat.

## Chapter 14:

## Justice Alfred Moore (1755-1810)

In many ways Justice Alfred Moore followed in the footsteps of his father. We this in that his father was a captain in the Army during the Revolutionary War, and he serving his Emerging new country as a captain also. Not only did Moore have a father who served in the war, but also a brother and uncle. Truly it was a family affair, and yet he would discharge and also participate in a militia later on in his journey. Educated at Boston, he would begin studying law in North Carolina at the tender age of 20 years old.

Unfortunately, Justice Moore is rated as one of the worst justices due to his only writing a decision one case the whole time he sat on the high court. Justice Alfred Moore was appointed to the US Supreme Court by President John Adams and served as an Associate Justice. Due to no fault of his own, Justice Moore was also susceptible to sickness and this might have played an effect on his few written decisions as well as his short time on the Highest Federal court—that is 5 years.

The Case known for Justice Moore's opinion was *Bas v. Tingy (1800).* The particulars of this case dealt with the payment for recaptured vessels from the French during the Quasi worth. A preliminary law required a 1/8$^{th}$ payment, and a later more sophisticatedly written law required ½ payment of the recaptured vessel. In this particular case there was a discrepancy in what both parties wanted in payment for the recaptured vessel, Eliza due to the discrepancy in laws. It seems obvious that the majority of the Justices went with the ladder law. Moral to the Story: When considering a dispute or question of the law, look to the most recent legislation or statues.

One final case that was decided during Justice Moore's term on the bench,yet he did not give opinion on was the case of *Marbury v. Madison (1803).* This case dealt with the issue of judicial review, thus establishing a precedence where US supreme Court could invalidate

Congressional decisions, if by determining, State and Governmental laws and statutes be unconstitutional. Moral to the Story: In all things pertaining to the Law, Government and State, stick to the Script; that is, the US Constitution.

## Chapter 15

## Justice John Marshall (1755–1835)

Justice John Marshall was born in Virginia and grew up to serve in the continental Army. He held a number of positions before his appointment to Justice on the US Supreme Court, not to mention Chief Justice on the Court. He was a diplomat, attorney, as well as Secretary of State in the Adams administration. As Chief Justice, he held his position longer than any other Judge on the US Supreme Court and sat through and gave opinion on a number of cases in which we will consider herein.

Similar to the case *Marbury v. Madison (1803),* many of the issues dealt with in the following cases established and validated Federal Courts Governmental authority over that of the States in matters pertaining to the Constitution. The case of *Fletcher v. Peck (1810)* was one of the first cases where Federal Courts deemed state law unconstitutional and was considered the preliminary case in establishing that the Native American territories no longer fully belonged to Native Americans, from a legal stand point.

A second case that applied the contract clause from the Constitution was the case of *Dartmoth College v. Woodward (1819).* In this case there was a dispute between public and private charters as well as an issue of the President being voted out and responsibility of appointing Trustees to the Board given to the Governor of New Hampshire. Federal ruling declared that the first private charter that was established before the creation of the state of New Hamshire would hold preeminence over any public charter. Thus, this ruling led to boosting the American Free Enterprise System as well as Corporate business growth and expansion.

A third case that ranked federal powers above the state as well as Federal Courts having ultimate authority even in giving Congress power or the federal government to legislate laws that are not fully expressed in the constitution but that will further Congressional powers as in sprit of the Constitution. I think I have that right. This case dealt with a Second National Bank that was constructed in Maryland but had its charter elsewhere. Maryland attempted to levy taxes on "all" banks without their state charter, but in court it was argued that this Second US bank was being targeted by the state and thus the "necessary and proper" clause was invoked from the constitution ruling in favor of the federal powers over the State. Thus, State powers can not target federal institutions and levy state taxes. This was the case of *McCulloch v. Maryland* (1819). Moral to the Story: Federal Government always wins over State and Local Courts and Government, especially in matters dealing with Money. LOL.

# Chapter 16:

## Justice William Johnson (1771–1834)

Justice William Johnson was born in South Carolina and passed through a number of occupations before he ascended to the seat of Associate Justice of the US Supreme Court appointed by the third President of the United States, Thomas Jefferson. Justice Johnson was the first Republican on the US Supreme Court and was often a dissenter to those opinions scribed by his Justice colleges on the court, thus he was eventually nicknamed, "First Dissenter." Justice Johnson attended Princeton University for his undergrad career and afterward graduated from Law School.

As mentioned above the majority of Johnson's cases were written dissents; however, he did write the majority opinion on two of the mostly minor cases heard during his tenure on the bench. The one of these two cases dealt with an embargo on all foreign ships that came after the Chesapeake–Leopard affair in 1807. Prior to this Embargo of 1808, there was ongoing conflict on American Eastern shores and British ships carrying influencers that posed threat to American sailors by way of impressment; that is, the forcing of American sailors to serve in the British Royal Navy.

This was obviously problematic and further of these actions was not tolerated by the Young American Government, hence the **Embargo Act of 1808**. After this act was in place the scenario arose where one ship in particular was held under the statutes of the act, and the owner of the ship, Adam Gilchrist filed a writ of mandamus at the council of another government official for the release of his ship and thus the case proceeded. This is the case of *Gilchrist v. Collector of Charleston* (1808) and in the final judgment, the writ of mandamus was not granted to the plaintiff; reason being, the circuit court did not have the right or authority to enforce the writ of mandamus. Moral to the Story: Don't sail foreign ships into a country you just lost a war with, especially if your intention is to turn their soldiers.

There was another case in which I am not quite clear on, but it seems that there was another law in which allowed the State to confiscate, imprison, and confine any "negroes" on foreign vessels that entered into our ports. In this particular case a Caribbean Sailor was imprisoned and there were some efforts to have him released, but to that matter, I am unsure. For further details on this case, look up: Elkison v. Deliesseline. Moral to the Story: Unjust laws to control Blacks whether they were slaves or free where wrong.

# Chapter 17

## Justice Henry Brockholst Livingston (1757–1823)

Justice Henry Livingston served in a number of positions throughout his governmental career. Born a resident of New York, he attended what is now Princeton for his undergraduate studies, graduating and thereafter making his way through the study of law, being admitted and passing the bar in 1783. He started his call to duty being an officer in the Revolutionary Army, then went onto public service in the judicial arena as Appeals Judge in the New York Courts until his appointment to the US Supreme Court by President Thomas Jefferson. Sources also report that he served as type of Ambassador to the Spain.

In terms of his judicial career, there was one case in particular that he wrote a dissent on as he served on the New York Supreme Court. This case, Pierson v. Post; judgement given in 1805 was about a hunter who spotted a fox and kept pursuing eventually crossing into Post's land. The sign did not restrict Pierson's pursuit, and he eventually killed the fox and took the pelt for himself. Posts levied prosecution against Pierson stating that the pelt belonged to him because Pierson failed to acknowledge or respect his property sign. Sources state that the research prepared for the judgment in this case had to delve into the history of the determination of claiming wild animals as property, as well as, the history of men claiming property which went back to the antiquity of the 13th century in "how property was properly possessed of human being."

## Chapter 18

## Justice Thomas Todd (1765-1826)

Justice Thomas Todd was born and raised in the new colony of Virginia. He would eventually become an Attorney after his time at the Liberty Hall Academy where he also served as a tutor to the underclassman. After graduation, he pursued and studied law, helped with the formation of Kentucky, and served on the Supreme Court of Virginia. He was appointed as a US Supreme Court Justice by President Thomas Jefferson and opinioned a number of cases.

A few trivial facts on Justice Todd's politics; he had more of a Jeffersonian bent and consistently ruled mostly with Chief Justice Marshall in his written opinions. Records report that he dissented once out of a number of years and cases on the US Supreme Court, and further, he was actually branded the Supreme Court's most insignificant judge by one major Critic. In his tenure, he never wrote any Constitutional opinion, Simply judicial interpretation.

In the case of *Preston v. Browder,* the Nonintercourse Act was upheld which was an act that sort of covered six different acts or cases which had to do something to do with not alienating native American lands; Moreover, any purchase of Natives land had to be disclosed to the federal government, as each colony had it's own statues that regulated native lands; ie. Reservations. Furthermore, in the case *of Preston v. Bowder*, one nonnative entity tried to eject another nonnative entity and both circuit and Supreme courts did not allow the ejectment, referencing the Nonintercourse Act. Moral to the Story: Under normal circumstances, the law won't uphold the infringement of one entity upon another entities lands native or nonnative in America.

In the case of *Watts v. Lindsey's Heirs et al.,* Justice Todd wrote an opinion on a case regarding title laws that frustrated many Kentucky citizens. He explained and put things in laymen's terms so to speak. Moral to the story: Do your Real Estate Homework.

## Chapter 19

## Justice Gabriel Duvall (1752–1844)

It is unclear as to where Justice Gabriel Duvall attended school for his undergraduate studies, yet sources record him studying law and serving on the House of Representatives. He was appointed to the US Supreme Court by President James Madison in 1811. Serving in the Courts around 25 years he lived until the age of 92 and yet sources report that he made no significant change in Constitutional Law. The court at the time that Justice Gabriel Duvall served was primarily a Marshall Court, as he was the Chief Justice, yet Justice Gabriel as an Associate Justice authored 15 majority opinion to such cases and dissented only once from Justice Marshall in the case of *Mima Queen and Child vs. Hepburn* (1813). Herein, we will discuss a few of his cases.

Starting with the dissenting case first, apparently in the case of, Mima Queen and Child vs. Hepburn (1813), the issue of conflict was whether or not to admit the "hearsay" testimony of the daughter of an ex-slave confessing that she was born free. One ruling on the court was that hearsay testimony is considered incompetent as evidence and does not substitute for "witnesses which can prove with their own knowledge." I'm assuming this ruling was the majority opinion as Justice Duvall gave dissenting opinion to this case. Moral to the Story: Slavery was wrong in the first place, possibly a necessary evil, although cruel, breeded racism and contempt, corruption and unjust laws, and precipitated subtle and overt ills that exist in remnants of society even in this day and age.

The case we will consider first is *Freeland v. Heron, Lenox & Co. (1812).* This case had to do with two different merchants from two different Countries- namely, England, and America. Sources record that Justice Duvall went with the English clause on this case which state in so many words that when two merchants have had dealings with a set account for at least two years then those dealings are settled, and further that each parties silence implies acquiescence to the set deal, burden of proof being on the party with dispute? I think I got this right, to my understanding. Seems that this business contract is sort can be likened to say a common law marriage between marital partners or a type of civil union, only between business partners who don't speak up to change any part of the dealings within a two year time span. Moral to the Story: Speak up or forever hold your peace.

In a third case, *United States v. January (1813)* deals mostly with the repayment of bonds issued and if there be two bonds issued that the debtor has a right to pay them back in the order in which he feels best with no fear of repercussion. Moral to the Story: Entities have a choice of order in which they pay bonds.

In another instance where Justice Duvall wrote a majority opinion, is the case of *Crowell v. McFadon* (1814). In this case one party under the embargo Acts confiscated or held the vessel of another party. The issue as far as my reading, was not necessarily a matter of national security; nevertheless, the ruling included a clause stating that no ship be released under the embargo act without express permission of the President. In spite of this wording in the majority opinion, the overall ruling was for the plaintiff to trover the equivalent amount of goods. Moral to the Story: Although our Nations interest be safety and security when it comes to our ports of commerce, we have to be careful not to bully valid and legitimate international businesses, though taxes and tariffs be appropriate measures of international business acumen and etiquette.

Another case which was similar to that of the bonds case deals with the matter of insolvency and bankruptcy and the entities right to consider the United States a priority in creditors in repayment only in certain cases where the debtor has committed some "notorious act pursuant to law." In all other cases, debtors may choice who they pay back first. This is the case of *Prince v. Bartlett (1814).* Moral to the Story: Commit no "notorious act" against the United States of America.

In some other case, *United States v. Tenbroek (1817)*, it dealt with the matter of distilling spirits for liquor and the law required a license to do this business. The issue, if I am reading correctly, is that all distillation that happen before the law was written or enacted was fine, but thereafter, any distillation of spirits without the license would be considered an infraction. The penalty for breaking this distillation of spirts law was $100.00 back then which would be the equivalent of $1948.00 today in 2020. Moral to the Story: Don't practice distilling without a license.

In another interesting case opinioned by Justice Duvall, that of *The Neptune* (1818), it seems that proving registration for ships could be a hassle for foreign Captains with sloppy file keeping systems. One London ship owned and operated by a Captain Myrick, committed libel, or in what today's terms would be possibly considered fraud by stating that the vessel Neptune was registered out of North Carolina, when in fact there was no US registration of the ship at all, if I am reading the case correctly. It appears that he made a fuss before the notary republic and end up dying from unknown cause's days later. The vessel confiscated or forfeited to the United States. Moral the Story: Don't lie about the registration of your vessel; especially in a time when tension between your country is high with the Host country; ie...the United States of America.

In the case of *Boyd's Lessee v. Graves (1819),* essentially it is a case where to respective parties or entities agree to hire a surveyor to draw an invisible line of division between them and respectively observe this line as it is drawn between to plots to be observed and serves as a boundary maker in case of ejectment. Moral to the Story: The key to unfair zoning laws maybe bipartisan hiring of surveyors.

Another interesting case that Justice Duvall had majority say in writing an opinion was in the case of *Parker v. United States, (1828).* In this case an adjunct and Inspector General of he Army was not granted his portion of double rations. The precedent is that it is at the discretion of the President of the United States of the America to allow or disallow those Army officers serving in two commands with those in command under him to benefit of two separate proportions of rations. Moral to the Story: He that hath, more is given.

In a final case discussed herein that Justice Duvall handled the matter of *Nicholls v. Hodges, (1828).* This case involved the Maryland Courts dealing with the deceased and the executor having claim on an estate. In these matters, if an executor has an right to the estate, their claim is just as valid as other claimants. The amount commissioned will be between 5 and 10 percent. Moral to the Story: Administrators are important.

# Chapter 20:

## Justice Joseph Story (1779-1845)

Justice Joseph Story served on the United Supreme Court for approximately 33 years. He is most known for handling two cases in particular; *Martin v. Hunter's Lessee* and *United States v. Amistad Africans* case. Justice Story also published a title by the name of *Commentaries on the Constitution of the United State.* In was known as a conservative Justice who had as much influence as Marshall on American Law and was a major advocate for private property rights.

Justice Story attended Harvard University as an undergrad and was admitted into the Phi Betta Kappa society. Interestingly enough, he had seven children and only two survived to adulthood, one of which was a writer and artist who also has a work of art that stands in front of Harvard Law Library as well as he, Joseph's son, published two volumes of the life and works of his father, entitled *The Life and Letters of Joseph Story vol. I and II.*

Justice Story was appointed by the President James Madison who filled the seat of William Cushing who had deceased 14 months prior. Holding the record even to this day and year of October 12, 2020 as the youngest Justice to be appointed to the United States Supreme Court; the young and vibrant age of 32 years of age.

As we will see in the case as we discuss *Martin v. Hunter's Lessee (1816),* Justice Story was an advocate of the Constitution being the supreme law of the land in every state and made distinction between how the constitution in fact was framed not by the "sovereign states" but "by the people, for the people," and this fact should diffuse into all states thereby alleviating the problem of every state having its own individual rules of operation. I do not think this is the common practice today, though it may be the rule. It is my understanding that every state has a certain leeway and jurisdiction to govern, rule, and conduct the business affairs of that state, of course within the limits of the Constitution. In this particular case it is a matter power, jurisdiction and judicial review. From my understanding seems that there was an act to allow certain loyalists land to be confiscated after the American Revolutionary War. Certain entities tried to re-acquire their land and was met with heavy hand from the local courts, thus they appealed the matter to a higher court of appeals. Seems the matter went all the way to the US Supreme Court; State courts contesting that US Supreme court had no authority over the matter, and thus the State judgment reversed in Justice Story's majority opinion for reasons mentioned above; reasserting the supreme power of the US Supreme Court over State and local courts. Moral to the Story: Appeal to the Court; and you just may win.

In the *United States v. Amistad Africans (1841)* case it seems that Africans who had been illegally captured along the Coast of Africa were aboard the Amistad ship and thereby through a rebellion, killing both the captain and the cook. The ship continued to sale south the Atlantic until it reached Cuba. There, the ship was sent North to the Africans unawares being captured by US ports in Long Island, New York. Hence the case of the free Africans v. the United States proceeded; those group of individuals with the aid of American Counsel, winning their case, setting precedence to abolition of slavery. They were eventually sent back to Africa at the government expense as sources say with American Missionaries in Sierra Leon. Moral to the Story: Justice can prevail with respect to Race, Culture, and Economics, in the American Judicial System.

## Chapter 21:

## Justice Smith Thompson (1768-1843)

Justice Smith Thompson served for four years as the United States Secretary of the Navy before continuing his service in government of 20 years on the US Supreme Court, from 1823 to 1843 till his death. His undergraduate career was completed at Princeton University, and he was considered a great opponent to the Marshall Court as he sat on the bench. He was appointed to his position by President James Madison.

The first case of discussion is that of *Antelope.* It appears that the there was a ship in the Atlantic Seas off the coast of Florida containing African Human Cargo—slaves. Well, to my surprise there was an act passed in 1808 that made the importation of slaves into the United State illegal. Interestingly enough, the Emancipation Proclamation did not come to the scene till approximately 1863. Either way, with regards to the Antelope ship, it was actually captured by a Portuguese Pirate, whom when claiming the precious human cargo in court to be his property; it was dismissed upon Judicial review for lack of evidence. The majority of the Africans were shipped back to be settled in Liberia and 30 others were claimed by Spanish claimants, being forced to serve as slaves in Florida. This complicated ruling was not necessarily made by Justice Smith Thompson, nevertheless, one of the cases of the Marshall court during a time frame in which he was an Associate Judge. Moral to the Story: Slavery; still wrong, even when hijacking ship.

A second case that we will consider while Justice Thompson was on bench but was actually decided by Justice Marshall; a ruling to uphold the state courts decision, is ***Willson v. Black-Bird Creek Marsh Co.,*** (1829). In this case Wilson was sailing his sail boat in the waters of Delaware, and breeched a damn that was built by the Black-Bird Creek Marsh Co. The issue was brought to court by the damn building company; and their argument for validating their architectural structure was that there was a state police law that in so many ways commissioned them to clean up; health and hazard issues. Secondly, there was no Congressional legislation that would legally prevent the building of such a structure. Wilson countered in his defense that the damn was built for a private company for profit and that it inhibited the free sailing of such entities as himself. The Court ruled in favor of the plaintiff, and this decision was further affirmed by the US Superior court under the basis that there was no federal laws that prevented such actions.

## Chapter 22:

## Justice Robert Trimble (1776-1828)

Justice Robert Trimble was born in the same year the America declared her independence from Great Britain. He grew to become an Attorney, Congressmen, District Judge, and US Supreme Court Associate Justice. Justice Trimble was appointed by President John Quincy Adams to the United States Supreme Court as an Associate Judge and wrote the majority opinion for the *Ogden vs. Saunders* case. Furthermore, it is said that Justice Trimble had the shortest term on the Supreme Court, approximately 1 year and 3 months. One other case that was litigated during his time of Associate Judge, though he had no necessary direct role in deciding to my investigative knowledge, was *American Ins. Co. v. 356 Bales of Cotton*.

In the case *American Ins. Co. v. 356 Bales of Cotton,* bales of cotton were shipped and wrecked and ended up in Florida. Apparently the bales were recovered and moved to various points across the east coast; New York and Charleston, and ultimately fraudulently sold. It is ambiguous to me upon reading the litigation summary as to what percentage of the proceeds from the salvaged cargo was awarded to the salvers verses awarded back to the claimants for the lost material. Moral to the Story: Have insurance, and file your claims promptly.

## Chapter 23:

## Justice John McLean (1785–1861)

Justice John McLean started his education according to sources in a classical style. He went on to complete his matriculation through his undergrad career at Harvard and then studied Law in which he was admitted to the Bar. Positions held by Justice McLean were Congressman, Ohio Justice, and US Supreme Court Justice. He was also pursued by the various parties for a Presidential nomination. In addition, Justice McLean served as head of the Postmasters General and was appointed to the US Supreme Court by President Andrew Jackson. One of the cases that he wrote a dissent opinion for was *The Dread Scott v. Sanford* case.

In the very controversial decision of Dread Scott, that upheld the fact that the US constitution was not meant to include Black American citizens weather slave or free. Upon reading this, as an African American Male myself, as well someone at least somewhat informed of the racial History of the United States of America, my reaction was one of shock and appall. I knew there were racist laws of segregation, and even discriminatory laws such as the 3/5$^{th}$ clause, but to uphold a idea that insinuates that the constitution does not even apply to Blacks is just down right injustice.

Further details of this case disclose that Dred Scoot was taken by his owner from Missouri to a Free State, deemed free, and then upon his return to Missouri, was still considered a slave. He appealed his status to the local and state federal courts, but to no avail, all their decisions including the US Supreme Court decision deemed Dread still a slave under Missouri law, and for the reasons mentioned above,--namely that blacks were not considered or included as citizens when the framers drafted the Constitution. And thus the American Civil War of 1861 and won by the Union in 1865 and the 13th and 14$^{th}$ amendments added to the Constitution which considered anyone born in the United States a naturalized citizen (14$^{th}$) and the abolition of slavery, except in punishment for a crime(13$^{th}$). Moral to the Story: Sometimes injustice is countered with Civil War, when continued litigation is met with unjust decisions.

## Chapter 24:

## Justice Henry Baldwin (1780–1844)

Justice Henry Baldwin was born in Connecticut and attended Yale College for his undergraduate career, and would eventually graduate from Litchfield Law School. He went on to open his own practice as well as published a newspaper. He was appointed to the US Supreme Court and sat as an Associate Justice for some 14 years and before that was elected to the US Congress, a position in which he resigned from due to ill health. He was nominated to the court by President Andrew Jackson and some sources report that he was suspected to have problems with mental illness, although he served on the Supreme Court until his death.

Three cases which were significant during his tenure on the bench were; *Magill v. Brown, Worcester v. Georgia (1832),* and *Groves v. Slaughter (1841).* In the case of Magill v. Brown, Justice Henry Baldwin asserts his position for the US Supreme court as well as the law of the land after the Civil War, "We must take it therefore as a grant by the people of the state in convention, to the citizens of all the other states of the Union, of the privileges and immunities of the citizens of this state." This was the rhetoric used by Justice Baldwin, Washington, and Justice Story in similarly relatable cases. Essentially it is a highlighting of the Privileges and Immunities Clause in the constitution stating that all naturalized citizens should have access and the benefit to the privileges and immunities of all others in each state. Moral to the Story: Being an American Citizen privileges one to enjoy the benefits and privileges of all the other states.

In the case of Worcester v. Georgia (1832), which was a case of Soverignty and the

Cherokee tripe in the state of Georgia. Apparently two missionaries were arrested who were in Cherokee lands and were arrested under a statute that stated white men were not to be in Cherokee territory without license. Twice this happen and the first time these men asserted that the law did not apply to them because of their status as federal agents. The Second time they were arrested and jailed, and although offered pardon decided to appeal to the US Supreme Court. Georgia stated that it would stand ground with it's opinion irregardless of a Supreme Court decision. Nevertheless, the Majority opinion came down in favor of upholding that the stattues when applied to the Cherokee, were unconstitutional when applied to the Cherokee tribe. This would infer that the men were arrested illegally, and could continue their business. Notwithstanding, Justice Baldwin wrote a dissenting opinion which he did not turn in supposedly, In his position he stated that Cherokee nation was subject to state of Georgia in so many words. The majority opinion stated that the Cherokee tribe and territories were soverign in so many words, subject to the judicial authority of the courts, if I am understanding accurately.

How this translates into the various Native American Tribes and Reservations, Casinos and Resorts today, I am not sure. Moral to the Story: Despite colonization, various Native American Tribes and their Tribal lands were acknowledged and protected by Judicial Supreme Court laws.

In the Case of *Groves v. Slaughter,* which was somewhat complicated, we have one entity who made a purchase of some human cargo..ie slaves for a certain amount. As they wrote the bill and the amount expected to be payed the other party declared that under a Missouri constitution that the bill was void because of the law. The matter was taken to federal court and then further appealed to the US Supreme Court and opinions of the justices stated in so many words that slaves were considered property, and further that there was protection of owners moving into free states with their slaves, protecting slavery of the South, and lastly some verbage about congress not being able to control the actions of the several states penned by Justice Baldwin. Moral to the Story: The purchasing and selling of human cargo was a complicated animal back in the day and had far reaching judicial repercussions.

# Chapter 25:

## Justice James Moore Wayne (1790-1867)

Justice James Wayne was borne in Georgia and in his lifetime and political career served in the Army during the War of 1812 and later became an Attorney, Politician, Mayor and Associate Justice appointed by President Andrew Jackson. He studied law after completion of his undergraduate studies at Princeton and was classified as a Democrat.

Justice Wayne heard a wide variety of cases as he sat as an Associate Judge on the US Supreme Court. The cases ranged from slavery, taxes, reform, interior improvement and other matters of state. Primarily he was opposed to the building of more highways and canals and yet an advocate of the deepening of rivers and harbors. He was opposed to Native Americans having their own lands and thus forced them west. Finally, although he was from Georgia, he considered himself a Unionist.

In this case, *Louisville, Cincinnati & Charleston Railroad Co. v. Letson,* it concerned a matter if a man named Letson who acquired a legal contract with a the Railraod company for expansion of a certain road in a certain area that was left unfulfilled. Therefore, because of the breach in contract Letson sued the Railroad Company although there seems to be some ambiguity regarding both parties having members in different states. Partly for this reason the Courts ruled that the lawsuit was unjustifiable and out of the proper jurisdiction. Furthermore, from this ruling, incorporated companies in their particular state could be considered citizens there. Moral to the Story: The importance and relevance of Jurisdiction in the Federal Courts when deciding cases it seems is more important than the actual evidence or details of the individual cases.

## Chapter 26:

## Justice Roger B. Taney (1777-1864)

Justice Robert Taney held a few other positions besides his seat on the US Supreme Court. He was also appointed by President Andrew Jackson as Attorney General and served in the State department as the Secretary of Treasury. Justice Taney was born into a wealthy slave family who owned a plantation in Maryland, which would explain his pro-slavery sentiments later on in his judicial career. He was educated at Dickerson college and then pursued the study of law and admitted to the bar.

In this first case that we will consider, the matter of *Charles River Bridge v. Warren Bridge*. Apparently there were two bridges being built 100 yards from each other. The first Bridge that won a contract with the State to begin building sued the second bridge building company under the reasoning that the State and given them a monopoly. Ultimately the matter went up to the Supreme Court and Justice Taney said in so many words that such an issuance and state backed monopoly would not be good for future infrastructure, and thus the continued building of both bridges by the two separate companies continued. Moral to the Story: State issued Monopolies are not good for future industry or infrastructure.

In the matter of *Briscoe v. Bank of Kentucky*, this case regards the legality or constitutionality of the usage of certain bank notes or bills of credit held by a certain bank. In a preliminary case there was a ruling that state banks were not allowed to issue interest bearing loan certificates, deeming them unconstitutional. In a Secondary case, the contrary was deemed constitutional; essentially that all bank notes, loans, and certificates could be circulated by the state as money thus giving the state more control of the banks. Justice Taney had a ruling in the majority opinion that seconded this matter, moreover these matters were consistent with President Jackson's Economic Plan, whom witch sources say Justice Taney was to be politically aligned or allied. Moral to the Story: The circulation of bank notes helped stimulate the economy back as it does today. Furthermore, Banking and currency is political.

In another case dealing with slaves and slave owners, the case of Prigg v Pennsylvania (1842), where there were a women and à child recaptured by a certain previous slave owner and brought to Maryland under the slave fugitive law, but not in abidance of the Pennsylvania law. There were two main opinions on the court, one by Taney, as chief Justice, and another by Justice Story. Apparently, there was no law preventing slave owners for recaturing their slaves, yet and still under the fugitive slave law, the state could not assist or hinder this process. Moral to the Story: During the times of Slavery, even if one broke away and got Free, they could still legally be recaptured. A harsh reality of American History.

# Chapter 27:

## Justice Philip Pendleton Barbour (1783-1841)

Justice Philip Barbour was born in Virginia and attended William and Mary College, and later he took a year to study the law and was admitted to the bar and practiced for eight years. Politically he was a House Speaker and sat on the District of Virginia Federal Court. He was later appointed by President Andrew Jackson to the US Supreme Court as an Associate Justice.

There were a number of cases that Justice Philip Barbour sat on the court for, but we have herein already discussed these matters. One case we have not considered is the matter of *Holmes v. Jennison, (1840).* In this case there was a man who was detained by way of indictment against his will apparently for some infraction committed in the providence of Canada, if I understand correctly. There were plans to extradite this man so that he could be tried for felonious murder, and he later prosecuted a writ of error, being a both a citizen of Vermont and the province of Canada. Moral to the Story: Dual citizenship has its benefits and downfalls, nevertheless an indictment for felonious murder are normally inescapable.

## Chapter 28:

## Justice John Catron (1786–1865)

Justice John Catron was appointed as an Associate Justice to the US Supreme Court by President Martin Van Buren. Justice Catron studied law and was admitted to the Bar in 1815. In terms of cases that Justice Catron tenured or wrote opinion on, we have already herein discussed the case of *Dreadscott v. Sanford.* Notwithstanding there are the cases of, *Bank of Augusta* v. *Earle* , *Piqua Branch of the State Bank of Ohio v. Knoop*, and *Ohio Life Insurance and Trust Co. v. DeBolt, (1853).*

In the case of *Bank of Augusta v. Earle*, in this very convoluted case Justice Catron ruled on the majority side that banks can operate nationally and furthermore that state could prevent or prohibit an entity from doing business within the state so long as this exclusion is stated directly. Moral to the Story: It took time for banks to gain the scalability and fluidity of currency on a national and eventually international scale that they enjoy today.

In the case of *Pique Branch of the State of Ohio v. Knoop,* the bank wrote into their charter a clause stating that the bank was exempt from State taxes. Furthermore, because of the charter, it was argued that this is a "contract with the state" and there for must be kept under Article I Section 10 of the Constitution. Justice Catron ruled on the dissenting side of things asserting the point that legislative and Federal powers are Sovereign and not subject to Corporations. This ruling is fascinating considering it allows for corporations to essentially write whatever they want, including the exemption of state taxes in their charters or "state contract" and it will be upheld by the Constitution. Moral to the Story: Corporations have a unique power to the write exemption clauses in their charters; if gone unchecked might seem unjust.

In the case of *Ohio Life Insurance and Trust Co. v. DeBolt, (1853)* it was another instance of essentially taxation and American Corporations. The universal issue of whether or not corporations had more power than the state initially wanted to or was willing to give came to question. There was a storming for American Corporations to find their role within the nation. Moral to the Story: The massive corporate wealth that some companies brought to the scene in some ways competed with Federal Powers.

## Chapter 29:

## Justice John McKinley (1780-1852)

Justice John McKinley was born in Virginia and ultimately grew to read the law and was admitted to the bar and practiced in Louisville, Kentucky. He also served in the Senate and was appointed to the US Supreme Court as an Associate Justice by President Martin Van Buren. Two cases in which Justice McKinley was sitting on the US Supreme Court for or right around the time that he held tenure as an Associate Justice were the cases of *Sheldon v. Sill*, (1850) and *Hotchkiss v. Greenwood*, (1851).

In the case of Sheldon v. Sill, (1850); it was a matter of limitation of federal powers in the circuit court by the legislative branch under the auspicis of the Constitution. Apparently, according to the Constitution, the legislative body possessed the powers to decide what types of cases would be heard by the inferior federal Courts. Moral to the Story: The US Governmental System; Legislative, Judicial, and Executive holds massive political power, has many heads and more governmental and bureaucratic tentacles that pervade the national infrastructure; yet there will always be the checks and balances that balance each head and Office;--a democratic hierarchy or shall we be more proper and say republic.

The second case of Hotchkiss v. Greenwood was one of patent laws and more specifically dealt with the scenario of one creating a better doorknob. Apparently in the past doorknobs were made out of porcelain and clay and this new technology was brought forth manufactured from clay, porcelain, and iron; in that they were united by the shank and spindle. This new invention showcased the ingenuity and creative talent of the gifted and skillful and therefore deemed patentable material. Moral to the Story: Men's extreme talent should be acknowledged, protected, and awarded in Society.

# Chapter 30:

## Justice Peter Vivian Daniel (1784–1860)

Justice Peter Daniel was born in Virginia and subject to paid tutors for a rigorous home schooling program. He eventually attended and graduated from Princeton and then continued his education by studying the law and being admitted to the bar. In his political career he served the State Department as a Lieutenant Governor in the state of Virginia in the year of 1818. Finally, Justice Peter Daniel was nominated to the US Supreme Court by President Martin Van Buren. Justice Daniel sat as Associate Justice upon the Taney court, and primarily for the majority of his opinions ruled in dissent of the majority opinions. In terms of his justice and politics, he advocated slavery and despised the gaining power of the federal government.

A number of the cases from the Taney Court we have already briefly discussed. There are more left to be highlighted, one being; *Swift v. Tyson* and a second and third being, *Luther v. Boren*, and the *Passenger Cases*.

In the case of Swift v. Tyson, it mainly dealt with local federal courts having the power to use state law or "common law" in their cases on issues that the state legislature had already spoke or litigated on. For cases in which there was no legislative record of them ever addressing the issue, then state law need not be used, and the default constitutional law applies. Moral to the Story: Congress has the ability to litigate and authorize judicial power over local federal Courts.

In the case of *Luther v. Boren*, there was as certain individual by the name of Marin Luther who rebelled against the charter of Maryland, in his own matter advocating the idea of an expansion of voter rights to more people. He attempted to use the "Equal protection clause" in his defense and ultimately the Supreme Court ruled that this was a political question issue and in need of being decided by either Legislative or Executive members of government. Moral to the Story: Even the US Supreme Court has the necessary ability to defer to their Judicial and Executive Colleagues when dealing with awkward or class action political cases that pose difficult or unwanted territory.

In the matter of the Passenger Cases;--namely *Smith v. Turner; Norris v. Boston (1849).*

These cases dealt with states having the right to impose taxes per passenger of the boats that were coming in to the Eastern ports. The Court ruled against this phenomenon yet not in a majority opinion, there were 8 separate opinions. Moral to the Story: States didn't always get away with being greedy with taxes.

## Chapter 31:

## Justice Samuel Nelson (1792-1873)

Justice Samuel Nelson was born to a wealthy family in New York. He was educated as a youth and then went on to attend Mulberry College in the North East. After graduation he decided upon reading the law and after his admission to the bar in 1813, decided to practice after one failed partnership and another joint venture, he stepped out on his own and had a successful real estate and commercial practice. Justice Nelson was appointed by the governor to the state court in New York and eventually sat as chief Justice of that local federal court. Eventually Justice Nelson would be nominated by President John Taylor to the US Supreme Court. Justice Nelson's total Federal court career was 27 years, and within this tenure, we will cover a few cases in which we have not already discussed.

In the case of Ableman v. Booth; the main issue at hand was the fact that State court can not overturn or have no judicial authority over US supreme federal court. This would seem intuitive for us considering where we are in this study. It seems we have already established the fact of a hierarchy of courts both superior and inferior in ranking authority and jurisdiction. Nevertheless, in this case, there was a riot or mob invigorated apparently by a certain individual by the name of booth for the recapture of a escaped certain slave. Well, Booth was jailed and released from custody and the Marshall took the matter to the high court under the constitutionality of the whole matter, but to no avail, Booth's release was effectual and permanent. What made the matter political was that the state of Wisconsin courts refused the authority of the Supreme court, by not sending the record. So, the Supreme Court decision was written without a record, and part of the opinion stated, in so many words, that state courts were not to usurp Supreme Court powers or authority in these ways and matters. Moral to the Story: Sometimes those bringing matters to prosecution lose their cases even when matters seem unjust. Imagine appealing a matter to a higher court and winning your case, only to not have the matter recognized by the inferior courts of the land. I think I am in line when I say, such was the case in the matter of the abolition of slavery and the years of Jim Crow laws.

## Chapter 32:

## Justice Levi Woodbury (1789-1851)

Justice Levi Woodbury held a number of positions before his appointment as Associate Justice to the US Supreme Court. Not only was he Governor of New Hampshire, but also served in the Senate as well as held positions of Secretary of the Navy and Secretary of Treasury. He also held his own legal practice for a number of years and sat of the State Supreme Court in New Hampshire. His early years found him at an specialized Academy school. His collegiate years were spent at Dartmouth College where he graduated Phi Beta Kappa. Justice Woodbury attended Law School in Connecticut and as aforementioned, went on to pass the bar and open his own practice.

In the case of Jones v. Van Zandt, Justice Woodbury asserted that the Fugitive Slave Act was indeed Constitutional and furthermore that slaveholders where protected by this sinister clause written into the Constitution. Woodbury further argued that slavery was a political concept that individual states needed to decide their position. The Fugitive Slave Acts themselves being laws that protected slave-owners in their recapture of slaves who traveled from slave states to states where slavery was illegal. Moral to the story: When the laws of the land were unjust and authenticated by some Superior held document, there were no consequences to the belittled people of the land being mistreated, enslaved, and even recaptured in the event of their escape. Thank God laws have changed.

Aside from the aforementioned case, Justice Woodbury had influence on some other major topics during his tenure on the US Supreme Court as well. Namely-- Construction clauses and Commerce clauses written in the Constitution with respect to the *Contract/Banking* cases and License *Cases*. More directly put, Justice Woodbury had a hand in writing opinion on liquor licenses cases. In the License Cases in which Justice Woodbury deferred to the states to allow themselves to make their individual decisions as to whether or not they would allow the purchase and selling of Spirits or run along with prohibition on certain days. In the matter of the Construction clauses, certain contracts held between banks and their permission to circulate legal bank notes and what not. Moral to the Story: All US Supreme Court Justices have substantial power to influence present and future decisions on matters serious, political and social brought to their attention. The opinions they write and judgments they give have long lasting effects on the courts and the land hopefully to the benefit of society, but as history has shown, at times to its digression.

## Chapter 33:

## Justice Robert Cooper Grier (1794-1870)

Justice Robert Cooper Grier was born in Pennsylvania; he graduated with a BA and went on to become a sort of Lecturer/Instructor at his alma marten. Later he served in the position Headmaster; a seat that had been previously occupied by his father. Justice Robert Grier had an interesting political ideology over the years. I imagine that his ideals changed because of his support for the blockades on confederate ports in staunch support of the Union Army right around 1863. Interestingly enough, or ironically, some 20 years before this date, as he sat as a Supreme Court justice he wrote along with the majority opinion in the *Dread Scott case*. Furthermore, sources report that he was known to argue that Blacks or slaves "were never meant to be citizens of the United States;" moreover, "that the property of slave-owners was protected by the Constitution." Thus, the evil empire of slavery, the slave trade, and their masters were protected by law, and further, by the very Framer's Constitution that would eventually be amended to give liberty and protect the civil rights of all United States Citizens. In this vein, it seems that as history ebb and flowed, Justice Grier may have amended his ways to the point that he supported the Union.

One other case that Justice Grier wrote an opinion on was the, *Cook v. Moffat* (1847) case. In this case, one party declared bankruptcy in Maryland because of the insolvency laws of his State, thought that he could travel to another state without having to worry about the debts he had to individuals and businesses from other states outside of Maryland. Well, as the story goes, two individuals from another state considered the matter in court and Justice Grier ruled essentially that States could not rule bankruptcy on debts beyond their jurisdiction. Moral to the

Story: Americans can't run to other states to hide from their debts; they follow you, at least back then anyway.

A second case that Justice Grier made decision upon involved industry and commerce, that is the case of *Fredericksburg, and Potomac Railroad Company v. Louisa Railroad Company* (1852). In this case, you had a railroad company that had a contract with the state of Virginia to carry passengers for thirty years. Over time, another railroad company sought to build a track that focused solely on steel, coal and other freight items. The rout of the second RR company was close to the first, and thus they thought to bring lawsuit against the second. In the ruling Justice Grier ruled in favor of the second RR Company that sought to expand the market place; namely the Louisa Railroad Company was allowed to continue to build and service the Virginia businesses in a free market place, free from the monopoly of the Potomac Railroad Company. Furthermore, (PRC) was not disallowed from also transporting coal, steel, and other freights along with their contracted persons to transport for 30 years. It is unclear as to whether or not LRC was also allowed to transport people. I assume not, considering this was specific to PRC's) contract with the state of Virginia. Who Knows? Moral to the Story: America has always encouraged competition in the marketplace, even in the face of selfish greed from certain individuals and companies.

## Chapter 34:

## Justice Benjamin Robbins Curtis (1809-1874)

Justice Benjamin Curtis was born in Massachusetts and was the first US Supreme Court Justice to leave the bench on the account of moral principle. A member of Phi Beta Kappa and a Harvard Graduate; he attended Harvard Law and upon completion of his program was admitted to the Bar. Shortly thereafter, Justice Curtis attached himself to a private law firm in Boston.

Justice Curtis was appointed to the Supreme Court by President Milliard Fillmore. He heard a few cases including the Dread Scott Case as he was one of the two dissenting opinions in that ruling. He is another that I presume amended his ideology somewhat over time, reason being, in earlier case dealing with the freedom rights of a 6 year old girl brought by her mistress who incidentally had to stay with the mistresses father due to the mistress's illness. The father of the mistress; Ave, had to battle with charges declaring the little girl, "Med" being essentially abandoned and a necessary asset, or excuse me, ward of the state as asserted by the Boston Female Anti-Slavery Society whom filed an writ of habeas corpus against Ave accusing him in so many words harboring a slave in a free state. I could only imagine what type of rumors spread fire as this 6 year old black girl suddenly was shacked up with Ave, whom I assume was a semi older white male in the free North.

This was the case of, *Commonwealth v. Aves*. The Boston Female Anti-Slavery Society advocated for little "Med's" freedom, but Dad Ave argued essentially that he was just holding property for his daughter whom he was to return when she was well and better. Justice Curtis was one who ruled dissent of the Chief Justice Lemuel Shaw, whom ruled Med free and to be given to the State. Moral to the Story: As time progresses; common sense, good and sometimes shrewd reasoning, and compassion will hopefully continue to rule and even more so infuse the Justice system that true judgments with mercy when necessary will prevail.

In another case, Justice Benjamin Curtis wrote opinion that essentially stated that federal powers control commerce in the event that "national unity" is needed, in other times these powers are administered by the states. The name of this case is, *Cooley v. Board of*

*Wardens (1852).* Moral to the Story: When needed, federal powers take control; especially in those matters of finance and commerce.

## Chapter 35:

## Justice John Archibald Campbell (1811–1889)

Justice John Campbell was an extremely smart young man who was considered a child genius and talent and graduated college at the tender age of 14. He applied himself to the Military Academy and after these years of learning and service were completed he was ready for Law; which he studied and was admitted to the bar at the ripe age of 18. Apparently Justice Campbell Only served a short time as a US Supreme Court Justice due to his leaving to serve in the Confederate Army and was jailed in a Military Detention Facility for six months, and afterwards went back to his private practice of the Law.

Many cases Justice Campbell chimed in on were of the dissenting opinion. One case in particular, *Dodge v. Woolsey (1855).* In this case, Ohio state adjusted its constitution surround the issue of banks being tax exempt and soon thereafter, certain shareholders brought issue to court concerning this matter. According to Justice Campbell's dissent, he felt that if corporations were protected by the Constitution that individual citizens or the people would never have recourse or a voice for that matter in the midst of corruption. He was a Jacksonian democrat and felt in so many words that more government was needed to step in to regulate big corporations and banks to prevent massive power, control and corruption ruling over the people. Moral to the Story: Seems that the same issues fought back then are the same issues we deal with today, especially in light of the recent court proceedings with multi-billion dollar corporations such as Amazon, Facebook, and Google. Not to mention Bank bailouts in 2008, and FBI investigations of government and political leaders that are still in the press.

In a final case that we will herein discuss that Justice Campbell wrote opinion on, again considering the Contract Clause of the Constitution. There was a church that was deemed exempt in paying taxes by the state, then after a few years there was a state wide tax put forth to every organization and all corporations. The church felt that its first exemption still valid, and took the matter to trial in the case of *Christ's Church Hospital v. County of Philadelphia.* Justice Campbell ruled in so many words that the state needed to be able to keep the power to exert taxation at every level, because this is what kept up the Commonwealth. Moreover, the state needed to remain in control to assist in corporate development. Moral to the Story: Essentially, Justice Campbell wanted to keep the authority of the State, that is federal powers, and be sure that corporations did not exceed their limitations as far as corporate loopholes, kickbacks, cronyism, corruption, and all the other insider fun that businessmen and politicians deal with in their territory of industry…LOL.

## Chapter 36:

## Justice Nathan Clifford (1803-1881)

Justice Nathaniel Clifford held a number of key level positions before taking his seat on the US Supreme Court. He also attended a number of schools and Academies before his study of the law and admittance to the Bar. He would go on to hold a position in the legislative branch as well as serve as the Attorney General for the President. So it would seem proper that he capped off his career with a tenured US Supreme court seat, although this position be appointed by the President himself.

Justice Clifford was appointed by President James Buchanan even though his appointment was held up by the Senate vote, as they balked at his history of pro-slavery politics. In terms of his political philosophy on Constitutional law, it appears that Justice Clifford mainly advocated a separation, or more accurately put, a distinction in federal and state powers, with federal powers having preeminence.

Justice Clifford's notions for federal powers having authority were exercised in his implementing his opinion based on the Legal Tender Acts (1862). In one particular case that saw its way around the various state local, appeals, and the Supreme Court was the matter of *Hepburn v. Griswold* (1870). In this case Hepburn made effort to pay Griswold with a tender that essentially expired because of a new bank note law. Griswold demanded payment in the new tender US bank note, but Hepburn brought promissory note to Court which cleared the debt in the state local court. Griswold appealed to the Kentucky Court of errors which reversed the decision, and Hepburn, in kind, appealed to the US Supreme Court which ruled in favor of Griswold. Moral to the Story: Federal Supreme Courts had final say in the exercising of legal tender. The question is, what Federal Courts will say about new block chain technologies, cryptocurrencies, and the digital currencies of today and the future. Will they be regulated? Taxed? How will these new technologies change our Society and even the World and Global Economies, if at all? Moreover, how has the economic landscape already changed because of such conceptual and potential disruption?

Justice Clifford was not as known on such a grand scale for his interpretation of Reconstruction writ, nevertheless, sources report that one of his phrases written in a case that dealt with the matter of the separation of races on steam ships; *Hall v. DeCuir* (1877), might have been the kindling to the prominent phrase "*separate but equal,*" in the *Plessy v, Fergusson* cases. He stated that "*equality is not identity,*" in his assertion to reinforce separation of races on steam ships. Moral to the Story: History tells us that what may seem right in one era, may not hold true in another. Yet morals and values should not change, or should they, or more contemporarily put, should it be or tolerance that that builds over time. Or, is this the vicious and deceitful slippery slope that allows all manner of subversive ideology to creep in.

## Chapter 37:

## Justice Noah Haynes Swayne (1804–1884)

Justice Noah Swayne was born in Virginia and attended an Academy of sorts for his preparatory schooling. He was pre-med in college and due to an Unfortunate death of one of his Professors; he decided to leave in pursuit of the study of Law. Eventually admitted to the bar in the state of Virginia, it is from this point that given his anti-slavery sense of ideology, he relocated to Ohio. As Justice Swayne's career progressed, he was elected Attorney General and also to a position in the House of Representatives. He rubbed shoulders with various judges and politicians, including Justice John McClean, which had something to do with his emerging as a Strong Republican, and one of the first republicans who was ultimately nominated and appointed to the US Supreme Court as an Associate Justice.

In one case dealing with bonds and whether or not constitutional state laws in Iowa could impede payment; Justice Swayne ruled in the Majority opinion a resounding No. This is the case of *Gelpcke v. Dubuque (1864)*. Apparently, some contracted entity was trying to get out of paying previously agreed to stakes and was using state constitutional law as the reasoning and backing. "No," said Justice Swayne, in addition to some flowery rhetoric surrounding the issue of how when the state set up the "alter of sacrifice, truth would not be immolated." Moral to the Story: State Constitutional laws could not and should not be manipulated by any entity to get out of payment to previous agreed to contracts.

One other case in which we will briefly touch on that Justice Swayne took Majority Rule in was that of ***Springer v. United States***,(1881). In this particular there was one, an Attorney who reported some approximately $50,000.00 for his income on his tax forms. He owed approximately %10.00 percent of his income in taxes and refused to pay, and thus the government filed suit against him and levied some of his properties for sale. Thereafter a writ of ejection was in play and Springer was ejected from his property in which he brought lawsuit against the government. There was some matter of confusion between dates and Acts of when taxes could be assigned, but in the end, Springer was still on the hook for the taxes he owed and the ejection was upheld. Moral to the Story: Tax evasion is a federal offence and carries serious consequences.

## Chapter 38:

## Justice Samuel Freeman Miller (1816–1890)

Justice Samuel Miller was born in Kentucky to farmers and yet would go on to earn both Medical and Judicial Doctorate degrees. He attended Transylvania Medical School also in Kentucky and after his graduation took nine years to study the law on his own and subsequently was admitted to the bar. His political ideology was more aligned with the abolitionist and he associated with the Whig party. Justice Samuel Miller was ultimately appointed to the US Supreme Court by President Abraham Lincoln just before the War and many of his decisions fundamentally aligned with Lincoln policies and politics. Justice Miller authored over some sixhundred Supreme Court opinions in just under three decades on the court.

In this first case we will discuss entitled, ***Bradwell v. State of Illinois***, 83 U.S. (16 Wall.) 130 (1873), it was essentially about a women's right to practice law in the state of Illinois and her initial denial. Interestingly enough, the state of Illinois initially argued that the law or the bar would be harmful for this woman to apply herself to, because it would "ruin her femininity." The backing of this logic stemmed from coverture laws which asserted that women had no legal standing apart from their husbands. The women's lawyer, Bradwell, argued that she could practice under the privileges and immunity clause, but to no avail, as the US Supreme Court ad well as Justice Miller's opinion upheld the state of Illinois' decision, claiming that this particular clause did not protect the women or afford her the opportunity to practice law. Not in the State of Illinois, in 1873, anyway. Moral to the Story: Not only was racism crafted into the law of the land, but also and obviously sexist and gender biased laws that gave men the upper hand;- namely White or Anglo males, those who were more like the framers. Both minorities-namely African-Americans and other people of color, as well as women would have to legally maneuver throughout history to overcome many of these obstacles and barriers that inhibited their overall success and quality of life.

It's just the way things were back then, and sadly enough, remnants of these systemic manufacturing errors still exist in the fundamental architecture of society even today, Yet, despite our adversarial and sometimes sordid history we all look forward toward a future of life, liberty, and the pursuit of happiness where even those of us esteemed low in sociologyeconomic, and even in political class can truly enjoy the fruits, benefit, and freedom of our high ambitions and labors and exercise our full God given rights as well as our American citizenship; in whatever joys or pleasures that may be or lead to.

In other hard decisions, and cases to be heard, Justice Miller held the line argument that the fourteenth amendment did not have the power nor the authority to stop private individuals from their preferential discrimination against blacks; yet and still-certain criminal acts of violence promoted by the Ku Klux Klan and other private groups, the federal government had full jurisdiction to protect black voters. Issues like these come up in the United States v. Cruikshank and other Civil Rights cases. A dangerous and unjust ruling in my personal opinion. Although, I was not there and did not witness what actually happen, but apparently there were two mobs, both armed, and at the end of the day two white males indicted for murdering over 200 individuals at the polls.

Interestingly enough, these men got off, and the rulings by the Federal judges suggested that all American citizens are essentially under two governments, the government of their state and that of the country; state and federal, and that men had the right to defend the right of their state. Now, I don't presume to know all the politics and details of what really happen during this slaughter, but it did happen in the South some 13 years after the signing of the Emancipation Proclamation. I would assume there was still high tensions from the Civil War, though this does not really excuse the murder of 200 lives, unless both mobs were attacking each other, then I guess it would be justified. Moral to the Story: Who's Who? Who knows what really happened, and who really sits in the seats of power?

## Chapter 39:

## Justice David Davis (1815-1886)

Justice David Davis held a number of positions besides Associate Justice on the US Supreme Court. He also was a Senator for the state of Illinois and served as President for the Senate for two years under President Abraham Lincoln. Notwithstanding, before these positions of glory, came the the trial of youth, as Justice Davis was said to be born to a well to do family in Maryland and went off to college in Ohio at Kenyon University. After graduation, it was off to Law school at Yale Law School, and then off to practice and begin a political career in Illinois. At one time or the other toward the end of his career on the US Supreme Bench, Justice Davis resigned his position to retake his position as Senator of Illinois. Also, after the assassination of President Abraham Lincoln, Justice Davis was instrumental in moving forward with decisiveness and strength in organizing the Electoral Commission.

In terms of cases that Justice *(1866).* In this very involved case, it dealt with whether or not military tribunal courts could be used to try citizens when ordinary courts were still open. In short, the ruling of the US Supreme court stood on the side of civil liberty and declared that using a military tribunal was unconstitutional except in a time of Marshall Law where civilian courts are not operational. Yet and still, there is a huge back story on this, and I can see the reasoning of trying these three individuals in a military tribunal. Essentially their actions were military as they were charged with conspiring and planning against the US government. Of course this was during the Civil War, and they were planning to aide Confederates, as well as "incite rebellion." Milligan and his associates were originally sentenced to death by hanging, but by way of a writ of habeas corpus being filed to the US Supreme Court, the writ was upheld and Chief Justice Chase had mercy on the defendants, decreeing the tribunal unconstitutional and thereby releasing them from custody. Justice Davis delivered the majority opinion on this case which further explained how military tribunals were only necessary where civil authority had been overthrown. Moreover, he argued that such courts should be contained to "military operations, where war really prevailed." I guess I can see both sides of the argument; I mean, we were at war, civil war, and these men were conspiring. And on the other side, it was a horrific civil war, and these were brothers and fathers of the same nation fighting and killing each other, and these particular tried men just so happen to be on the losing side, so maybe mercy was necessary. Moral to the Story: The American Judicial System is a Master that can take or give life. If ever in a fight for one's life, be sure to know the law, means of appeal, and justifiable arguments to fully defend one's case.

## Chapter 40:

## Justice Stephen Johnson Field

Justice Stephen Field was born in the state of Connecticut and ultimately studied law and was admitted the bar. Because of the unique time in history in which he came into development and success in opening his law practice career along with his brother;--The California Gold Rush somewhat attracted him and it was during this time the he relocated West. This is not to say that he was panning for gold nuggets and dust, sources don't say; but he did reopen his legal practice in California and it saw growth in the community. Although he was thought or known of at times as sort of petty and mean, he actually had a hand in, as he was appointed to a sort of mayor post in Marysville California, establishing a penal system of a whooping post, as there were few jails to house those who would commit crime on the gold rush front. Among his attributes off the court, so to speak, as an Associate Justice, he had a dual with another Associate Justice who sat on the Supreme Court. Both men decided to keep their pistols holstered.

Justice Stephen Field was the second longest serving Judge on the US supreme court. He tenured through Chief Justice's Chase and Taney's rule and even at recommendation of some of the other Justices during a time when he was becoming senile and unable to keep up with his caseload, he refused and pushed one to sit for 34 years. One might think his stubbornness was a disservice to the Court; herein we will discuss a few cases that he considered.

The first case I'd like to mention is that of the case *Munn v. Illinois (1876).* This case dealt with the matter of federal government having the power and ability to get involved with the private sector when their products or services involved or affected the "common good." So, more specifically in this case there was this price ceiling set by the government on maximum rates that private companies could charge for transport and storage for agricultural goods. One company in particular out of Chicago, Munn and Scott, was charged as guilty and essentially non-compliant as I'm assuming they ignored the price cap set by the government. They appealed their case to the State Supreme Court of Illinois on the grounds that the law was unconstitutional and promoted "depravity of private property." Secondly, they firmly believed that their civil rights to do as they pleased with their company, especially with respect of setting

prices for their services. The Illinois Supreme Court ruled in favor of the state. Moral to the Story: The Private Sector can legally be regulated by federal powers when their business affects the general welfare of the public. This fact holds true for the farming industry when provided with subsidies and economic price ceilings or floors placed on specific goods like oil, like in the 70's during
President Nixon's time in office. Seems that it all comes down to understanding a few fundamental principles of economics; supply and demand, quantity of goods provided, deadweight, taxes and the whole gamut.

A second case to be considered is that of *Penoyer v. Neff*. In this case, you had an individual by the name of Neff who hired a lawyer by the name of Mitchell to obtain for him a land grant from the state of Oregon. Oregon at the time was giving away parcels of land to be developed, and Neff prepared himself to file the necessary paperwork. In the passage of time, the paperwork was submitted and Neff acquired the property, worth just under $20,000.00. Mitchell, the trickster of a lawyer that he was, turned around and sued Neff for legal fees in arears. The suit was made public and Neff never showed up for court, and therefore a default judgment ruled in Mitchell's favor. Subsequently, through a series of legal maneuvers, Mitchell acquired the land through auction and deeded it to a man by the name of Sylvester Pennoyer.

It is at this point that Neff decided to counter sue for his property and brought Pennoyer to the State federal court and won. The nerve of Pennoyer to appeal to the Supreme Court and lost his case and the Court considered Neff and the technicality of *quasi in rem* jurisdiction and ruled in Neff's favor.

## Chapter 41:

## Justice Salmon Portland Chase (1808-1873)

Justice Salmon Chase possessed the unique distinction of the privilege of serving in all three branches of government. He was a Chief Justice on the Supreme Court, legislated policy in the Senate as an elected official, and helped manage the budget as Secretary of the Treasury in the President's Cabinet. His life started in New Hampshire, as this is where he was born, and then progressed to Dartmouth College, and then to his study of the law and opening up a practice in the state of Ohio. His moral philosophy was to have an anti-slavery sentiment and he opposed the expansion of a Southern ideology and the actual fact of an evil economy of a slave workforce moving into Northern territories.

A bit more background about Chief Justice Salmon Chase; he was appointed by President Abraham Lincoln and was as direct contrast philosophically and politically to the Chief Justice Taney whom he succeeded on the court. Sources also mention that he appointed the first African-American lawyer; John Rock to defend cases before the Supreme Court. John Rock's resume was quite impressive, as he was the first African-American to obtain a medical degree; he was also a lawyer and a dentist.

The first case to be mentioned is that of *Texas v. White (1869)*. It had something to do with the Confederate State legislature illegally selling bonds held and owned by Texas during the Civil War. The Reconstruction government of Texas brought suit against these powers and Chief Justice Chase ultimately ruled in favor of the state of Texas retaining the bonds or the payment. In the opinion statements, key points that Justice Salmon brought up were that the state of Texas was part of the Union and that, in so many words, she was Constitutionally and "indissolubly" bound to the other states in a "perpetual union." This relationship overrode any Confederate ties and therefore those bonds that were illegally sold had to be, as aforementioned, returned or repaid. Moral to the Story: Union ties between the states are constitutionally bound and this legal relationship threatens all other subversive actions that would try to maneuver against this bond. Therefore, other legislative factions cannot supersede US Supreme Court powers, jurisdiction, or authority.

One other controversial case in which Chief Justice Chase gave decision was that in the case of *Ex parte McCardle*. In this instance there was a man who was publishing subversive and "incendiary" material posing threat to Reconstruction laws established by the Legislative branch of government. This was a big no no, and he was subsequently apprehended and put into custody by way of the Military Reconstruction Act of 1867. One might say today, that this gentleman was exercising his first amendment right to free speech and press. Not sure where or how the line is drawn between free speech and treason, in light of some of the things that have been said in media, song, and spoken word over the years. Nevertheless, this individual in custody had a lawyer who filed habeas corpus in the Circuit court and lost. They appealed to the Supreme Court and still a release was not granted under the decision given by Chief Justice Chase. The California twist to this case is that the legislative branch under article III, section 2 of the Constitution restricted the Supreme Court's jurisdiction in this case. This is ambiguous to me as to the reasoning why. Moral to the Story: Should this man be considered a political prisoner of the Confederate States or a Treasonous Subversive? Where is the line drawn between free speech and the promotion of treasonous thoughts, ideas, and actions?

## Chapter 42:

## Justice William Strong (1808-1895)

Justice William Strong was born in Connecticut and attended an Academy school for his pre-collegiate training. Groomed at Yale University and a member of Phi Beta Kappa Society, it was evident that Justice Strong would study law like so many of his colleagues and political predecessors. Justice Strong served as a democratic councilman, and although he was prepared for judgeship he was actually the second choice of President Ulysses Grant, and his first Supreme Court appointee suddenly died.

In terms of Justice Strong's judicial philosophy he ruled in favor of states' rights and against the Civil Rights act of 1866 which was primarily an act that confirmed full citizenship for African-Americans; notwithstanding some may have disapproved because it gave African-Americans the right to testify against Whites in the courts of Law. We will discuss two cases in particular that highlight Justice Strong's politics.

The first of the cases is that of *Bylew v. United States (1872).* In this case, you had a murder that took place with an axe involving two white males and four African -American victims. The case was a US Supreme Court case due to the state of Kentucky appealing to the federal courts defending the two White males by highlighting their state law that disallowed African-Americans, or more properly for that time, "Negroes" from testifying in court against White men, as well as from serving on juries. The US Supreme court ruled in favor of the conviction of these men; Justice Strong writing a dissenting opinion suggesting that in so many words, if the Court backed the Civil Rights Act of 1866 by validating testimony given by African American victims in this case, that it would set a precedent and the Federal Courts would become inundated with testimony from African-Americans against White males. Moral to the Story: From Justice Strong's dissenting opinion, it can be inferred that there was a concern that certain court judgments or decisions would open up the floodgates for justice to be served everywhere. Why would this have necessarily been a negative thing, considering it could promote justice, is the question that I would have liked to present in answer to Justice Strong's dissenting opinion. Albeit, possibly a court docket management nightmare if this thing caught on in the African-American community; nevertheless, would not it have had a positive affect on society and racial or prejudicial violent behavior amongst the citizenry in general overtime, as harsh punishment and convictions against hate crimes would have possibly served as a deterrence to future acts malicious and unwarranted violence.

A second case we will discuss is that matter of *Strauder v. West Virginia.* In this case and its companion cases, the subject matter primarily dealt with certain defendants—namely African-Americans, being able to be entitle to a jury of their peers. Certain laws prohibited or discriminated in jury selection process in which those of certain race where excluded. Actually, it was more a technical case about certain cases on equal rights being "removed" to the Federal Courts. Supreme Courts ruled that in such cases where State powers are unable to "remedy" denial of rights cases, this cased fall under the jurisdiction of the Federal Courts through the appeals process. Moral to the Story: There is a method to the madness.

## Chapter 43:

## Justice Joseph Philo Bradley (1813-1892)

Justice Joseph Bradley started off at a young age as a teacher at heart. Sources report that he was sponsored by the Dutch Reformed Church to attend to the study of ministry at the prestigious Rutgers University. After he completed his undergraduate program, he held the job of an Academy Head Master and went on to pursue his personal interest in Law. After some practice, President Ulysses Grant took notice and nominated him to a seat on the US Supreme Court as an Associate Justice.

Upon taking an overview of a few of Associate Justice Bradley's opinions, one would say that he opinioned on the wrong side of history if we take the issues that were at the forefront and bring them into perspective of how common sense contemporary thinking would rule today. Regardless of political affiliation, the notion that women were not suited for law or to their ambitions outside of the home is almost criminal even though he he used the "God Argument" that a women's place was only in the home and to be a wife and mother. Moral to the Story: Well, I believe that these two occupations for women are definitely a high calling, but also, to have the choice of career, given the fact that there are so many effective, productive, and necessary female attorney's, out in the world today testifies to the sheer error of this old mode of thinking.

Another instance of a possible skewed justice ruling that Justice Bradley stepped in to decide was in the case of the Coifax Massacre. If the reader will remember we discussed the case where those gentlemen were released from custody after some 200 Blacks were found dead at the voting poles. Now, there was controversy between who started the gun fight or some other technicality about the two mobs being under military jurisdiction, but Justice Bradley ruled on the side that the Supreme Court should not meddle in the affairs of paramilitary and group attacks, which allowed for further increased paramilitary actions happening in the South so much so that the results of these actions were the forced removal of Republicans from office, further disenfranchisement of the Black vote, and support to the Democratic takeover of state legislatures, not to mention increased instances of Jim Crow laws so reported by specific online Sources. Moral to the Story: It seems that some Justices were more politicians with biases and certain leanings as any other Councilman or Representative official. These partisan biases that were not to enter the Judicial Branch of Government sort of tainted pure judgments and allowed for certain politics to dictate the consciousness and key elements in important decision making of our Supreme Court.

## Chapter 44:

## Justice Ward Hunt (1810-1886)

Justice Ward Hunt was born in the state of New York and attended the Oxford and Geneva Academies for his pre-collegiate grooming and education. It was Union College for undergrad and then Litchfield Law School in Connecticut for his Graduate studies. Justice Ward Hunt was admitted to the bar in 1831.

In terms of his famous or notorious rulings, it is more known that Justice Hunt mostly ruled in concurrence with the majority opinions on the court. There were a few cases in which he dissented and one in particular that gained notoriety and that was that of the case *The United States v. Susan B. Anthony.* The late 1800's was a time of sort of gaining inertia for the time of women's suffrage in America; nevertheless, this courageous women, Susan B. Anthony found it within herself to vote on the premise that it was her constitutional right, only to be arrested and tried. I'm not sure if this is what put her on the $1 coin; nevertheless, according to one source, Justice Hunt basically was running a circus court surrounding her trial. Please excuse my irreverence, but it is reported that he would not permit her to testify, but took her testimony that was given upon her arrest, commanded the jury to return a guilty verdict, and read the opinion that he had written before the trial had even started? She was fined $100 which she adamantly declared that she wound "never pay" and thus Justice Ward in a silver lining to the story granted that she not to be jailed for her declining to pay. Interestingly enough, it was the election inspectors who allowed Susan B. Anthony and her troop to vote, whom were apprehended (the election inspectors that is) and jailed and ultimately pardoned by President Ulysses Grant. It is unclear as to how long the election inspectors were in custody, but regardless of the fact, it makes one think of all the commotion surrounding the election cycle today with the controversy between President Trump and incoming Joe Biden and allegations of voter fraud across the United States.

Moral to the Story: Movements don't gain momentum over night or become ultimately effective with one single news covered event or even civil case, but the constant dripping of and wrangling for justice is what causes change. These truths are proven evident by the examples of abolition, suffrage, and even the civil rights movement which were not moments in history of pure coincidence, but planned and strategic maneuvers by individuals and organizations attacking the stalemate of status quo through tactical and well thought out procedures.

## Chapter 45:

## Justice Morrison Waite (1816-1888)

Justice Morrison Waite was born in the state of Connecticut, and served as the Chief Justice of the US Supreme Court for 12 years. He practiced as an Attorney at Law after his attendance at Yale University and was known as an adversary of slavery, yet he ironically fell on the side of the majority to overturn the *Civil Rights Act of 1875*. He served as a Chief Justice of the Court his court oversaw some just under 3500 cases. There is no way to go through each case in this vehicle herein, yet we will select a few that speak to his program and philosophy of judgment.

One case in particular that stood out when reviewing some of the cases heard under the Waite Court was that of *Reynolds v. United States (1878)*. Apparently Reynolds, a member of the Latter-day Saints Church, had a mind to test the procedure of law, and exercise his first amendment right; that is to practice bigamy. He was so enthused at his undertaking that he provided the Prosecutor's office with eye witnesses of his second marriage, while the first wife still living, and thought with great assurance that he would be protected by the fact that he was a male member of the Mormon church earnestly practicing and exercising his "freedom of religion." Well, things went sour, and he was convicted under the law in the Utah State Courts, in which he and his attorney appealed to the US Supreme Court The Supreme Court, under Chief Justice Waite's ultimate opinion upheld the inferior State Court's conviction, with the exception of the hard labor part of the sentence, which came along with the two year imprisonment. Part of the reasoning of the State court was that Reynolds knowingly broke the law or in the grand jury's words, "the want of understanding on his part that he was committing a crime---did not excuse him." So, it seems that his social experiment backfired and he was found to have criminal intent. Moral to the Story: I guess when some laws are expressly spelled out and certain actions deemed as criminal and illegal, they are best left untested or challenged unless one is ready to pay the penalty of a sentence, which may include imprisonment, fine, or hard labor. Yet and still, throughout history, certain laws regarding civil rights had to be challenged in order for progress to be made and to get to a point or state of equality in respect to individuals and certain racial groups being regarded by the law.

This next case that we will take a brief overview look at happens to deal with the issue of cruel and unusual punishment and how certain capital punishments were justified or preserved by the $8^{th}$ amendment of the Constitution. In this case, a premeditated murder was transacted by a Wallace Wilkerson. The background of the individuals seems to be unclear as to their relationship but that they were in several heated altercations before the event. The judge in the case gave Wilkerson, in the *Wilkerson v. Utah (1879)* case, the delightful option of execution methods, which were hanging, decapitation, or firing squad. Well, the story goes, after one year of waiting for a pending execution, Wilkerson appealed to the court, arguing that the nature of the firing squad was "cruel and unusual" and that it violated the $8^{th}$ amendment. The Supreme Court would hear none of this argument, striking the appeal. Moreover, this case's opinion was used in a later case; the reasoning suggesting the "humanity" of lethal injection against the Old English methods of burning, beheading, and disembowelment which was where the methods that the $8^{th}$ amendment were actually referring to as cruel and unusual. Moral to the Story: Capital Punishment has always been a touchy subject in the political sphere and sometimes even lately omitted from the platform of conversation. Lethal Injection, Electrocution, Gas chamber, Hanging, and Firing Squad; the latter two still seem to be a bit archaic although possibly the quickest and less painful way for one to Meet their Maker. In fact, after further thought and consideration, they all do seem to be deadly ways to transpire and possibly serve a purpose of invoking fear in the individual criminal about to face execution. Not sure of the statistics on which methods are used most in US capital punishment sentencing.

## Chapter 46:

## Justice John Marshall Harlan (1833-1911)

Justice John Harlan was born in Kentucky and served in several capacities for the US State department. He was an Attorney, served as Attorney General of Kentucky, as well as an Associate Justice of the US Supreme Court. He was known for dissenting in most of his opinions so much so, he was tagged, "The Great Dissenter." Some of his political or judicial philosophy led him to oppose the emancipation proclamation and yet he was a strong Unionist, served in the Kentucky Infantry, as well as advocated for many civil liberties in his cases. Some of his notable dissenting opinions where civil rights were being limited were cases such as *Plessy v. Ferguson,* as well as the *Civil Rights Cases.* Much of his philosophy centered around increased government strength, along with a strong consideration for those who were in lower social and economic classes.

As mentioned, Justice John Harlan was a dissenter in the *Plessy v. Ferguson (1896)* case. The details of which are captivating to say the least. In this case, you had Mr. Plessy who was "7/8$^{ths}$" white and found breaking separation laws by finding his seat in a place other than with the black passengers. Horner Plessy was officially charged with boarding the "whites only" train in New Orleans, Louisiana's in direct violation of the Separate Car Act. Of course Plessy appealed to the State Supreme Court which delightfully heard his case and up held the decision. Mr. Plessy was faced with a conviction sentence of a $25 fine and proceeded to move his case forward to the United States Supreme Court in which he was met with another unfavorable decision. Yet, one silver lining from all this was Justice Harlan's dissenting opinion on the case. He stated that the "US constitution is color-blind, and neither knows nor tolerates class among citizens." The truth to this statement would be left to be seen in those thousands of cases heard thereafter; those both related and unrelated to race or class; notwithstanding, the *Plessy v. Ferguson Case (1896)* would go down in history known as the "separate but equal case" and although never officially overturned, was in many ways eroded by future civil rights cases. Moral to the Story: Within in the history of documented Supreme Court Cases, those dealing with segregation and Civil Rights Acts and even various unconstitutional racial or unfair laws; even great effort and good fight did not always precipitate the desired result. Yet and still, something about the moral or ethical code, fortitude, and character of man could be understood. Moreover, that no man is good, but God and that inwardly, innately we are evil and our evil is detected by the laws we create and the things we do. This is not to say that there is no good in our laws or the men who framed the governing Constitution of our Republic, or that even that the men and women who are bent on breaking and challenging such statues have no virtue, but that we acknowledge the subtle residence of greed, envy, thirst for power, cruelty, unjust, and even overall immorality and the overall depravity of man in our Earthly System. Oh, but there is also good done and heroic works accomplished now and has been throughout the history of the Courts. Hopefully throughout the epochs of time, we find that we progress from glory to glory intellectually, judicially, and even in our government and technology with God in our active mind and memory.

In a second case that we will consider, we will discuss the state seizure of private property and how federal regulations mandated that there be "just compensation" for any private property seized. In the case of Chicago, *Burlington & Quincy Railroad Co. v. City of Chicago (1897),* the state of Chicago had it in mind to widen a certain street and in doing so confiscated property of certain individuals as well as some areas owned by Chicago, Burlington & Quincy Railroad Company. In the trial, the jury ruled in favor of the citizens who lost their property in the ordeal receiving proper financial recompense and as for the railroad company, they received 1 dollar. Of course the railroad company proceeded to take their case to a higher court feeling that they were shafted and rightly deserved more. Justice Harlan wrote on the case as it was heard in the US Supreme Court. I should not fail to mention that the reason why the Rail Road company did not get their full compensation was because the State Court ruled that the due process of law was kept by allowing the RR company to appeal the courts first decision. This was essentially a technicality, and Justice Harlan addressed the issue in his opinion as Chief

Justice on the case declaring that due process must have "substance" which included just compensation. This was to be the process whenever States took over private property and used it for public use. The rightful owners, whoever they were, were to be properly paid out. Moral to the Story: Any time State or local governments take from local citizens or even private companies or corporations, with respects to private property; those diminished entities should be rightly compensated.

## Chapter 47

## Justice William Burnham Woods (1824-1887)

Justice William Woods was born in Ohio, my original place of birth. He would eventually attend what is now Case Western Reserve University and complete his undergraduate studies, only to progress his academic career onto Yale where he studied law and latter would practice with a firm and pass the Bar. He was a Military Veteran, as he philosophically aligned with the Democratic Party, yet agreed with Union ideas and fought in the Civil War.

Justice William Woods was nominated to the Federal level of Judgeship twice. The first time to the Federal Circuit Court in which he served in the 5th Circuit and was nominated by then President Ulysses Grant. His second nomination was an obvious promotion, as he was nominated to the US Supreme Court as an Associate Justice by then President Ruthford B. Hayes. Ironically, sources report that Justice Woods had more of an impact in his Circuit tour than on the US Supreme Court. We will consider a few of the cases when he sat on the US Supreme Court here within.

This first case, *Ex parte Crow Dog*, deals with a at type of Tribal Sovereignty, as it addresses a murder between two Indian men, one named Crow Dog who apparently murdered a Sioux Chief by the name of Spotted Tail. As the story goes, the matter was immediately handled by the Tribal Council on the Reservation and Crow dog paid his restitution to the family and was considered done with the issue by the Indian High Council. Notwithstanding, the federal courts got involved and Crow Dog was taken into custody only to file habeas corpus, on the grounds that he had already been tried on the issue. The US Supreme court released him on these grounds yet there were future statutes legislated to restrict Tribunal Council. Moral to the Story: Sometimes we don't realize the power of major organizational Councils. I think of the Catholic Church and how it has handled many of its Priest's past cases of child sexual misconduct by moving their preist to another perish instead of immediately turning them over to the authorities. I'm not sure if this is still the practice, but it is another example of a type of Sovereignty held by a major organization.

In a second case where Justice Woods was present during its time being heard; we have the matter of *Hurtado v. California (1884).* In this case, another act of murder, this time dealing with a man, Joseph Hurtado, his wife, and their close associate, Jose Estuardo. As the narrative goes, Hurtado attempted on numerous occasions to prohibit the adultery, and further prevent himself from going to the extreme by first sending his wife away to stay with family and then secondly roughing Estuardo up at a bar. His final measures were to fully take matters into his own hands and commit murder, for which he was taken into custody and tried without a grand jury. Here lies the dilemma and the issue that perturbed some in the legal community, Hurtado was tried, convicted of murder, and sentenced to death all without a hearing of "24 of his equals and neighbors" (Dissenting Opinion by Justice Harlan). The main issues were the question as to whether or not Hurtado's 14$^{th}$ amendment rights, that is *due process* were violated not. There were other technicalities surrounding the *indictment clause* of the fifth amendment; yet and still, majority Supreme Court ruled that Hurtado's due process right was in fact not violated. Moral to the Story: There is a difference between Vengeance and Vigilantism; and further, both may have its consequences when brought to the light of the law; moreover, one may receive more justice than mercy.

## Chapter 48:

## Justice Stanely Mathews (1824-1889)

Justice Stanely Mathews was born in the great state of Ohio and fared well in his early life and young adult years. So much so, that he attended Kenyon College, met a future President whom he would later keep an acquaintance with along with founding a prestigious literary club with many great literary scholars and American leaders whom frequented the social organization. The name of this club was the "Literary Club of Cincinatti," and it appears that it was more than just an ordinary book club, but a place for leaders and intellectuals to come together, discuss the topics of the day, fraternize, and engage culture. Justice Stanely studied Law and was admitted to the Bar; in addition to these things, he also edited a newspaper that had an abolitionist bent.

Turns out that inwardly Justice Mathews was a strong patriot, as he resigned his civil service position as a Federal Attorney to take on a military position serving as a ranking officer under whom would eventually be President Rutherford B. Hayes in the Union Army. After two years of service, he returned to civilian life as well as his practice and found himself involved in

Congress. Both Interesting and Fascinating how providence would have many of our past countrymen who were leaders and governing officials follow a similar trajectory in their scholarly life and career. Many Presidents, Politicians, Attorney's, Justices, and Leaders studied law after graduation; some took on military service, and others were involved in some type of civic or government work before they landed in their Federal Careers. Some had altruistic, divine, or religious interest, and others I would assume were self-calculating nationalist who believed in ruling and protecting their country.

Justice Stanely Mathews was nominated to the U.S. Supreme Court by none other than his longtime friend, military officer, literary buddy, and close associate President Hayes. Sources say there was some miner issue surrounding the fact that Justice Mathews had such close ties to the Railroad because of his years serving in the capacity of council and representative to the industry. A few cases that were heard during his tenure we will consider here within.

In the case of *New England Mutual Life Insurance Co. v. Woodworth* we encounter a situation where one has an insurance policy that has not been paid, and the insurance company's reasoning for not paying was that the claimant moved to another state, or more specifically, that the claimant should have filed suit in the same state as where the policy was originated. The narrative is actually more detailed. It was the beneficiary's wife that took out the life insurance policy in Michigan, and then died in New York, and then the Husband moved to Illinois where he filed lawsuit against the Insurance company for refusing to pay. Ultimately, the Supreme Court ruled that the insurance company had to pay on the grounds of *simple contract debts.* Essentially that instruments like insurance policies are to be paid for the "assets where the debtor resides, irregardless of where the policy was originated," in terms of geographic location. Moral to the Story: One might consider it common place for a party in a peer-to-peer interaction to refuse to pay on a business deal or word of mouth transaction. Nevertheless, one would assume it to be far less common, one would think anyway, for a major corporation or big business to refuse to pay a smaller party; moreover, breech a contract on technicality and persist in court on these technicalities instead of general principle. On the contrary, maybe this kind of thing happens all the time. The point is, according to the rule of law, financial abuses of this kind and sort should not be.

In a similar case that had the inverse outcome, in that the Supreme Court decision was for the insurance company to retain their payment due to a technicality in the contract which prevented the beneficiary from being paid out. In the case of, *Drennen v. London Assurance Co.*, we have a gentleman who purchased fire insurance policies, not one, but two policies in the state of Minnesota. According to sources, there was an incident, and a substantial amount of cash was to be paid to the claimant under the condition that the property was still held in tow, title and all, with no attempt to sale or transfer. Well, such was the case, that Dennen in his defense claimed that he had a partner within his firm named Arndt who the property was transferred to. This line of argument did not hold up during trial, in which the US Supreme Court determined that there was no "partnership" and therefore no payments would have to be ensued by the London Assurance Insurance company. Moral to the Story: Technicalities, Technicalities can work for or against the plaintiff or the defendant especially in contract cases where certain statues, limitations, and restrictions are spelled out. One does best to understand the details, and loop wholes of their specific contracts; Career, Military Service, Mortgage, Lease and Car financing and agreements, Plea Bargains, and Probation Sentences and Securities and Business Partnerships, but then again, not everyone has the general language of the law, various property and intellectual, civil rights, or a Law degree. So, what are we to do when most folks also have no time or do not want to take the time to read and understand what they are signing? Especially when pressured by the One on the other end to hurry up and get one with it, because time is a wasting. Fortitude, Patience and Diligence are both virtues for these matters.

## Chapter 49

## Justice Horace Gray (1828-1902)

Justice Horace Gray was born a resident of Boston Massachusetts, and being the brainiac that he was, wind up attending Harvard College at the tender age of 13. Sources report that he graduated in a timely matter and continued his graduate education at the prestigious Harvard School of Law. Due to his love for knowledge, research and attention to detail, Justice Gray somehow fell into the position of an advisor to the governor of Massachusetts, as he painstakingly edited over some 15 volumes of court documents. After this work and experience, Justice Gray was appointed to the State Supreme Court and soon thereafter, just about a decade's time, made Chief Justice of the Massachusetts State Supreme Court. This was not the end of his ascension in holding federal government positions. When President Chester A. Aurthur took office, he would eventually nominate the well-known Justice Horace Gray to the United States Supreme Court as an Associate Justice.

Justice Horace Gray served his time on the US Supreme Court while Justice Melville Weston Fuller was Chief Justice. Herein we will only highlight a few of those cases, as the number of cases heard on the Supreme Court during those years was extensive as it is today. One interesting case that sort of brings the to mind the Hollywood Film "Catch me if you Can" starring actor Leonardo DiCaprio playing convicted felon and FBI agent Frank Abagnale who posed as a Pilot, Lawyer, and Medical Doctor and wrote fake or fraudulent checks all over the United States of America. Interesting and engaging movie, but it only relates to this next case in the sense that the plaintiff in this case practiced medicine with his Father and Grandfather for a number of years in the state of West Virginia without the proper credentials. It must also be said, I don't think anyway, that his intentions were to be a fraudulent Medical Doctor, but just to be a part of the family business in which he grew up in. Eventually, there was an Act passed in 1881 requiring those that practiced medicine to have obtained at least one of three requirements: 1).Diploma from reputable college, 2). Certificate showing at least 10 years practice, or 3). Successful passing of a state-administered exam. In Frank Dent's case; ironic he has the same first name as the character played in the aforementioned movie; nevertheless, he through self-determination attended an eclectic institution titled the American Eclectic Medical College. Unfortunately, even after Mr. Dent presented his diploma as a certificate of completion and began to return to his family medical practice, he was arrested by Chair of the Medical Board in West Virginia. To make a long story short, Both State and Supreme Court ruled in favor of the state medical board, even when the Court was presented with the due process clause argument of the $14^{th}$ amendment under the grounds that Mr. Dent had the civil right to practice his vocation.

US Supreme court ruled essentially that because medicine was such a profession that required a significant body of knowledge as well as delt with the life and death of other human beings, that the necessary state requirements must be followed. Moral to the Story: Sometimes to truly take on the Family Business, one must go to school, and an Accredited school at that, to be fully legitimatized in the eyes of the State. Even though years of experience may qualify after a certain number of years, one needs the official documentation as proof they have mastered or are at least proficient at their craft or vocation.

A second case during the time that Justice Horace Gray was an Associate Justice of the US Supreme Court was the case of *Hans v. Louisiana (1890).* In this case we have a situation where a citizen of the state had sought to bring legal action against his State due to the fact that he was the possessor of bonds issued by the State of which he felt were going to be deemed unsolvable an unable to be redeemed for the matured price. These efforts were deemed futile in light of the fact that federal law stipulated that citizens could not bring suit against another state. Nevertheless, the Justices on the case did not fail to mention in the discussion part of the opinion that the Framers had not considered individual citizens suing and bringing up charges against their own state in the Federal Courts. Moral to the Story: Looks like according to these rulings that the State can somehow get out of paying interest due on bonds. I guess the reasoning behind this would be that these bonds are just like any other financial instrument; there is a risk involved, and private investors must make these allowances beforehand; moreover, do their own contingency planning without considering suing thier State as one of those options.

## Chapter 50:

## Justice Samuel Blatchford (1820-1893)

Justice Samuel Blatchford was native to New York, and finished his undergraduate degree at what is now Columbia University. He took on a number of positions before getting into business with his father his uncle who were both attorneys and eventually opened his own law firm sometime after successfully being admitted to the bar. In terms of positions with the State Department, he served as a sort of US Ambassador to the Papal States although sources record him as a Presbyterian. Justice Blatchford was nominated to the US District Court by President Andrew Johnson, which speaks to his readiness considering this was this was his first official appointment. He later was nominated to the US Supreme Court by President Chester Arthur where he tenured and wrote over some 425 opinions and 2 dissents. We will discuss a few of those cases herein.

The first case we will discuss is one of personal injury or better put, a denial of worker's compensation, and the rule of law on when companies have the right not to pay their employees for such tragic injuries. The case was heard on the US Supreme Court in 1893, that is *Kohn v. McNulta* and ultimately the ruling was that when workers are fully experienced in their position and sustain injury, and further, "there is no neglect or extenuating circumstances on the company's part", then compensation does not have to be paid. In the details of this case, we have a worker Kahn, who worked as a type of operator, or "switchman" and had one of his upper extremities crushed while trying to pair two freight cars. The jury of the District Court on this case actually ruled that the claimant should receive $10,000.00, but somehow through the fact that there was no actual "cause of action" or through no fault of company did this tragedy happen, the jury decision was dismissed, hence Kohn appealed to a higher court. The Supreme Court decision was the same, with a detailed Opinion even after a defense from Kohn that the equipment he was operating was brand new and the company had not made him aware of these changes. The Court ruled as first mentioned above, and declared that the due to the claimant's experience the minor changes in equipment should not have put him in any position that he could not "cope with." Moral to the Story: Personally, I think any Personal Injury Attorney worth his salt would have had a field day with this case. I'm just a layman to the law, but this judgment does seem a little harsh if in fact the equipment was new and Kahn had not been properly trained. Good Companies these days are so careful to train their employees so as not to be considered negligent, that I think if a situation like this happened in these modern times the award decision might have been different, and in favor of Kahn. Notwithstanding, on the contrary, the caveat in the opinion is that the judgment considered that the claimant was an "experienced worker." I guess that would hold some precedence, but who determines how far experience transfers to new technology and new equipment. It would be like an old, experienced and certified Car Mechanic having to work on top-of-the-line cars with new computer software and technologies foreign to his training. Although he be experienced and truly certified, if he wasn't trained on the new equipment or new technologies and having to rely on his obsolete experience alone, how can he succeed without error or even injury to the car or possibly himself? So, seems the liability would lay at the company's feet for not properly training and recertifying all of their Employee Assets.

In a second case, unrelated to the first, we have the matter of *Elk v. Wilkins*. And whereas from today's standpoint it would seem that this case should be matter of dual citizenship or some type of multi-national citizenship status, it is actually a matter of being denied full US citizenship by the United States Courts on the basis that Elk was a Native American, and his Legal allegiance was to his Tribe and their Jurisdiction; even despite or in light of his US birth, renouncing his tribal allegiance, and attempting to dwell among white American citizens. One might immediately jump to the conclusion and call these rulings "racist" or even "unjust" as they were considered to be laws that excluded Native Americans from US Citizenship and were later corrected or adjusted by the Indian Citizenship act of 1924. Yet and still, after second thought, there probably were certain rights and privileges that came along with being bound to the Native American Legal Jurisdiction within the United States. Although it must have seemed unfair not to be considered full US Citizenship in one's native land, the possibility that one could probably flee full criminal penalty by being extradited to his Tribal Courts might have been a thing that happen on occasion. Not sure, I'm speculating; but it would seem that their courts would be more lenient than the US judicial system toward their own tribal members. So, in a nation within a nation, where the peoples actually feuded over territory and land, I guess it may seem not fully "just" but justifiable and understandable from the colonizers perspective why the American Government was slow to allow full citizenship to Native Americans, whom may have posed a threat. Moral to the Story: The passage of time has a way of Healing and Correcting History. Look at many Native American peoples and tribes today. I presume to be no expert, but in the State of Arizona where I live, there is a Native American Hospital, and Reservations and Casinos, Educated Youth who graduate college, Generational wealth, and those who receive special benefits and payments from the Federal Government. All these positive things do not make light of the ramped alcoholism, drug use, domestic violence and incarcerations, that still plague their community, as with many communities.

## Chapter 51:

## Justice Lucius Quintus Cincinnatus Lamar (1825-1893)

Justice Lucius Lamar held a few positions before his recommendation and appointment to the US Supreme Court. He was born native of Georgia and would ultimately attend what is now
Emory University. His post graduate years seemed to be a bit disjointed as he served as a Mathematics Professor, practiced law, and established a cotton plantation. Perhaps he was overly focused on his economic preservation. Nevertheless, he was promoted as an elected official and served as a Democrat in the House of Representatives. It could be said that Justice Lamar owned just over 30 slaves and resigned his position of Professorship to serve as an confederate officer during the Civil War. He was a special Liaison to France and a sort of Ambassador to Russia during this time. This sort of background sort of built his judicial philosophy as he was known as an adversary of Reconstruction, did not agree with the Black Vote, and was known to advocate for the idea, "the supremacy of the unconquered and unconquerable Saxon race." He was nominated by President Grover Cleveland to the office Associate Justice of the United States Supreme Court. Herein we will consider just a few of the cases that were heard on the Supreme Court while he served as an Assoicate Justice.

The first one being quite interesting and delving into the relm of the Government seizure of property, or more properly put, dealing with the concept of "*Escheat*," and this is when an individual or entity has ceased to exist and has not properly put in place a legal beneficiary or heir to receive the inheritance or transfer of property and/or that estate. Under these circumstances, this wealth, no matter how large or small, falls into the care, ownership, and responsibility of the State and Government to confiscate, maintain, and or sale and make dispose of. In the controversial case of *Late Corp. of the Church of Jesus Christ of Latter-Day Saints v. United States* we have an example of the aforementioned dilemma. In this matter it seems that the LDS had property worth an upward $2.8 million, and only a little under $400,000.00 worth of assets were seized by the Utah State officials. Part of this sudden seizure seemed political considering thier practice of polygamy which was illegal and this practice was discontinued by the LDS church and promoted thus in thier 1890 Manifesto. These happenings led there being a congressional enactment that released LDS formally ceased assets back to the said church. It must be noted that the Chief Justice who dissented on the case highlighted the fact that it was right that the Congress criminalized the group practice of polygamy; notwithstanding, to prosecute the church through confiscating thier assets because of thier criminal actions was wrong. Moral to the Story: The LDS church seemed to have overcome this Escheat while others today have thier property seized and Foreclosed because of nonpayment, death without beneficiary, or even imprisonment. These homes are auctioned off and sold through the HUD program for sometimes 50% of the houses value, by banks who would rather keep the profit than manage the property. On the note of these levied charges being political, who knows, although this tactic seemed effective in manipulating the LDS church to amend her polygamous ways.

The next case in which we will touch and expound upon is that of *Ross v. McInyre (1891)*. In this case, we have a scenario of expressed American law exercised over foreign sailors on US ships in international waters or in countries in which America has "extraterritorial jurisdiction." More specifically, a Canadian sailor was upon an American ship and killed a man; for which he was at first sentenced to death. Notwithstanding, President Rutherford B. Hayes made an interjection to the sentence and gave the very unlucky fellow a life sentence of hard labor in the Federal Penitentiary. The Canadian man, John Ross accepted his mitigated sentence and later sought to be released by filing a habeas corpus on the grounds of his foreign citizenship, his birth place being that of Prince Edward Island. The Supreme Court dismissed his motion, on the fundamental principle that Ross was subject to US governing powers and jurisdiction the moment he enrolled on a United States ship. Moral to the Story: What kind of nation would we be if we let all international criminals escape thier just sentence by fleeing to their own countries after the offence was committed. My thoughts immediately jump to hateful acts of Terror, committed both at home, that is, State Side, and abroad. The controversy of those sitting in Guantanamo Bay, and past prosecutions of those who have committed such Grevious acts of hate and terror. In many ways, mercy does not seem just for such individuals, and yet for arguments sake, is it all a matter of perspective? I think, either way you look at it, mass murder of innocent people on the basis of extreme religious causes is wrong, and those who commit such acts, whether deceived or conscious of their actions should be prosecuted and brought to justice, whether that sentence be capital punishment or a life of imprisonment.

## Chapter 52:
## Justice Melville Fuller (1833-1910)

Justice Melville Fuller was native to the state of Maine and a key piece of trivia, both his paternal and maternal grandfathers were Judges. He attended Harvard University for a year, but graduated from Bowdoin College with honors. He would eventually go back to Harvard for Law school but only attend for half a year, according to sources and leave without graduating in 1855. Ironically, he eventually would become not just an Associate Justice on the US Supreme Court, but the Chief Justice reigning in the Fuller Court. He would oversee *Plessy v. Ferguson*, *Pollock v. Farmers' Loan and Trust Co.*, and *United States v. E.C. Knight Co.* just to name a few of the more prominent cases that he sat Chief Justice for. In line and up until this accomplishment, Justice Fuller also served in the House of Representatives for one term, edited a newspaper, and was president of the Illinois State Bar. He was ultimately nominated to the US Supreme Court by President Grover Cleveland.

The first most spoke of and I believe well known was the separate but equal case, *Plessy v. Ferguson (1896).* Of course, this was some two decades before *Brown v. Board of Education (1954)* so integration had not yet happened, and segregation of schools, churches, business offices, and even government buildings was the norm. Not to let you the reader down, but the Plessy v. Ferguson case is actually widely considered a misjudgment on the grounds that it considered blacks inferior and upheld the law that "separate but equal" was in fact just, even though most facilities were in no way close to equal in quality or even in aesthetics. The reasoning of the court was that "blacks could not expect all the social norms and distinctions of society to change simply on the basis of race." Well, during that time, that may have seemed like a pretty logical argument, if you were White and didn't want to be bothered by those exslaves. On the other hand, if you were Black, Negro, or Colored, as we were so politely called before the politically correct term of African-American, and you were seeking upward socially, equality in education for your children, tired of being treated second class, and desired a good opportunity for economic sustainability, these were some of the obstacles that you would have had to overcome. The funny thing is, Plessy was what was called an "octoroon," that is someone who was only 1/8ths Black and 7/8ths White. Who knows, had he been any darker and tried to sit in the whites only car, maybe he would have been beat, lynched or arrested instead of having his day in court considered the social climate and behavior of that day. It's funny how even today, our neighborhoods still seem segregated, most churches, some business centers, and the gap of wealth continues to widen between the rich and the poor. And I honestly ask myself, is it a question of race, or more so a question, these days, of hard work, ethics, self-determination, ingenuity, and business acumen. I don't doubt that the ills of racism and discrimination, still exist out there in the world, but I no longer feel that it is an excuse for mediocrity or defeat; and I say this taking an honest hard look at myself. More often than not, it is our own actions that causes our undoing. I feel and believe there is opportunity for everyone to succeed and do something in America if we look to God and inward to ourselves and apply those gifts and

talents innately planted by the hand of our Creator and given to us to be developed, if we would only patiently stay the course.

Yes, some have it easier than others, but such is life, to wine and complain, would only make one a poor sport. I can't say that I have been perfect, but to blame one's ultimate economic defeat and on the "System" or "The White Man" I think is a bit of a cop out. For sure many clever minded individuals and other than white peoples have used the same system for their overall benefit, social upward mobility, education, financial welfare, and befriended the White man instead of considering him the enemy of their demise and had better lives. This does not dismiss or ignore history or certain current atrocities of misguided and hateful individuals against blacks, but why not free oneself from Hatred, so as not to be mentally, economically, and physically stuck and move forward in a Spirit of forgiveness, drive and self-determination. In my opinion, these thoughts fair better than the Negativity of anti-establishment, subversive, and overly aggressive actions that only further divide and promote generational hatred and resent on all sides. So, Moral to the Story: Segregation was a major thing of the past and is seen in remnants of society even today. Not officially, but the unspoken norms, of where people live, and who belongs and who's neighborhood, seem obvious, but then again, one cannot and should not be prosecuted for being successful. So, in light of these things, I think the solution is that all people do their best, learn how to overlook the hurtful past, and make no excuse for failure. I paraphrase the proverb that says, "the just falls seven times, but the Lord delivers him out of all of them." Meaning that, and not to sound cliché but, it's not that we fall, or fail, or even get tired from the journey, but that we get up, keep going, and never give up.

The next case, *United States v. E.C. Knight Co.* We have a major suger refining company that is becoming massive behemoth of a manufacturer and distributor by acquiring smaller companies. The federal government took not ultimately ruling that power belonged to the States to regulated their own manufacturing woes, and only when interstate commerce was affected, then would Congress get involved. Chief Justice Fuller gave the majority opinion and essentially ruled that that which belongs to commerce is under federal powers and that which belongs the "power to control manufacture" is under the jurisdiction and "policing" powers of the State. Moral to the Story: One would think that in the individual's quest for Life, Liberty, and the pursuit of Happiness, that they would be able to grow, expand and acquire all they could manage, as long as they were paying their taxes, a legally sound company, and not performing acts of mischief against any individuals, local, state or federal governments. Yet, we see today, bemouth companies like: Amazon, Facebook, Google, Microsoft, and Apple have had their day in Court.

## Chapter 53:

## Justice David Josiah Brewer (1837 – 1913)

Justice David Brewer's parents were Missionaries far from home, and this is why he was born in the Ottoman Empire, in the city of Smyrna. He returned state side just intime to attend and graduate from the prestigious Yale College and for his post graduate studies he would finish up at Albany School of Law. Sources report that his early career was nomadic as he jumped around after trying to start his own law practice, and then from various Circuit Courts in Kansas for a number of years until he found himself nominated by President Benjamin Haris to the United States Supreme Court. Justice Brewer's jurisprudence philosophy was that of "for the people" as he advocated for people's rights and even looked upon the immigrant and those considered foreign with compassion. One unique case that we will herein discuss, as we will only discuss two from many, was that of Church of the *Holy Trinity v. United States (1892).*

In the case of the Holy Trinity v. United States (1892) it essentially delt with a technicality that of whether or not a foreign minister was considered the same as an ordinary foreign laborer. This distinction was important because there was a law enacted in 1885; The Alien Contract Labor Law, which prohibited, "the importation and migration of foreigners and aliens under contract or agreement to perform or service of any kind in the United States, it's territories, and the District of Columbia." Interestingly enough, the Court ruled that the minister was not to be considered a foreign laborer, although he was indeed a foreigner. Part of the reasoning for this case was the idea of following the Spirit of the Law instead of strict adherence to the Rule of the Law. It was thought that perhaps the Congress did not think, consider or intend for this law to cover Christian Ministers. Moral to the Story: How often is the concept,

*The Spirit of the Law* used in today's judgment in cases. How often do the Courts of today miss apply or get spot on those judgments, and how often through discernment we see how America was a different country back then with different norms and social constructs and social contracts that don't always fit in modern society. The solution is not that we change all the laws, but with caution, from my layman's perspective, we perceive what is just and right for this epoch.

A final case that we will herein discuss is that of *Muller v. Oregon (1908).* This case did not deal with women's rights per say, but more so the State's jurisdiction and authority to inspect businesses and make sure that women's rights were being preserved and respected. In this particular case, there was a situation where the women employee was made to work just a little over 10 hours in one day at a public laundry mat. The controversy surrounding this case is that Oregan state law stated that women were only allowed to work up to a certain amount; lesser hours that is than men. Another main issue of the case, was whether or not women had the capacity and/or should be given the "liberty" to negotiate e their own contracts. The Courts ruled in favor of upholding the conviction against Muller on the grounds of a bunch of language essentially stating in so many words that women are the weaker vessel and dependent upon men. Moral to the Story: In light of events in the progression of women's rights and liberties since 1908, there have been humungous leaps and bounds. There are women CEOs with their own companies, they vote, they go to war, they hold positions on all levels of government, including the Highest Courts. Although the county has yet to see a women President, there was just sworn into office a women Vice President Kamalah Harris. I think any man or court would have a hard time telling a woman that she couldn't work more than ten hours in a day if it was in her mind and desire to do so. Surely given the fact that many women hold MBAs, JDs, PhDs, and MDs; it is obvious that they can negotiate their own contracts.

## Chapter 54:

## Justice Henry Billings Brown (1836-1913)

Justice Henry Brown was born in Massachusetts and attended Yale College for both undergrad and his graduate studies, capping off his Law School tenure with a semester at Harvard Law. He was admitted into the Bar in Michigan and held two major state positions before his career started in the Judiciary. As he started his own law practice he would serve as Deputy U.S. Marshall, and Assistant United States Attorney, Est. Dist. Mich. His specialty during his own practice was admiralty law. He was later appointed to the District Court in Michigan by President Ulysses Grant. It was the President Benjamin Harrison who appointed him to the US Supreme Court, philosophically known as Republican, he opinioned a few major cases in his contribution to US Jurisprudence; herein we will consider a few, namely *Holden v. Hardy (1898),* and *Lochner v. New York (1905).* Although it must be noted that he wrote the majority opinion on *Plessy v. Ferguson (1896),* a case we have already considered, which solidified racial segregation as well as Jim Crow laws where blacks were treated as second class citizens; moreover, although there would be still remnants of this treatment afterward, legally things stayed the same until *Brown v. Board of Education (1954)*, in terms of desegregation.

The next case we will discuss briefly is that of *Holden v. Hardy (1898)*. It is a labor law case in which the Supreme Court decided that certain state maximum hour labor laws were indeed unconstitutional. The inverse of this idea being that putting a limitation on hours that miners and smelters could work was within the realm of the way things should be, and of course legally consistent with the constitution on the basis of the due process clause in the 14th Amendment. This clause concerns the government depriving a person of life, liberty, and property without proper *due process*. It was actually Justice Henry Brown who wrote the majority opinion on this case and in his line of reasoning he stated essentially, my interpretation, that because of the employer's position of authority, that of the hirer; the hiree would essentially always bend to the will of that authority disregarding their health. He further stated in so many words, that in these cases where employees were ill exercising their good judgment for selfinterest and health, it is the duty and responsibility of Congress to appropriately interpose. Moral to the Story: Any business that maintains "sweat shop" worker conditions for their employees is in danger of certain legislation and laws being enacted on the behalf of the employee that will possibly affect the bottom line of that business's revenue, production, distribution, and payroll model. Such disruption should have warned future businesses models to present the best environment and treatment toward their employees to rid of being held in contempt for lack luster or inhumane work conditions. I think of jobs where minimum wage pay seem like a cruel and unusual new age form of slavery. This may seem extreme, but, as mentioned in the opinion by Justice Brown, the employee's position limits them to the will of the employer, if they so decide to keep this position for their substance and livelihood. Furthermore, the compensation received, if it be minimum wage, is insufficient for today's current market place. One can be creative, frugal, and content within any station, yet and still, the laborer is worth thier fair wages.

A second case that we will consider that was heard during the time Justice Brown sat on the Supreme Court is that of *In re Neagle.* In this matter, US Federal Marshall David Neagle shot and killed a man as he was approaching the Justice Stephen J. Fields whom he was appointed to bodyguard. Apparently, there was a prior dispute a disagreement between the approaching man who was shot, David S. Terry, and the Justice Stephen J. Fields. To prevent a sudden attack US Marshall David Neagle opened fire and killed the man, or the alleged threat. Both he and the Justice were arrested, Justice Field later being released while Mr. Neagle was detained. It was the San Joaquin Sheriff who appealed the writ of Habeas corpus for Neagle's immediate least, as the case would go to the Supreme Court. The Supreme court actually confirmed the lower courts discission, ruling in a language that stated in so many words that Executive authority had the right to be exercised, in its own "necessary and proper authority." Essentially stating that those Federal officers operating and acting in the realm of their authority in their offices are immune from State prosecution. Moral to the Story: Sometimes within the scope of the job and the duty to protect, federal officers must be equipped, prepared and take decisive action. These actions include and are not limited to excessive force and use of power at the expense of criminals, terrorist, and alleged threats to national security, those foreign and domestic. So of course, having the weight of this responsibility, the government would benefit to protect our own and not allow State prosecution to interfere with Federal affairs. With all that being said, sometimes power is abused and there must be accountability of some sort. Unfortunately, there have been increased death from in our cities from our local police officers attempting to do their jobs, but in bad judgment and misguided decision making, have executed a number of black men. I have not considered the details of each individual case, and this is no blanket judgment on all policemen or white officers, but the stigma of racism persists within our city precincts because of this matter of black men being shot and killed. Some are mentally ill, some may even be deserving of jail and harsh sentencing, but it would be the duty of those deadly officers to apprehend and detain those persons, and hold their fire unless excessive and deadly force is absolutely necessary to remain lawful in the eyes of the overall General Public and the Black community.

## Chapter 55:

## Justice George Shiras Jr. (1832-1903)

Justice George Shiras was born in the state of Pennsylvania and did his undergrad work at Yale College. He would continue onto graduate studies at the Yale School of Law, and leave before graduation to start a practice in Iowa and continue reading and studying the law on his own. He ultimately became a Corporate Attorney representing many corporate giants in his region and some of the nation's top industrials were his clients. Justice Shiras was nominated to the US Supreme Court by President Benjamin Harrison after some over 37 years of private practice in which he never judged a case. There was a touch of nepotism as he recommended by his cousin whom was the Secretary of State. His political philosophy ranged from striking down income tax to upholding racial segregation as constitutional. He opinioned more than 250 majority decisions and 14 Decents in a little over a decade with his time on the US Supreme Court. We will consider briefly only two of his over 200 cases.

The first case we will discuss is significant that is the case of *Pollock v. Farmer's Loan & Trust Co.* This case primarily delt with income tax, and was adamantly opposed by Justice Melville Fuller would actually write the majority opinion. The details of the case involve a history dating back to the first tax that was posed during the American Civil War. This tax was dismissed in 1872, and then in the 1890's Congress levied the Wilson-Gorman Tariff Act which lowered tariffs and started taxing the asset classes we recognize today; such as, income, corporate profits, gifts, and inheritances. In this case, Chief Justice major reasoning for writing this decision against property income being taxed was that there was not a fair amount being "apportioned" among the States in terms of representation in the United States House of Representatives, which to me is ambiguous reasoning. Nevertheless, this case was indeed substantial because it actually prevented Congress from levying taxes for another two decades because the "apportionment" requirements were unfeasible. Later came the Revenue Act of 1913 just before World War I. Moral to the Story: Federal, State, and International taxes in many ways are necessary and useful for any Sovereign State or Country; the Federal Government to Operates a budget and this revenue levied funds the military and government infrastructure, pays State employees, build roads, government institutions, buildings, bridges, and State and Federal programs such as Food Stamps and Social Security. Not that this is an exhaustive list of federal billings, but Tariffs also play a role. That saying that Business is the Business of America rings true, and in business, finances are a bottom line. Not that I understand it all, but even our international debt to Gross Domestic Product ratio derives from some calculated idea to seek our ultimate profit as we sell debt to other nations, and buy theirs.

These entanglements we would hope ultimately would render a peaceful trusting relationship abroad among nations as we be financial bed fellows. Less we change our trending strategy and remain completely financially independent of all nations, cutting ourselves off from trade which flies in the face of the fundamental economic principle of expertise. In short, taxes and tariffs are profitable and I think necessary for strength and prosperity in any nation given that those in leadership are fiscally wise and manage well giving back to the people not excluding the Infrastructure and extension of the State. International trade can also be beneficial as long as it continues to meet our self-interests whether that be financial or philanthropic.

The second case we will herein consider is the matter of *Coffin v. United States.* It is actually a very involved case with multiple indictment counts rendered upon the Coffin family and another defendant, being charged with *aiding and abetting* a past Bank President in Bank Fraud. The language of some of the opinions surrounded whether or not the Coffin family were actual officers and the legality of them being solicited for them to commit the crime of bank fraud. At the heart of the case raises the issue of *Presumed Innocence,* which goes hand in hand with R*easonable Doubt,* two fundamental principles of court proceedings in determining guilt. The articulation of the opinions in the case detail how the presumption of innocence is a proof and evidence working for the accused, while reasonable doubt is another proof working against this evidence, in so many words. Moral to the Story: In the history of trying individuals in the court of law, presumption of innocence along with the concept of reasonable doubt, have been tools used in the determination of guilt. This would be a great accomplishment of Justice if it were true. We find in history that although the tools and judicial instruments were ready and available to determine fair verdicts; not in all cases were these utensils used and furthermore, in some cases, siting at the head of the table were Fathers with racist ideals and motives toward the alleged negro criminals, while apparently, if we are honest with ourselves, many white alleged criminals were treated as sons with the love from a benevolent Father, given full grace, mercy and often times pardoned from their heinous crimes and sins. Of course, these truths give rise to a whole other modern idea of possessive investment in whiteness, which has its own political ramifications, that I do not care to discuss less because it seems to be the popular topic of the day that is over purchased and saturated in the market place of ideas. Yet and still, injustice is entangled within the history of our Justice System, and today; with modern day DNA tests, and the progress of Forensic Science, many falsely accused have been brought to justice, released from the pits of prison, and given new live after years of banishment from society. And today, I can firmly attest that whites are not the only persons who receive the Mercy of the Courts.

## Chapter 56

## Justice Edward Douglass White (1845-1921)

Justice Edward White was born in the state of Louisianna and attended the College of Immaculate of Conception, what is today still a Jesuit School of Teaching, although he ended up finishing his undergraduate studies at The University of Louisianna. He would fight in the Civil War as a Confederate Soldier and later Served as a Louisianna State Senator, as well as a State Supreme Courage Judge. His jurisprudence career was heightened and then accelerated by his appointment to the US Supreme Court by then President Grover Cleveland, as he was again promoted to the position of Chief Justice by past President William Howard Taft. In terms of his jurisprudence philosophy, he was Whig party affiliated and ruled on the side of keeping things as they were in the case of *Plessy v. Ferguson*, upholding the constitutionality of separate but equal. Although there seemed to be a change in heart, as he would originate the language that would strike down many of the "grandfather clauses" in Southern States. Finally, he also authored the opinion on certain Selective Draft Cases. Herein, we will consider a few of these cases and examine certain details, along with my provocative "Moral to the Story:" commentary.

The first case we will consider is that of *Guinn v. United States (1915)* which was the case in which "grandfather clauses" were struck down because of their unconstitutionality against the 15th amendment which prohibits discrimination against voters due to race or color. At the heart of the grandfather clauses was the idea to register as many illiterate white voters and, keep them voting while keeping black voters out. The clause gave certain privileges to voters who had grandparents who were from foreign countries, served in the military essentially before the Emancipation Proclamation. This type of filter almost immediately prevented all blacks from voting whos grandparents were mostly slaves before 1866. In addition to the grandfather clauses, there were difficult literary tests given at voting centers, where blacks were challenged to read and write any part of the constitution. Many illiterate whites themselves would be unable to pass these tests, but due to the grandfather tests, they were able to vote. Thus, the case of *Guinn v. United States* that happened in 1915 seemed to start a tide toward change in the political climate even though many states found ways to discriminate against black voters after the fact. It would still be a long journey to end disenfranchisement, as even in modern times certain groups claim that certain zoning rules and other issues are the remnants of voter discrimination existing in contemporary society. Moral to the Story: We can infer from this case and prior cases such as *Plessy v. Ferguson*, that at one point in history there was a social agenda to keep whites and blacks separate and things unequal even after the days of slavery. This seems obvious, yet and still, here we have the facts. In addition, from this specific case, we can also see that there were those who wanted things to change, or who for whatever purposes felt that enough was enough and certain judicial, social, and even economic practices were unconstitutional, unjust, and flat out wrong, and made efforts through using the power of their position, authority, education, and inner philosophy to move things toward a more egalitarian state.

A second case we will consider involves the details and rules of the pardon phenomenon. In the matter of *Burdick v. United States (1915)*, the parameters of accepting a pardon were set in order as well as the fact that a pardon could be rejected by the detained person whether that specific pardon carry with it conditions or not, even in the event of a capital sentence. The precedent for this reasoning was set in order by *United States v. Wilson (1833)*. In the details of the case we have a New York Tribune editor, George Burdick, who was allowing sensitive Treasury Department information to be reported. Apparently, the State Treasury Department had a mole, or a rat, whatever the rodent was that was leaking State department secrets. (LOL). Regardless of the fact, Burdick refused to reveal his source and was heavily fined and jailed until he disclosed this information. President Woodrow Wilson offered him pardon with the hopes of his testimony; a clever strategy to shake out a name. Moral to the Story: State Employee Whistleblowers and Media Reporters are often faced with highly controversial decisions to be made; that is, whether to report a matter to the general public because of its dire importance and risk criminal persecution, or to keep thier contract responsibility of keeping maters of national security in the circles for which it belongs and can be utilized for our nation's self-interests and protection. Interesting, that there seems to be a thin line between those who have committed such acts, as to whether or not they be Heroes or Traitors who committed Treason who exposed State Department Secrets. I think the challenge of leaving such violators unchecked only opens to door to more persons exposing the State Department and Federal Government inner affairs. And yet, prosecution in some way's seems harsh for those who sought to be Robinhood types, bringing knowledge to the people. Notwithstanding, those who sold US secrets to other nations for self-interests, in my opinion, deserve their judgment in full.

## Chapter 57:

## Justice Rufus W. Peckham (1838-1909)

Justice Rufus Peckham was born in the great state of New York, in the cold month of December, in the year of 1824. He ended up attending The Almany Academy with aspirations to become a lawyer as his father. With single-minded grit and determination, he studied the law on his own and practiced for ten whole years. It was toward the conclusion of these certain career shaping and career prepping years that he was selected to serve as the Albany District Attorney as well as High Counsel to the City of Albany and although he studied on his own, he also held tenure on the Albany School of New York Law School Senior Executive Board while sitting as Associate Justice .to the New York Court of Appeals. Justice Peckham was ultimately nominated to the United States Supreme court by President Grover Cleveland. Apparently, Justice Peckham authored over 300 Supreme Court decisions while dissenting just under 10 times. History tells of his jurisprudence philosophical leanings as being more conservative than liberal, as he sided with the majority in *Plessy v. Ferguson*, although he was an advocate for consumer welfare, and was considered by certain sources to more than likely favor Chinese litigants in the plethora of immigration cases that flooded the court. We will consider only two of the many cases for which he sat.

In the case of Ex parte Young, we have disgruntled shareholders of a railroad company who sues his sate and state Attorney General on the grounds that the price regulation of the railroad and the laws to enforce those laws were too harsh. They did not agree with the laws surrounding the railroad pricing as well as those laws that would enforce them by jail time. In the case proceedings it was actually the Attorney General, Young who after being sued as to have an injunction against him that he would not be able to enforce the law, he was held in contempt of court when belligerently arguing his case. An ironic turn of events in that the civil servant who worked for the State was penalized to the point of being detained by the State of Minnesota. Some of the other legal factors that played a role in this case was that the shareholders of the railroad company based their claim upon the due process clause of the fourteenth amendment. And young argued for his protection the caveat in the 11$^{th}$ amendment which stated that the State could not be sued citizens of other states. Moral to the Story: Greed, although may profit the reward of great financial increase; at times, the costs of exorbitant behaviors, that is breaking the law, necessitate the consequences of inconvenient sentencing, which can be prevented. Although the race of exponential profits seem fitting for the private sector, for government agencies and entities, the plight of the people must be considered. Thus, hiked up rates and laws that punish those who don't pay seems unjust. Such is the case with certain mandatory insurances, DMV Emission laws, and in some cases HOA fees and regulations, although HOA fees more pertain to the private sector the main point of the issue is that one would think taxes be the only mandatory fee. Nevertheless, the costs of medical billing without insurance and death, without the same, does reason for having certain premiums to cover these serious and expensive life inevitabilities.

The second case in which we will discuss, considers the matter of double jeopardy. There have been many Hollywood productions that delve into this phenom; yet, in real life, this matter really exists. In the case of *Ball v. United States,* we have two men who were convicted of murder and appealed to the supreme court to have the decision reversed on the basis that the indictment was "insufficient." The men were indicted a second time in which they again appealed to the Supreme court and the court reversed the conviction upon the double jeopardy clause. Moral to the Story: Quite simply, can't be tried of the same crime twice. Or can you, if there be a repeat offender, does this judgment apply? I think repeat offenders of the same type of crime even get harsher sentences having prior convictions. And yet, in today's age, I guess it depends on the city, town, or locality one resides in.

## Chapter 58:

## Justice Joseph McKenna (1843-1926)

Justice Joseph McKenna was born in Pennsylvania, home of the Pittsburg, Steelers and where Steel country is. Not to mention, the location where the original framers drafted the constitution in 1776. Furthermore, it is the location where Benjamin Franklin opened the first public Zoo. Justice McKenna, like his city, was extremely unique, as he was one of few persons served on each branch of the Federal Government. That is, the executive, legislative, and judicial arms in which he was the Attorney General, Seved on the House side of Congress, and accepted his appointment to the US Supreme Court. Justice McKenna traveled to the Westcoast to attend a Catholic College and was admitted to the California bar at 1865. Very prolific in his authoring majority opinions, Justice McKenna wrote over some 610 majority opinions and just under 150 dissents. We will only consider two of such cases in this forum.

The first case we will herein discuss deals briefly with an epidemic that still exist today, and that is that practice of human trafficking and prostitution. This specific case upheld what is technically called the *White – Slave Traffic Act* or the *Mann Act*; and fundamentally what the Supreme Court case, *Hoke v. United States (1920)* did was uphold the Mann Act as it stipulated its jurisdiction boundaries prevented them for regulating prostitution on one level, nevertheless, when it comes to interstate travel and transporting women for the sake of prostitution or other "immoral deeds," then that's when the Supreme Court's jurisdiction kicks in. Essentially, it is the rule of the state to judge whether or not it will consider prostitution a practice of a civil right and liberty or an offence. Moral to the Story: When State lines are crossed for the purposes of prostitution, with women in tow, the lines of legality have officially been crossed. On the other hand, between two consenting adults, the practice of such seems to be a fuzzy grey area, although there have still been convictions levied from State to State.

The second case we will discuss delves into the relm of free speech and that is free speech attributed to the film industry. Although, the case seems to be more about economics and business, as there was a state law passed in 1913 in Ohio that regulated all films to first be approved by their state committee and pay a fee, or fall under the risk of being arrested for showing an unapproved film. As the dust began to settle amongst the quagmire of this case, the plaintiff, Mutual Film Corporation argued and defended the merit of their creativity and that such regulation or restriction to the basis of censorship was a violation of their Freedom of Speech, essentially. Moreover, there were other raised arguments that authority had been illegally allocated by the State to the Censor board, and further that the interstate commerce violation of the Dormant Commerce Clause was violated. Ultimately the ruling on the case surrounded the fact that the film industry is a for profit industry that was not beyond the regulation of government or censure. Furthermore, their free speech should not be protected all on the basis of the fact and possibility that film could be used for evil. Moral to the Story: It's ambiguous to me as to the follow up case of these matters, because although it seems just that certain matters must be approved, it seems unjust in the same vein that free speech be hindered. Unless something is completely profane, treasonous, and propagating some evil foreign agenda that can do devesting global and national harm, why not let people tell their creative stories without restraint and as far as the imagination will carry them. This seems to be the current thinking given the range of genres present in the film industry today. For even the profane, the treasonous, and the foreign agenda gets displayed. Or maybe, I just haven't recently been to the movies.

## Chapter 59:

## Justice Oliver Wendell Holmes Jr. (1841-1935)

Justice Oliver Holmes was a native of Boston, Massachusetts; and by his father being Doctor, he naturally grew up in an intellectually challenging and vigorous environment. Always asking questions and challenging known thoughts he attended Harvard College and would write down his own theories; commenting and challenging the writings of other intellectual giants such as Plato, having life time friend of the family, Ralph Waldo Emerson to edit his papers. One source records Emerson's comment on one of Justice Holmes's early papers on Plato's, "idealist philosophy, saying that, "if you strike a king, you must kill him." His inner values and philosophy led him to be an advocate of the Abolitionist movement in Boston as well as a man of war, as he would leave his undergraduate exercises to enlist in the militia, and return back to Harvard College for Graduation. Fortune being on his side, Justice Holmes escaped death and was discharged from the Battalion due to a severe case of dysentery.

Justice Holmes was coerced into the study of law by his father and eventually completed his studies at the prestigious Harvard School of Law, after which he opened his own practice. His specialty was in admiralty and commercial law in the state of Massachusetts. Justice Holmes was nominated to the US Supreme Court by President Theodore Roosevelt; Shortley after the appointment there was a rift in the relationship because of Justice Holmes authoring a certain opinion on a particular case *Northern Securities Co. v. United States.* This case was a highlight for President Roosevelt and he felt strongly that the company Northern Securites had been in violation of the Sherman Anti-Trust Act. This and more we will herein discuss. It also must be said that Justice Holmes held the record for the oldest Justice, retiring at the ripe age of 90 years old.

In the case of *Northern Securities Co. v. United States (1904),* at its heart it is a case of attempted acquisition, pride, and greed. Or maybe, better put, it is a case of simple business principles and a test of American Market Place competition at its best. The market place being the two Railroad companies and a securities company by the name Great Northern, Northern Pacific, and Northern Securities Company. In this racket, although the case mentions no coercion on or intimidation, we have the Owner of Great Northern RR who merges with a RR company owned by JP Morgan; namely, Northern Pacific. These two combined forces and set their eyes on the run and highly profitable Chicago Burlington, and Quincy RR Co. (CB&Q). These were running smoothly accept for the two newly merged companies did not consider that a rival RR Co. From the south would also seek to bid on (CB&Q). Not having a contingency plan, when the RR. Co. From the South began to purchase shares of their competitors RR. Company, Northern Securities Co. Began to purchase their own shares of their company at a greater volume, thus being the ultimate leader in the Northern securities race, possessing the lions share, they were also able to purchase (CB&Q) out right, owning a significant and respectable amount of track and Western, Northern, and mid-Western territories, Where the legal conflict arose, is that Northern Securities, Co. Was allegedly in violation of certain Antitrust laws under the *Sherman Act of 1820.* This act was legislation stipulating the rules of free competition among those engaged in commerce. This precipitates more specifically 1) anti-competitive agreements 2) and unilateral decisions that would cause a company to gain a monopoly in any given market. The Ruling was that the merger between JP Morgan and Great American was unlawful. Moral to the Story: If government allowed monopolies such as the above to exist, we would be under a plutocracy; a ruling of the extremely wealthy and oligarchs would of major corporations would control the business of the country and allocate the wealth. Or is this just some controversy babel that would never come true.

## Chapter 60:

## Justice William R. Day (1849-1923)

Justice William Day was born native of the state of Ohio. He was one of the few government leaders who held position in two of the three branches of government, the first being under the executive branch; Secretary of State during the Mckinely presidency, and along the Judicial Arm; Associate Justice on the United States Supreme Court. His background and education actually consisted of a Bachelor of Science as opposed to one in the Liberal Arts arena, although he would take up the study of Law after graduation and be admitted to the Bar in 1872. His Judicial philosophical leanings as inferred from what type of law he practiced; criminal defense, and corporate law were ambiguous considering he also aligned himself in the business of politics with Republican politicians. Although, as a US Supreme Court Justice he authored over some 435 opinions where he helped support the government against major corporations of his day such as Oil, Tabacco, and Rail Road companies. We will consider a few of the cases he authored herein, namely; one dealing with antitrust measures, and another considering Justic Day's defense for the Fourth amendment, more specifically, illegal search and seizure.

In the case of ***Standard Oil Co. of New Jersey v. United States,*** a company owned by John D. Rockefeller, this major corporation was essentially split up into several smaller companies by the federal government due to its alleged monopoly in the oil industry, acquisitions, mergers, bribery, and price manipulation of low rates that put other oil companies out of business were among the racket of practices that precipitated the companies rise to test the Sherman's Antitrust Act of 1890. Such Anti- competition practices by the conglomerate of a company got the attention of the federal government and after the case was over, the progeny from the asexual split not only multiplied the number of powerful oil companies across the face of America, many of which are still around today, but also multiplied profits, more so than when there was one major company Standard Oil Co. Those new companies that had Standard Oil Co. As their Fiscal and Structural father, were; ExxonMobil, Marathon Petroleum, Amoco, and Chevron to name a few. Moral to the Story: Sometimes being summoned to the highest court in the land is not necessarily a bad thing, the results from constitutional judgment, as jurisprudence history tells us, can be profitable, although change and regulation may have to be adopted.

In this second case, a matter of private privacy, illegal search and seizures, and procedure, the plaintiff in error, defendant Freemont Weeks fell on the radar of the local precinct as he was in suspicion for transporting lottery tickets through the mail. Local officers illegally went into his home without a warrant, and confiscated all materials in relation to the charge and released it to the US Marshalls. Sources say that the officers entered as second time with Marshalls in tow to seize additional letters and incriminating evidence. In the finality of this case, ***Weeks v. United States, (1914)*** had the ruling that all the evidence collected during the illegal search and seizure was should not be admissible to the court because proper procedure was not followed, ie. No search warrant. These matters fall under the language of the fourth amendment, which the local precinct and US Marshalls violated. Moral to the Story: The Law of the land is a like a maze that has open doors and dead ends, and loop wholes that lead to the reward of settlement, acquittance, or a verdict of guilt depending which side one is one, the Prosecution, or Defense. And the rules of navigating this maze play a role in the success or failure of reaching the desired verdict. In this case, it was the lack of having a warrant that prevented the defendant from ultimately being convicted of a matter that violated the criminal code. In another case, it might be a piece of evidence that forces the judgment of a sentence. The point is, it seems that, the Rule of Law is a deadly, life changing and affecting game that rewards those who Study.

## Chapter 61:

## Justice William Henry Moody (1853-1917)

Justice William Moody was a native-born Massachusettsian and attended an Academy for his high school career. His parents were fairly wealthy, owning a number of farms in the local community. After graduation young Justice Moody went off to Harvard University to complete his undergraduate studies, and then it was Harvard Law in which he left early to start real life training and was admitted to the Bar in 1878. Interesting enough, Justice Moody also served as Secretary of the Navy for two years under President Theodore Roosevelt's administration and had a hand in the building of Guantanamo Bay Naval Base in Cuba. Serving as the Secretary of the Navy was essentially a launching pad for Justice Moody that aimed him at even higher State Department positions; US Attorney General and ultimately the US Supreme Court. On the Supreme Court, Justice Moody authored over 65 opinions and a hand full of dissents. His Jurisprudence philosophical leanings, the short time he was on the bench, delt with business liability and employee-employer interrelationships, and increased federal control along with protection against self–incrimination.

This first case that we will discuss was kind of vaguely reported even from the various sources that I looked it up. Essentially it is a case of removal, or attempt of removal and the prevention of the denial of certain constitutional rights. More specifically, in the case of *Tinsley v. Trent (1907),* there was a dispute concerning interstate commerce and the way certain cars in a locomotive where manufactured, with or without "couplers" as pertaining to the safety of the way in which cars on the line hitched with each other not needing manpower to go between the cars which was a safety hazard and risk under the Safety Appliance Act of 1893. The purpose of the case was to promote good safety in business and manufacturing of tools and equipment to not put employees in danger and "protect lives and limbs of railroad employees." Moral to the Story: This safety Appliance act leads me to think of some of the OSHA compliance statutes that certain companies have to follow. Maybe it's the Safety Appliance Act make over or Remix. The old proverb says, "There is nothing new under the sun," and the familiar adage which may seem cliché, though rings true says, "Pay attention to History, because, or it will repeat itself."

In this second case of Louisville & Nashville Railroad Co. V. Mottley, we have a case of jurisdiction as well as a settlement compensation being taken away or dismissed due to the technicality of jurisdiction. More specifically, the Mottley couple were injured in a train wreck and were compensated with free passes, to be renewed annually. In 1907, the Mottley's and their passes were revoked and this is the reason that they pursued their case a number of times. It was first dismissed by the Supreme Court on the grounds that there was no constitutional law broken and therefore the Supreme Court did not actually have jurisdiction, therefore the case was dismissed. The Mottley's persisted to take the case the state Kentucky Court which approved their cause, in which the RR. Co. Resisted this decision with a final blow from the U.S. Supreme Court which out ranked, the lower court and ruled in favor the RR. Co., ultimately denying the renewal of the passes. Moral to the Story: It seems that compensation from cases where plaintiffs were injured and settlements were agreed upon are not necessarily indefinite. Just like money runs out if not invested and managed properly, benefits can also change when laws, statutes, organizational structure of companies and/or administrations change.

## Chapter 62:

## Justice Horace Harmon Lurton (1844-1914)

Justice Horace Lurton was born native of the 'ole state of Kentucky. He majored in Law even in his undergrad years at the University of Chicago, and continued his education at Cumberland School of Law. It was at this time that he found himself deep in the helms of War during the America's Civil War as he was to be a prisoner of war as he was captured by after his release, and pledge of allegiance, he went on to private practice and eventually would sit upon the Tennesse State Supreme Court. Not to mention his permanent seat upon the United States Supreme Court by President William Howard Taft, whom of which was a friend of Justice Lurton according to sources. In terms of opinions authored and numbers on dissents with the other Justices on the court; these numbers evade this author, yet and still, Justice Lurton served a significant role in that he authored one case that delt with Federal Government say so in state location of finance, as to put all states at an even playing ground. We will look further into this case and one other as to complete this section, hopefully uncovering more wisdom to our knowledge about Federal and State Fiscal and economic policy.

So, in the case of Coyle v. Smith (1911), which was essentially a matter of semantics and jurisdiction; less of language and its effects and more of constitutional powers and jurisdiction; the problem lies in the Oklahoma being brought into the Union and at its inception as a Unionized state being restricted in terms of determining where it's seat of power and authority will be; ether Guthrie, or her special choice of Oklahoma City. Ultimately the Supreme overruled the Enabling Act and her restrictions and gave Oklahoma full power and equal footing as other states to choose where it's central city of administration, business, and power would be. Moral to the Story: Parents have to determine when their children have reached an age of accountability and responsibility, that is the age of awareness when their capable of making decisions for themselves and bearing the brunt of the consequences for those choices whether good or bad. The truth of the matter, this power is released to the child not all at once, but gradually and little by little as the child grows older and wiser, they are endued with more freedom and strengths to do as they will. Likewise, God gives power to man, and though the governing bodies of our Superior Court System be no God to the Inferior Courts, or even parents for that matter, but Guiding Counsel of Supreme Authority, it can be understood how federal powers must be given to the States on certain decisions as to sure up their Adulthood, or Maturity, given that they all be governing bodies of hopefully wise men and women who can by all means manage themselves and their particular state affairs.

In the second case we will discuss, we have an Italian man living in New York who confessed to the murder of his wife in Italy. It is the case of *Charlton v. Kelly (1913)*, and the honorable Justice Horace Lurton authored an opinion. The conflict at hand was that not only did Charlton openly confess to the homicide, but that the Italian courts wanted his extradition expedited. Meanwhile, Charlton applied for his release from custody through habeas corpus, which was eventually suspended, warrant being issued for his arrest and his extradition being approved by the U. S. Secretary of State. Apparently, there was a Treaty between U.S. and Italy at this time; notwithstanding, Justice Lurton included in his opinion that the extradition, though it be a breach in the extradition treaty, was waived, and the US and Italy remained in treaty. Moral to the Story: Murder is Murder, and though there be various levels, and reasons; such as premeditated or self-defense, involuntary manslaughter and all the other kinds, not to mention executions committed during War Time, which though I not be versed in all the laws of War, I presume to be pardonable in most cases. On a civilian level though, the murder of one's spouse in most cases is not excusable and the American Justice system would not stand by and let Mr. Charlton hide from the consequences of to be faced in his Mother country, not in the end anyway. Leads one to think before they commit such an act. On another note, we can go to the bible and see in the Old Testament how God instructed Israel to build certain cities on the boarders and outskirts of the land for those who had committed murder accidentally and needed a place to flee and refuge.

## Chapter 63:

## Justice Charles Evans Hughes (1862-1948)

Justice Charles Hughes served in a number of State department Positions before his nomination and appointment to the US Supreme Court. Those positions include Governor of New York, Secretary of State, United States President, Associate Justice in the US Supreme Court, and ultimately Chief Justice. An obviously impressive legal background and political career, one might ask how he managed to maneuver his way around and obtain these various high government positions; and secondly, continue to do the necessary work with vigor. Looking at his childhood and educational upbringings, one might consider him to be a sort of child prodigy, as he was a descendent from Wales, his father being an immigrant from that place; Justice Hughes actually first enrolled in College at the tender age of 14. It was Madison University at first, then Brown University and on to law school at Columbia Law. In terms of Judicial philosophy, coming from the perspective of one that matriculated through all these positions as well as held his own private practice for a number of years, he actually brought challenge to the New Deal in its inception and during the 1930's, yet over time, his liberal leanings upheld the Wagner Act and a state minimum wage law.

In this fist case that we will consider, it is one that deals with tax legalities and technicalities. In the case of Lucas v. Earl under Chief Justice E. Hughs Court, we have a man who only reported half of his income due to the savvy contract entered he into along with his wife. Somehow the wording of the contract that was written before certain tax laws stated that he and his wife were joint tenants; whereas the income from the jointly held property was only reported as half in Earls reported salary. The Bureau of Internal Revenue sought to get a total salary, in addition to his half of income from the property, also, the portion divided to his wife. Ultimately, Justice Hughes ruled in favor of the Tax Collector, as he is recorded so eloquently quoting the maxim, "The fruits cannot be attributed to a different tree from that on which they grew." Moral to the Story: Oh, the privilege of being married and filing taxes together, or separately, head of household, along with standard or itemized deductions. So many of us struggle with financial matters in our household, and yet also, for many of us it is a breeze, and both parties whether they be together or living separately have an understanding of their finances and submit accordingly. On the contrary, there are those persons in society, who feel it robbery that the government should exact taxes upon their hard-earned income. And they count it a light thing their living in a clean and orderly nation with cities and roads and universities, and libraries, and means of communication and travel, and healthcare, and retirement and disability income, and all the other benefits that come along with being an American citizen such as living in a safe environment for the most part free of terror because of our local and federal police agencies, and military organizations. All of these things and our Court system and governing officials and more require funds and salary, and rightfully so, though we be a nation in which the people give permission to the government to govern, in each particular office one would think should be individuals who seek the best for the commonwealth of the people as well as the nation, putting their motivations of state and country first, being elected and appointed to these various state department, legislative, and judicial positions for those purposes. So, the one who refuses to pay taxes not because of exemption or clever deductions, or some other legal loophole, but because of some gross animosity toward the State and through evasion because of a desire to withhold it all is none other, in my opinion. ungrateful for the privileges they daily indulge for being citizens of the great U.S. of A. I am not saying that tax laws are always fair, and that the disproportion and measures of ones bracketed income to be taxed are even always fully justified, but such are the ills of running a country and we should seek legislative amendments and adjustments until such equities are met.

In this second case that we will consider, still a matter held and tried in the Hughes court, is the matter of *Sorrel v. United States (1932)*, which is a case dealing in the matter of entrapment. The details present are a factory runner who happened to also be a rumrunner and an undercover government agent by the name of Martin. Both had been soldiers in the Army, same division, hence the conversation asserted by Martin, "Can you get a fellow soldier some whiskey." Sorrel's first notion was to resist the temptation to hustle up a bottle for five dollars, but after a few more guilt and pressure pointed request, he gave in to his presumed Army Buddy and got him a half-gallon bottle and was immediately arrested by Maritn for violation of the National Prohibition Act. In the ultimate ruling there was a petition for certiorari filed in which the defense of entrapment was made and won on the defendant's behalf. Moral to the Story: This sort of situation is really hurtful and all out embarrassing quite frankly. Two soldiers who served in the same division, one an undercover, and another a rebel and bringer of joy so to speak. Maybe I shouldn't comment, because it is hard to understand the nature of the prohibition laws during that time given the fact that all liquors and even marijuana is licensed and legal today, and can be purchased from the neighborhood corner store today. Not to mention many Scheduled drugs can be purchased off the street and on the internet quite simply.

# Chapter 64:

## Justice Edward Douglass White (1798-1847)

See Chapter 56

## Chapter 65:

## Justice Willis Van Devanter (1859-1937)

Justice Willis Devanter was born native to Indiana, and attended Cincinnati Law school. He attended to the State of Wyoming in the capacity of city attorney and eventually took an appointment as Chief Judge to the territorial court, and then Chief Justice of Wyoming Supreme Court. From that post he went on to private practice and also had dealings with the Union Pacific Rail Road. On the US Supreme court, he had more than a few cases in which he took part. He represented the Indian Americans, state poaching, and before this post he also served the State Department as assistant Attorney General in Washington, D.C. as well as lectured at George Washington Law School.

The First case we will consider in which Justice Devanter was present for, but did not necessarily author the main opinion is the case of *Blackmer v. United States (1932)*. In this very intriguing case, we have a tale of contempt by means of refusal to attend court, and an underlying story or backdrop of bribery and high contract manipulation at the highest order. Apparently, US history reveals the Teapot Dome Scandale, a scandal in which certain oil contracts were released from the control of the Navy to the Department of Interior and certain private companies with bribery incentives. Such action was unconstitutional because of the unfairness in not allowing other companies to properly bid for the oil and leasing contracts. Well, in the aftermath, as the indictments were going out, after a tedious investigation, Paris resident, Blackmer refused to show up for trial and testify as a witness after receiving his subpoena. This inaction on his part led to fines and further prosecution by the US Courts, and yet Blackner held his ground against the fines under the due process clause located in the 5$^{th}$ Amendment. Essentially, Blackmer didn't stand a chance after failing to complete his civic duty of giving testimony, as the court unanimously ruled against his defense; Chief Justice Hughes giving the majority opinion basically stating in so many words that, the US has supreme power and sovereignty to demand any of its citizens to return whenever public interest requires or be properly penalized, and secondly, it is the duty of every citizen to support the administration in justice whenever a testimony is required and they are properly and legally summoned. Moral to the Story: Although it's unpopular to tell on friends, when one is faced with criminal prosecution, they have to decide whether they will live up to their ultimate civic duty, or commit perjury.

In this second case we will discuss, it involves the use of Federal powers transacted on collective State Legislatures to implement the Social Security Act of 1935 in the form of granting unemployment to those qualified for compensation. The conflict belies in the question of whether or not Federal powers exceeded thier reach in regulating State fiscal matters, as States were to be considered "quasi-Sovereign." This is the case of *Steward Machine Co. V. Davis (1937)*. There were three major points being considered in all these happenings, the first being: 1) The use of federal government's spending power to regulate commercial economic activity. 2) The expansive view of general welfare. And thirdly, 3) Economic conditions during that time. Supreme Court Rulings ruled in favor of the justification of Federal powers to help support its citizens and have authority to prompt State governing powers to make necessary changes and budgetary policies to do so. Moral to the Story: What was going on in the 1930's is similar to what we see even today in first and second decades of the 21$^{st}$ Century. We have had bouts of recession and financial collapse from mismanagement and predatory lending of certain financial institutions creating new derivative "assets" that failed the housing markets, bank bailouts due to insolvency and debt, War, Nazism, and new generational unrest, Pandemic, rapid unemployment, and the Need for the government to step in as Roosevelt Did with implementing Social Security. Obama-Trump-Biden; all issued Stimulus checks and talks of Universal Basic Income are on the table, and around the corner. Is this Socialism, a Cry for help, or a Generous Democratic Capitalist Nation aiding the general welfare of its people?

## Chapter 66

## Justice Joseph Rucker Lamar (1857-1916)

Justice Joseph Lamar held of lot of colloquial qualities, who as a young adult and was close friends with the future President Woodrow Wilson. Sounds like a long story, but this friendship and even a bit of nepotism would find him in High seats of power later on in his life. He was born in Georgia, the son of an old Preacher, attended an Academy for grade school, an Institute for High school; he was use to the comradery and environment of an all-boys school. He would go on to attend Penn Lucy for undergrad and then Columbia for Law School. He was elected to the Georgia House of Representatives and then took an appointment to the Georgia State Supreme Court. Eventually he would also accept a nomination for the United States Supreme Court by former President William Howard Taft.

The first we will consider is not one that Justice Lamar wrote the opinion on, but he was present and it was Justice Charles Hughes who authored the majority opinion. In this case, the question of cruel and unusual punishment was up for debate. It is the case of Bailey v. Alabama (1911) and the apparently A. Bailey, a Black man won a contract on a job at $12 a month. He was given an advance of $15 and midway in the job stopped working. It is unclear as to why he had to stop or choose to discontinue the job; irregardless, no refund was issued to the employer and in the state of Alabama this was considered an attempt to defraud, or in the latin, (prima facie). The final ruling on this case is a bit unclear, as the Supreme Court found Alabama law that stated the one who did such an act as accept payment and defraud with intent and fail to complete the job was to be punished on conviction. That punishment is also unclear. Moreover, the United States Supreme Court found that charging a person criminally for taking money for unperformed work was likened to indentured servitude, and this was deemed illegal under the $13^{th}$ amendment, as it was a sort of barter system that required a person to work instead of be criminally found guilty. Moral to the Story: It's hard to find good workers. It's hard today in some aspects, and it seems that it was hard back then. And nothing pisses of an employer off more that someone who walks off the job. Can't say that I haven't' done this myself more than once. I've had my reasonings; didn't like the pay, felt like I was wasting time, or that I was supposed to be doing something else with my precious time, and not to mention the time I went crazy, but that's another story. This type of behavior is maybe ok for a young man, although it's not; and stick-to-it-ness shows character. But for a man with a family, this may show some irresponsibility; nevertheless, every case is different and Man will have his reasonings. The main point is, does one deserve to die, be harshly punished or be hung for this behavior. I'm not sure what the penalty or punishment was back in 1911 in the state of Alabama for committing such an act, but anything more than a fine and maybe a judgment to pay back what was owed in civil court would seem harsh and unjust.

In this final case that we will discuss in this chapter; it is another instance of jurisdiction in so many words, and federal and local precinct officers overstepping legal boundaries to obtain incriminating evidence against said plaintiff Fremont Weeks. The case is the matter of *Weeks v. United States (1914),* in which the Supreme Courts found it an unconstitutional thing to search and seize any evidence from a private residence without warrant. This in fact was considered a violation of the Fourth Amendment. And soon in the case of Mapp v. Ohio (1911) this president of the "exclusionary rule," was disseminated to the State Courts as well. The details of the case pen Mr. Weeks as committing some type of illegal activity with the mail and lottery tickets. Eventually, Feds and local precinct officers get a tip, and in religious, determined pursuit go to apprehend and confiscate all material evidence, only without a search warrant. This is the thing that made the actions of their investigation reprimandable in the court of law, dismissing the evidence on the technicality of the way it was obtained. Moral to the story: First of all, we can learn that citizens should not be playing around with State lottery tickets and the federal mail system in order to increase thier chances of winning. And secondly, we learn that in hot pursuit of evidence there are protocols and procedures to be followed, even by federal officers.

## Chapter 67:

## Justice Mahlon Pitney (1858-1924)

Justice Pitney was native of the state of New Jersey, went on to become an undergraduate at Princeton University and rubbed shoulders with future President Woodrow Wilson during his attendance and played a little baseball, or rather served as a sort of Director of the baseball program on campus. After graduation, it was back to work at his father's law practice, and after about three years of this kind of daily grind, he found himself running for the House of Representatives. He served two terms and later in his career was appointed to the US Supreme Court by then elect President William Howard Taft. Justice Pitney authored quite a few cases which exposed his philosophical leanings with respect to Jurisprudence. Herein we will discuss two such cases; one case we will not cover due to lack of available details is a case that delt which the Unions and their powers being limited when dealing with their employers and their incentives to implement strikebreakers.

A similar opinion authored by Justice Pitney was in the case of *Coppage v. Kansas (1915).* In this case, we have an employer that wanted his employees to sign a contract that would prevent and prohibit them from joining any labor union during the time of their term of employment. This scenario was elevated to the US Supreme Court and in the aftermath, the opinion on the case as authored by Justice Pitney, entitled Employers to write such contracts for their employers in order to protect thier companies. And the main reasoning behind this ruling, according to Justice Pitney, was that the contract did not deprive signers of any of thier "constitutional freedoms." Moral to the Story: Employers have the right to specify expectations and conditions to thier future employees. Employees also have leveraging power at the negotiating table weighted upon thier skill and demand status. So, just because a future employee may be discontent with a project contract, does not mean

In another case, also dealing with labor and law; the case of ***Holden v. Hardy***, (1898), in such case the majority ruling agreed that Utah laws which limited employees from working over a certain number of hours because of fatigue and dangerous working conditions were in fact just. Secondly the language of the author of this opinion Justice Billings, also made a distinction between this law and other laws that universal maximum hour rules that where in fact very unconstitutional given due process clause and the fourteenth amendment. Moral to the Story: Both ways considered in this chapter, whether employers can tactily construct thier contracts to thier companies benefit as long as constitutional rights and civil liberties are not tampelled upon, so to speak. And secondly, there are limitations to how hard an employer can be pushed. Just as the body has physical limitations, and pushing it passed a certain threshold make cause breakdown, but in the end makes it stronger. Well back then in the workforce, unlike the military, and maybe olympic trainees, sleep deprivation is not the goal and tired overworked workers could have led to on the job injury and possible death, which would be liability to the company.

## Chapter 68:

## Justice James Clark McReynolds (1862-1946)

Justice McReynolds had a colorful academic and professional career to say the least. He was born native of Kentucky and would eventually serve the State Department in the capacity of Attorney General, as well as US Supreme Court Associate Justice. His philosophical leanings were that of an overt racism and antisemitism type, and according to sources he adamantly opposed President Franklin D. Roosevelt's solution to the Great Depression in form of the New Deal. He authored over 500 majority opinions, of which over 155 were dissents, and of those 93 were direct dissents against the New Deal executive legislation. Other accomplishments attained by Justice McReynolds were that he was a Surgeon in the Confederate Army, attended an Academy as a young man and ultimately graduated from Vanderbilt University with the high rank of Valedictorian. Justice McReynolds continued on with Vanderbilt for Law school and practiced on his own while subsequently serving as an Adjunct Professor.

The first case we will discuss for this chapter is actually on in which the topic Justice McReynolds had written dissents on; however, this particular opinion or majority ruling was not authored by him, as it involved the Jurisdiction of States to allocate funds after appropriating taxes for unemployment insurance. The country was in a great epidemic of depression during the 1930's, whereas, unemployment numbers reached beyond 10 million and Senate, Executive, as well as other judicial and legislative officers were at a quandary as of what to do, or how to go about correctly solving the problem. Hence, many New Deal laws came down around 1937 and the Social Security act of 1935 helped alleviate some of the economic tension. The case of ***Steward Machine Company v. Davis***, *(1937),* essentially reinforced the Social Security Act of 1935, and also implemented a federal taxing structure that could be used by the states to raise and appropriate funds to ensure the unemployment compensation program. Dissenting arguments that attempted to counter these judgments fundamentally tried to paint the image that federal powers were in many ways coercing the State into these programs which action was supposedly a direct violation of the tenth amendment of the Constitution. Moral to the Story: Our country at various sordid and devastating times, has seen the overwhelming dilemma of massive and gross poverty, and in more recent times great recession. This is not to say, that there are few among the masses who by and yet remain prosperous, but that there be a great majority who even today in the midst of the Covi-19 Pandemic remain unemployed, death and pestilence in the streets, overwhelmed and filled to capacity hospital staff and facilities. And this is happening in America and Abroud, and not just the plight of Third World or what be considered under developed countries. The death and pandemic seem something out of an Albert Camus Novel, "The Plague," only the virus be not passed by rats but airborne through a high-tech viral machinery that seems to keep mutating into a more and ever-present deadlier strain. So, in light of these economic and health risks, solutions are developed, President Biden's 1.9 Trillion-dollar economic stimulus plan falls along the lines of President Franklin D. Roosevelts Social Security Act in many ways, except the stimulus check as of yet is not permanent income for the social welfare of the poor. Yet and still, some countries and even fewer American states have begun testing the idea of universal basic income and it has yet to be seen if this thing will catch on.

In this second case, the main issue is buried in the context of history, that is World War I as America fought Germen occupiers and laws at home, namely in Nebraska, restricting foreign language education. The US Supreme Court ruling in this matter, *Meyer v. Nebraska (1923)*, called out the law as unconstitutional and against the due process clause of the fourteenth amendment. It was Justice McReynolds who authored the majority opinion on this case, he essentially wrote in an egalitarian prose that peoples were entitled to enter contract, "marry, establish a home, and bring up children, to worship God according to the dictates of his own conscience, and generally to enjoy those privileges long recognized at common law as essential to the orderly pursuit of happiness by free men."

This seems to be the equivalent to the "American Dream," and ironically the deemed overt racist, and AntiSemite seemed to have quite a world perspective on breaking down international barriers toward education and the dissemination of economic knowledge. Although the case specifically delt with tearing down an AntiGermen legislation in Nebraska, there seemed to be a world affection flare to the authored majority opinion. Moral to the Story: We live in an ever-changing world, where it seems that are nations enemies and allies interchange over the decades and centuries of passing time. France, Germany, Russia, Iraq, Afghanistan, Japan, China, Vietnam, Korea, Cuba, and who really knows the complete inner workings and political affairs of Government and Statehood, except for those who be involved in it. The point is, as are world grows smaller because of the technology that binds us, and it becomes easier to travel through and surf on the internet both virtually and physically, we slowly become the epitome of a cultural melting pot. So, cultures and worlds clash and combine, strict rules and protocols attempt to keep boundaries and preserve certain cultural artifacts and heritages, but in the marketplace of ideas, business, and the celebration of diversity, cultural pluralism seems to be an American pass time. Immigrant-American children and young adults, eat Mexican food, benefit from Asian Technologies, attend schools to attain a Western Education, and may attend African American Styled Worship Services or no worship service at all. This is one example among many alternatives to future American Society; one of those alternatives being a completely assimilated all white culture hegemonic in its being, epistemologically destined to teach from a meritocracy perspective feeding the democratic republic machine.

## Chapter 69:

## Justice Louis Brandeis (1856-1941)

Justice Brandeis was a native of Kentucky, and a son of Jewish immigrant parents. Highly competent and an aptitude that landed him at Harvard Law School. He graduated at the tender age of 20 with a record-breaking GPA that was the highest the ivy league school had ever seen. As a lawyer, he was one that gravitated toward community as noted by media outlets. Also, he was known to do a lot of pro bono work and tackle community issues that affected the public as a whole. Examples stem from labor laws, workplace issues, railroad monopolies, assisted with creation of the Federal Reserve System, and brainstormed new ideas for the Federal Trade Commision. His jurisprudent philosophical leanings were that of "social justice" and he was known as a "militant crusader" for such matters; his moral authority giving him a certain clarity and respect amongst his peers, him being the first Jewish man nominated to the US Supreme Court. It was President Woodrow Wilson who nominated Brandies to the Associate Justice position.

The first case we will deal with, considers the market place of ideas, free speech, and the legality of propaganda spread to draft-age men during war efforts to encourage resistance to induction. It is the case of, *Schenck v. United States (1919),* in this case the Espionage Act of 1917 was forced while WWI proceeded. The Espionage Act was to prevent persons and groups from organizing campaigns against American Military recruitment efforts or interfering in any way with military operations. This law was not intended to eclipse Free Speech, but subvert the subversive individuals and groups that sought attack on the American ideal and the way American Military Might sought to preserve life. Further illumination, reveal that most of these individuals and groups were either Germen-American, Anarchist, Socialist, Communist, or whistleblowers and the like. Moral to the Story: Certain Individuals and groups who have their base in America; attend schools here, worship here, and raise their children here, have always astounded me with their anti-establishment, anti-American, or even Anti-Christ sentiments. It's like, If you Hate America that much, Go live elsewhere, instead of Trashing Our Great Nation. Not that there has to be one hegemonic way of thinking; for we all are different, with various upbringings, leanings, and proclivities, but it is the ungrateful nature and sense of dignified hatred toward one's own country that I do not understand. Even in the midst of such a horrifying history for people who look like me, African-Americans, there is still a sense of Pride, that I feel anyway, of being a part of This Great Story. It's like, we helped build this, fought in every war, served in great capacity to the needs of the people in spite of oppression, and yet arose in dignity and triumph as history would unfold; We are too The American Story, and claim Heritage to the Land and Culture, all the while not forgetting our African Ancestry.

The next case we will discuss considers the matter of privacy rights in regards to phone tapping conversations, and if this data acquired is legally admissible as evidence in court. Justice Brandies writes a considerable dissent on the case. In the case of *Olmstead v. United States (1928)*, Judicial review considered whether or not evidence obtained from wire tapped phone conversations without former judicial approval was a violation of defendants fourth and fifth amendment rights. In the final determination on the case, Justices would rule in a close 5-4 decision, that in fact wiretaps were not a violation of fourth and fifth amendments. Yet and still, this decision was later overturned by *Katz v. United States in (1967).* There are several cases that deal with the matter of privacy rights and wiretapping, but the details surrounding this case deal in the matter of a "major bootlegging conspiracy" and essentially an organized crime ring of some 70 persons who were indicted in this measure, Olmstead being a General manager type, to receive some 50% of the profits. The alleged conspiracy was to violate the National Prohibition Act, which enforced laws on possessing, transporting and the selling of spirits. Such elements written in the majority opinion talked about the fact that the wiretapping was different that a seizure of evidence in the home, because the wires that the conversation flowed on were outside the home. Justice Brandeis countered this argument by highlight the instance of the parcel service being a government agency, but federal agents do not illegally go through mail. That is, unless one is incarcerated or some type of warrant is obtained. Moral to the Story: Government Authority has certain rights and privileges to seek and search things out, although certain protocols are supposed to be followed to protect citizen's rights, in cases of national security or obvious criminal activity on a grand scale, snooping probably happens more than we think, or maybe it doesn't happen at all, and no one is really paying attention. Who knows? But companies like Google record our every movement, phone conversations can be restored and Credit/Debit cards record financial transactions, we have been in the Surveillance State for some time now, and I don't think any protest or legislature is going to take down the cameras or inhibit the technology that collects all the data from our lives. It's simply a matter of how this data is used, and that people's privacy is not exploited in my personal opinion.

## Chapter 70:

## Justice John Hessin Clarke (1857-1945)

Justice Clarke had a unique matriculation to the position of Associate Justice to the US Supreme Court. Along the way, he participated in politics, graduated from what is now Case Western Reserve University in Ohio and studied the law on his own, opting out of law school, preferring the guidance of his father, passed the Bar in 1878. Joining a corporate law firm that practiced for various big business and railroad interests, Justice Clarke began to grow and accumulate his wealth. He was appointed to the U.S. District Court for the Northern District of Ohio, immediately fulfilling a necessary vacancy by President Woodrow Wilson. Justice Clark fulfilled another vacancy as Associate Justice on the US Supreme court in 1916. His Jurisprudent philosophy was known to that of legal realism. As a "Progressive," and advocate of Federal and Local powers having influence over the regulation of economy. We will consider a few of these cases herein.

The first case we will herein discuss in many ways parallels that of The *Schenck v. United States* case as it also asserts the Espionage Act of 1917. In this case, *Abrams v. United States*, we have two individuals who were handing out literature and pamphlets that repudiated War efforts in Russia and sending American Troops to fight Against Soviet Russia. These two individuals were convicted on the basis of the language of their literature, which was obviously seditious and sentenced to 10 and 20 years in Prison. Their defense was that their Freedom of Speech was being violated, and this was overruled in the High Court of the land. Moral to the Story: Although the sentencing does seem a little harsh for passing out subversive material, in the grand scheme of things, the alternative could have been death for coming against the State during War Time. Not sure what this looks like today, when there are so many auxiliary organizations that have their separatist agenda's and actively arm themselves, equip themselves, openly recruit, plan events and even stage open attacks against the State, various precinct and local divisions, including the House from which our very Constitution dictates that Laws are passed. Nobody's getting 10-20 years for breaking and entering into the State Capital, but someone was shot, and a few lost their lives that day. Over 400 persons were charged with crimes.

In this second section, we have the *Smith v. Kansas City Title & Trust Co.* Fundamentally, it was a case of determining jurisdiction and whether or not District courts could uphold and implement the constitutional validity of the Federal Farm Loan Act of 1916. The plaintiff in this case was a banker who did not want to honor the Federal Farm Loan Act to the letter of the law, because in his opinion it was unconstitutional. He had the audacity to assert the claim that Congress overstepped its boundaries by legislating such an Act. The Federal Farm Loan Act was established to help small farmers compete with Big Corporate farms, and there was a whole formula as to how much these land owners could borrow, which was along the lines of halve the value of their land. It is unclear to this author as to whether the payment was in the form of cash or mortgage-backed bonds, or both. US Supreme court ruled that the Act as indeed constitutional. Moral to the Story: In my personal opinion, Mr. Smith was way out of line to not immediately honor the legislative Act that had been passed down from Congress. Instead he sought a lawsuit. Was he the owner of the bank? What was his deal? Maybe I'm missing something being naive to the time, history, setting, and any other contributing factors. But it seems that this scenario would be equivalent to Executive and Legislative Branches passing down laws authorizing Banks to give Paycheck Protection Program Loans to small businesses, and bank managers everywhere balking when faced with potential loan clients at their door. Moreover, some having the audacity to sue Congress or the Executive branch saying Congress and the President did not have the authority to legislate such policy. Just doesn't make sense to me.

## Chapter 71:

## Justice William Howard Taft

President William Howard Taft was the only person to both hold the office of President as well as Chief Justice upon the US Supreme Court. He was native to the state of Ohio and attended Yale University for undergrad. Justice Taft attended Yale College and Cincinnati Law School where he merited a Bachelor of Laws degree. He continued on to study and read the Law under his Father's tutelage. After Justice Taft completed his legal career with the Federal Department, he went on to Professorship at Yale. His jurisprudent philosophical leanings tended toward community though he was also sympathetic toward Republican ideals. He weighed in on lowering Tariffs and various Anti-Trust issues, and labor union issues.

The first case that we will discuss deal with trade restrictions and the limitations of the legality behind restraining trade. These matters are considered in the case of *Addyston Pipe and Steel Co. v. United States*, (1899), The ruling in this case mainly delt with Congress having the authority to prevent trade between private entities, which ruled they did not have; and according to the constitution, the framers only wanted Congress to get involve when State interfered with interstate commerce, according to the Commerce clause. Moral to the Story: Over regulation of trade, especially interstate trade was never the goal of the Framers, therefore Congress should not, and to my understanding, does not engage in such behavior.

This second case discussed is a case in which Justice Taft sat as Chief Justice, the actual opinion was written by Justice McReynolds. Linder v. United States (1925) deals with a physician being prosecuted for prescribing Schedule 1 drugs such as Morphine and Cocaine. The Doctor's reasoning was that the patient was an addict and physiologically his body needed the substance. He was first charged and His medical practice deemed illegitimate by the Federal government. The US Supreme court overturned his conviction and Justice McReynolds asserted in so many words that the Department of Justice has no control of the medical practice in the States. Moral to the Story: When it comes to recovery, handling addicted patients is an Art and a

Science. Some facilities allow clients to go through withdrawal without any substitute for the drug their chemically dependent upon, and other outpatient clinics simply provide a small dosage of an alternative to the narcotic such as methadone. The point is, Physican's on staff know their patients and what tools they need in order to properly treat the disorder of addiction. Many times, patients have display Co-occurring symptoms of Mentle illness that they attempt to selftreat with the illicit use of illegal drugs instead of taking their prescribed medication.

## Chapter 72:

## Justice George Alexander Sutherland (1862-1942)

Justice Sutherland had an eventful upbrining as he matriculated through the coursework of undergrad and Law School, and eventually arose to positions of elected representative in Utah as well as holding positions in the Legislative branch of the Senate. He would ultimately land in the high position of Associate Justice in the High Court of the land, and his ideals were normally conservative, although he had a fe w progressive projects that he persued. He was an English immigrant, who graduated from Michagan State Law School and openend up his own practice before getting heavly involved with both Justice and State Departments.

The following case we will herein discuss is one of Zoning ordinances and how government have the power or ability to regulate what lands will be used for insuarey vs. Private residential areas and so on. In the case of Village of Euclid v. Ambler REalty Co. (1926) , we have a situation where zoning ordinnces were just coming into being and there were massive influxes of such ordinancnes popping up all over the country including other countries in the world and Canada. In this particular case we have a subset of land that was seeking industry use, and the Reality Co., Ambler Realty, thought calculated that the industry use was devaluing the land in serveral ways and thus the ordinances was taking way Ambler's liberty and property without due process. During the actual Court proceedure the US Supreme court actual upheld the lower courts decision which was that Euclid Village was not moving unconstitionally by expanding into industry with their land, and that in fact, Ambler Co were basing their assumption of devaluation purley on speculation. Moral to the Story: This case was in fact was a different look or take on zoning laws then I had previously been exposed to. In the past, I had only associated zoning laws are ordinances with race and class areas of where certain groups of people were placed to live or could live and apply for mortgage loans to apprehend property, or registration districts of representation. So, today's study broadened my horizen a bit, in that zoning laws originated with ordincances to do different things, namely industrially expansion, with certain parcels of land.

The next case we will discuss was highly political and emotional case that still sparks depate amoung college intellectuals and those who seek to understand the racial history and sometimes unjust proccedural rulings of a country that was rooted in bias and a bigoted attitude toward Blacks that came along with the history and institution of slavery. In the case, not to be bias myself, but you have a situation where there are nine black boys charged with raping two wihte young women. In the details we find there were seven white men, the black boys, and the two young women on the train when a fight ensued. All the white men were thrown from the train and allegedly the two white women were raped. Wheather these rape events happened or not, the injustice or proceedure and the witholding of due process is what happen next. Also, it must be noted that in the aftermath, one of the girls redacted her claim that she was raped. The boys were held, not allowed to call parents, not given the right to counsel, and all sentenced to death within the same week, with the exception of the youngest boy of 13. So, in the State case, the ruling that the boys were convicted upon was deemed constitutional, but upon the young men appealing their case to the Supreme Court, Judgement came down that basically the young men were entitled to seek counce, thus the previous decision overturned. This was surprisingly the first time the Supreme Court had reversed a State trial on the basis of criminal procedural provision of the United States Bill of Rights. Moral to Story: The final conclusion of this trial is actually unclear to the author, because various sources report that the convictions were overturned, and other sources report that the death sentences were confirmed and carried out, despite the appeal. Some of the boys were given mistrial.

## Chapter 73:

## Justice Pierce Butler (1866-1939)

Justice Pierce Butler was born native of Minnesota, parents immigrated from Ireland. He was a unique selection for President Warren G. Harding, as Justice Butler's philosophical leanings and Jurisprudence was bent toward the democratic side of the house and President Harding was a Republican President. Justice Butler completed his undergraduate career at Carleton College, and studied the law, being admitted to the bar in 1888. Sources do not report him attending Law school, but that did not take away from his stellar legal career. He joined a law firm in which he became a partner in a short time. He also had his own private practice, not to mention the company owned by his five brothers whom he did work for. Justice Butler's specialty was Corporate law and representing Railroad companies and the interest of their shareholders. He actually won a 12 million dollar verdict for a Canadian Street Railway Investors. Ironically, although Justice Butler was a democratic by name, he actually adamantly resisted business regulation and New Deal welfare programs that would be supported by the Federal Government. Other decisions will be herein discussed.

This first case deals with the matter of allegiance to the country and the controversial political stance of pacifism from an immigrant women who had not yet be neutralized as an American Citizen. This is the case of, *The United States v. Schwimmer, (1929),* in which the federal government, after Ms. Shwimmer balked at the Oath of Allegiance, and refused to take up arms, if need be, to protect her new found land. She was Hungry born, there had to be many other factors that heated the situation, namely it was around 1930, which was the close to the inception of the rise of Nazism. Self-declared as a pacifist, her citizenship was denied by the highest court in the land, to her part she is quote saying, "My cosmic consciousness of belonging to the human family is shared by all those who believe that all human beings are the children of God." Justice Butler, in his majority opinion in so many words, spoke of how the Government has these checks in place to maintain allegiance and foster a sense of nationalism in its citizens. Furthermore, those who do not meet the standards and necessary qualifications find themselves burdensome, especially if when compelled to military service, they fail to comply. The dissenting opinion spoke of how Ms. Shwimmer's belief or faith in the Sermon on the Mount was stronger than others, and begged the question, should she be punished for this? Moral to the Story: In today's modern age of cyber attacks from far away lands like Russia, and en-bedded terrorist cells that disguise themselves in plain day, I think that citizenship and allegiance should be taken very seriously. Too many countries that pose adversarial relationship with the US have persons residing the the US who live comfortably, with access to resources, power, and influence, that could possibly subtlety change our American Landscape if not cause problems on a grand scale. Instances include recent espionage indictments of Chinese Americans at American Universities, the closing of various Chinese Confucius Institutes, Russian Hacking, Stateside Terrorist bombing. I am not suggesting that we revert back to a more dangerous time in our political history and take on such measures as internment camps like what happen to the Japanese Americans during WWII. That would be horrifying and politically devastating on all levels. But several questions of allegiance and testing the will to serve seem like an okay standard and bar to cross, to becoming an American Citizen, among other things.

In a following case in which Justice Bulter dissented but authored no opinion, we have a Connecticut Resident who trespasses a local record store to the point of breaking and entering and "lifts" a phonograph and begins to run; officers close on his tail in a heated chase. He is eventually cornered, pulls out a weapon, and proceeds to shoot, and kills two law officers. Palko, was apprehended approximately 30 days later and charged with $1^{st}$ degree murder, and sentenced to life in prison. Prosecutors, unsatisfied with the lesser charge of $1^{st}$ degree murder instead of $2^{nd}$ degree murder and the death penalty won a new case and got the sentenced they were after. Palko then appealed on the grounds of the fifth amendment, double jeopardy and misappropriated the privileges or immunities clause of the $14^{th}$ amendment. At the conclusion of the matter, it was Justice Cardozo who authored the majority opinion sentencing Palko to the death penalty in the matter of *Palko v. Connecticut (1937).* Moral to the Story: Double Jeapordy is a real thing, and criminals are not suppose to be tried twice for the same trial. Yet and still, I guess mistrials happen all the time, and Palko was deserving of his capital punishment sentence for murdering two State Officers in cold blood. Not sure what the judgment would be if the same were to happen today in the various counties and districts across the country especially given the climate, and modern day conflict that exist in certain cities between various precincts and certain political fringe groups. God forbid this action and deadly sin be repeated; notwithstanding, all things considered, the Devil's Question, quite possibly would be, would one who murdered not one, but two officers after a break-in,, theft, and chase, get the death penalty of the electric chair. It almost sounds barbaric, archaic, and cruel; electric chair, death penalty, capital punishment. Yet and still, so holds the responsibility of Federal Justices to exact judgments and at time, Do Harm.

## Chapter 74:

## Justice Edward Terry Sanford (1865-1930)

Justice Edward Sanford was born native to Tennessee and would turn out to be a heavily degreed man as he earned a Bachelors of Arts and of Philosophy from his hometown college, The University of Tennessee, and a Bachelor of Arts and Masters of Arts from Harvard University, and finally, a Bachelor of Laws degree from Harvard Law. His legal career involved him serving the State Department as Attorney General, sitting on the District Court of the Eastern District of Tennessee, the United States District Court for the Middle District of Tennessee, and ultimately the United States Supreme Court. His Judicial philosophy can be gleaned in a number of high-profile cases in which he either served as lead prosecutor when he was serving as the Attorney General, or from when he gave Opinion as a Federal Justice. Mainly, he was known to have conservative leanings, but also was instrumental in opening the door to broadening civil rights and liberties during the 1950's and 60's.

This next discussion is filled with political juice as it covers the case of *Gitlaw v. New York (1925)*. Another case in which the Espionage Act of 1917 and the Sedition of 1918 are of importance because we have a Socialist Bolshevik who is handing out what was deemed a "left wing manifesto" that provoked and incited unlawful overthrow of the government. The New York Criminal Anarchy Law was passed in 1902 on the heels of the President William McKinley's assassination by an anarchist in New York, which permitted people who seemed to be advocates of the overthrow of the American Government to be arrested in order to still the inertia and momentum of American Bolsheviks becoming a national movement and gaining more followers. Gitlaw's defense was that his writings were more so philosophical, political, historical analysis rather than a revolutionary bent. Prosecutors in the case reasoned differently, asserting that any words that incited actions that would cause readers or hearers to commit crime was punishable by law. It was Judge Sanford who gave the majority opinion in this case stating in so many words that the State may punish words or utterances that endanger or come against the very foundation of the American Government and seek to overthrow by illegal means. Moreover, these words pose threat to the safety and security of the American People and public peace of the State. Justice Sanford saw Gitlaw's political theory as a flame that could have ignited a blazing flame of unruly and destructive chaos across America, rather than simply "philosophical abstractions" of a strengthened mind. Moral to the Story: Revolutionaries that come against the State, in more instances than not, invite destructive, and life disabling trouble into their situation. This does not suggest that righteous causes should not be legally fought and advocated for, fore what would the purpose of living in free democracy be, if individuals and groups could not peacefully protest, speak, utilize the press, carry arms, and benefit from all the civil liberties that people are entitled to as law abiding citizens. But, times are changing, and there be many bad actors, and protests turn into riots, carrying of arms turn into people or officers being shot, and speaking so violently against the State seems to be a pastime of disgruntled, ungrateful, and unemployed Americans. That's not to say that there are not a fair share of Scholars who give accurate and precise analysis of Government Corruption or bring out instances of political bad behavior, but at least it's scholarly and civil. Personally, I believe, if everyone did what they were suppose to do, instead of talking about how bad things were and are, that collectively we all would be in a better place; Black, White, Asian, Latino, or otherwise. Sure there be social hurdles to overcome, sure certain pockets of injustice arise when "unarmed African-American Men" are shot in a disproportionate rate when compared with those from other races, and I'm not saying these things are to be ignored. But, it all seems so emotional, that it makes me wonder, do we incite this behavior against ourselves by being so negative. I'm not advocating people be fake, ignore facts, or be ignorant to the truth of history, but at some point, let's stop crying and bitching over it, and move forward with the business of the day. Maybe that's insensitive, and easy to say for someone who hasn't lost anyone to racial injustice, but, I have lived my share of life, and can say, even after experiencing a taste of the bitter pill of bigotry, American Nazism, and just down right rudeness, I think I would be a weaker man to allow that portion or pockets of my life experience to be my focus. But how did we get to that, the main point is, Revolutionaries against the State, who have no real righteous, or moral cause but Anarchy; in my opinion deceive themselves, and narrowly escape prosecution or judgment from the State only for a time.

This next case deals with racial covenants signed and implemented in all white neighborhoods and the legality of those covenants; furthermore, if they can legally uphold in court. In the matter of *Corrigan v. Buckley (1926)*, some thirty Washington residents signed a private document agreeing to not sale their home to any non-white individual, group, or family; it happen, that is a home was sold to a black family, and their contract was considered void because of the previous restrictive covenant. Despite laws that said racial segregation could not be enforced, the practice was rampid and evident in that primarily whites lived in suburban areas, and Blacks tended to live in the inner city. This decision was upheld by the US Supreme Court, and it was not until years later in *Shelly v. Kraemer (1948)* that racially restrictive housing covenants were struck down, which were rampid all throughout Washington. Moral to the Story: There's nothing wrong with wanting to be around your own kind, or people that look like, sound like, and think like you; nevertheless, when it comes to excluding a whole groups of people from property that they can afford, and merit the right to be in, simply because of racial prejudices;this seems unacceptable, inappropriate, flat out wrong. I guess if a family agreed to maintain a street neighborhood, or community and keep their property in their family, passing it down through the generations, this would not be illegal, but to purposely exclude others simply because of race and the idea that the property value will go down if "they" move in is a little absurd. Then again, I guess it just depends on what type of people you get in there. Notwithstanding, locking whole communities of people out of neighborhoods that they financially qualify to be in, denies them their right to life, liberty, and pursuit of happiness, which is unconstitutional.

# The Writings of Antonio Vol. V

## Chapter 75:

## Justice Harlan Fiske Stone

Justice Harlan Stone served in a number of high leadership positions before his ascension to Chief Justice of the United States Supreme Court. As an undergrad, he attended Amherst Coolidge, a native of New Hampshire, he went on to Columbia Law School and after graduation became the Dean. He served in the State Department during the second World War on the War Department Board of Inquiry. In addition to these positions, he also served as the U.S. Attorney General under The Coolidge Administration. Sources report that they were good friends at Amherst College. In the role of the Chief Justice, Hon. Stone reaffirmed the President's power to try Nazi saboteurs apprehended Stateside by military tribunals during the *Ex parte Quiri(1942).* We will herein discuss.

The first case we will discuss deals with eight Nazi spy's being captured and tried during time of war. The eight men were German American's who had recently traveled to Germany at the inception of WWII to attend a Sabotage School where they learned German Spycraft techniques, and deployed their newly developed skills upon American soil upon their return to the States. The conflict of the case lies in the that the appointed defender for the German Americans argued that the President did not have a constitutional right to set up a Military Tribunal using a previous case as precedent, which resolved that military tribunals could not be set up to try ordinary civilians. The prosecutor in the case countered that these were in fact German spy's, simply without uniform. All eight men were tried and convicted on four main charges; 1 violating the law of war, 2., violating Article 81 of the Articles of War; defining the offense of corresponding with or giving intelligence to the enemy., 3. violating Article 82; defining the offense of spying, 4., conspiracy to commit the offenses alleged in the first three charges. They were sentenced and 6 were executed by Electric Chair. The remaining were sent to the American Zone of occupied Germany. Such were the matters in the case of *Ex parte Quiri (1942).* Moral the the Story: I think for most military and government positions, people know what they are getting into before they accept a post an appointment. This is from the outside looking in, notwithstanding, one would think that the military of government contract signer has thought carefully about the consequences, potential risks, and fatal reality of being in such a dangerous job. This goes for any military or government agent who decides to infutrate with plans of sabotage another country, especially a country more powerful than their own. Such was the matter in this case, eight men knew what they had gotten into, being previous German-

American citizens, and deciding to betray the land that had accepted and neutralized them, America, for their homeland-Germany, during time of War.

In this following case, *International Shoe Co. v. Washington (1945);* we have a law mandating that all businesses pay a certain State unemployment tax. International Shoe Co., for whatever reasons did not pay their share of unemployment compensation to the state, and thus found themselves in court for the matter. The ruling came down that the company had to pay, even though this companies contact with the particular stare requiring the unemployment tax was minimal. Therein lies the tension or conflict of the case; even businesses that are registered in one state, but may operate in another, may still be required to pay unemployment compensation tax. Moral to the Story: Short and Sweet, business ca not really get out of paying unemployment taxes, irregardless or what state their business was registered, or operates

## Chapter 76:

## Charles Evans Hughes (1872-1946)

see chapter 63

# Chapter 77:

## Justice Owen Roberts (1875-1955)

Justice Owen Roberts was native to Philadelphia and graduated from an Academy Style Boarding School. For undergrad he attended the University of Pennsylvania and was a stellar Greek Student. Among other things, he worked with the newspaper on campus, and went on to attend the University of Pennsylvania Law School. After law school he joined a firm, and soon thereafter began to do work with the Attorney General's office. In terms of his judicial leanings and philosophical bent, Justice Roberts was more of middling, yet he had strong pinning in his discussions. Sources report that he advocated the constitutionality of President Roosevelt's New Deal, yet ruled against the Bill. He also ruled against the Japanese American Internment Camp also implemented by President Roosevelt of which we will discuss further herein.

This next case plays out at the inception of WWII and on the heals of the that dreadful day Pearl Harbor was bombed and we entered into conflict with not only Germany along with our British and Soviet Allies, but also against the Japanese Empire. Justice Hugo Black authored an opinion on this case, *Korematsu v. United States (1944)*, and in his final written statements he painted the picture that because of this horrific historical backdrop and facts, certain policies had to be implemented by the Military as to resist a West Coast invasion our Stateside Military bases and personnel not be compromised by clever Japanese spy craft, sabotage, or outright attack; I add and paraphrase. The internment camps, which all Japanese-Americans had to relocate to from the West Coast, uprooting many families, businesses, and otherwise happy US citizens is looked at by some Judicial and historical Scholars, hindsight being 20/20, as a Judicial blunder, and a "judicial stain" on jurisprudence. Yet and still, all things considered, given today's foreign political, ingrown threats, and homeland security quandary; one might beg the question, Were they so wrong, and did they do what they thought best given the dire circumstances? A moral, philosophical, and political decision, or was it simply Psychological and a maneuver of Combat Military Strategy. What am I saying? We face homeland threats of terror today, that range from cyber security measures that hack elections, to domestic groups that terrorize people, cities, and precincts for whatever reasons, and simply because verdicts didn't go their way, or "the way they should have gone", or because in their strong opinions, Justice was not served. At what point does the "Establishment" or our Government make broad and bold moves to put an end to the foreign infiltration and domestic chaos, or do we ever, or is it their job to do, or are we capable of doing such things? Philosophical and Moral questions for those who govern and have a true heart for the welfare of the people and the State, or whatever order that goes in. It almost harms me to think of it, but God forbid America has to go into some type of Marshall Law, not only because of the Covid-19 Pandemic, but because of wide spread subversive and/or terrorist groups that want to destroy the nation. Can't really see this happening, nor do I want our liberties as American Citizens infringed upon in any way; but, What If? And/Or does that lead to more dangerous conflict within our Nation and what is the Cost/Benefit? Moral to the Story: Fred Korematsu was a Japanese-American citizen who refused to relocate under Presidential orders during a time of War, and privileged himself to take this matter to the courts on the grounds of his fourteenth amendment right being violated. The Courts declared that this was not a matter of racial bigotry or discrimination, but Military authorities had deemed the exclusion of all Japanese Americans from the West Coast because of the "urgency of the situation."

In this following case, we have a rule passed down from the United States Supreme Court that affirmed racial desegregation and further confirmed the voting rights of all citizens, reversing or overturning the Texas State Law that allowed parities to create their own private regulations and policies, not excluding certain exclusionary policies such as white primaries. The use of white primaries excluded was implemented by Democratic Party and, for lack of a better way to say it, disenfranchised many African-American voters. After the Supreme Court Judgment was made, white primary laws changed not only in Texas, but other states across the nation as well. The name of this case is, *Smith v. Allwright (1944)* , and in this case Smith, a African-American Dentist sued the County election representative Allwright on the grounds that white primary laws were unconstitutional, more specifically, did the county officials of Texas and the State have the constitutional right to exclude black voters, and/or was that law constitutional in and of itself? Moral to the Story: Time enables Progress.

## Chapter 78:

## Justice Benjamin Nathan Cardozo

Justice Benjamin Cardozo was born native to New York and entered his undergraduate career at the early age of 15. He graduated from Columbia Law School and was admitted into the soon thereafter. Serving the Judicial Department as both New York Federal Appeals Judge, Associate and Supreme Court Justice position, his influence was great on the American landscape. Jewish heritage, Justice Cardozo came from a large family. Not only did Justice Cardozo author opinions on Supreme Court cases and otherwise, bur he also authored a few publications. One of them being, "The Nature of the Judicial Process, which was cornerstone in founding the American Law Institute. Appointed by President Herbert Hoover to the US Supreme Court, Justice Cardozo would use his years of private practice with his brother, his appointment as Chief Judge to the New York Appeals court as his foundation to build upon as he served the US Supreme Court as Associate Justice.

One interesting case in which Justice Cardozo was on the bench for, was that of Humphrey's Executor v. United States; power struggle, or political, structural struggle between President and his cabinet or administration and Congress. An Interesting layout of the alignment of power and the pecking order in American Government; furthermore, a review of what is allowed by certain executive offices. In this case President Hoover had previously appointed Mr. Humphrey as his Commissioner of the Federal Trade Commission. Upon the election of President Roosevelt, there was great tension, and the incumbent President wanted Humphrey removed from offices, asking him to resign twice. Sources report that there was lingering animosity or resent over Humphrey not being or showing enough open support for Roosevelt's New Deal. The Federal Trade commission allowed Humphrey's dismissal on grounds of negligence, yet the The US Supreme Court ruled that such a dismissal for a "quasi-legislative" and quasi-judicial officer was in-fact "improper" because the instance was politically motivated, in so many words. The judgment recommended that that a matter of this sort needed to be ran through some type of Congressional oversight. Moral to the Story: Politics often play a role in the government arena, or any industry for that matter, including families, churches, businesses, schools, militarizes, prisons, and all mater of organizations. In fact, usually when there are groups of people organizing for any matter, for whatever reason, there are certain unspoken rules of engagement and order. The more formal the group, the more explicit the organization and it's particular hierarchical structure. This is neither good or bad, but societal norm and I would say regular human social interaction. What's interesting, is how often times new and upcoming generations sometimes reject or battle against the structure, hierarchical and social norms, or status quo of the given day. This again, is neither good, nor bad; and I feel indifferent, because such action can be both good and bad. Justifiably some changes may indeed need to be made to the "status quo", and yet methods that don't work within the system, or legal-judicial-political labyrinth of a government system such as ours, can have deadly and detrimental consequences.

In this second case that we will herein discuss, a matter of harsh judgment, and incorrect procedures to obtain confessions that may or may have not been true. Coercive means to manipulate the suspect to confess to a crime can be deemed unconstitutional,and takes away an individuals due process. Yet Hollywood paints the picture of the clever scenario of "good cop, bad cop." And officers doing all the matter of evil to offenders in order to ascertain the Truth. In the specific case of *Brown v. Mississippi, (1936).* The details of this case are quite horrific as there was the murder of a black man on a farm. When the officer on the scene questioned the neighbors, who also were African-American, they were treated worst than human, and as guilty criminals, made to lay down while they were beat with a leather shard whip, and threatened to be hung from the neck if a confession was not made. These confessions held up in the local Court as well as the State Supreme Court, but were overturned and reversed by the US Supreme Court. The defendants ultimately were sentence with 1.5 and 7 years respectively, as oppose to death by hanging. Mind you this was circa. 1936; 16 years after the roaring 20's and just before WWII in the Deep South. Moral to the Story: I guess, no civilian really knows what goes on those black opp missions, or covert sting operations. The use of deadly force and pressure tactics to off balance the suspect or suspects is at times necessary. And many times all legalities may or may not already be in place before a major operation takes place. It becomes a question of doing the right thing or doing it the right way, from my civilian perspective, of how things may go on a battle field. Yet and still, for the local precinct officer, or FBI agent; whose jobs are just as important, in today's modern climate of high-profile cases and heightened sensitivity in the African-American Community from numerous deaths of Black men and women, I would think extra precautions would be followed to prevent unnecessary deaths of the civilian population as well as high stress legal lawsuits that destroy one's career. Not that our modern day Centurions should walk around doing their job in fear and on eggshells, for the Scriptures say, "he beareth not the sword in vain," but that they take note that times have changed, and they will be criticized for their every move, whether justified or not.

## Chapter 79:

## Justice Hugo Lafayette Black (1886-1971)

Justice Hugo Black was born native to Alabama. The youngest of eight, he originally was slated to attend medical school like one of his older brothers until prompted by his brother to become a lawyer instead. Hugo attended the University of Alabama School of Law after graduation and set off on his own to practice for a few years. Within his legal career, Hugo also became a Democratic Senator, and an Associate Justice to the US Supreme Court. His politics or Jurisprudence philosophy was one that supported the President Roosevelt's New Deal adamantly. On a deeper philosophical note, Justice Black was an avid reader of History, expressing the known sentiment, that History is necessary to understand as not to repeat past mistakes. He also believed that the Judicial Branch was not to be a Such a Supreme Power that such power lead judges to corruption, but that Supremacy should rest within the legislation; that the Constitution should and could be amended by the people; and yet to be acted within the bounds of that document. A natural born leader, Hugo resigned his positions to served in the Army during

WWII and was assigned to a post in Europe. He was in the 81s Field Artillery Division according to Sources. Finally, Justice Black advocated for African-American rights; one instance in particular as reported by sources is there was a certain black man who was forced into what was essentially "commercial slavery" after a time of incarceration.

One case in which Justice Black wrote a dissenting opinion was *Adamson v. California (1947);* a case in which a Mr. A.D. Adamson was charged with Murder of the 1st degree. He decided to not testify on his behalf reasoning that the persecutor would bring up his priors. Yet the Californai law stated that refusal to testify was essentially admission to guilt, and allowed jury to infer guilt, as so argued by the Persecutor on the Case. Mr. Adamson appealed the first decision saying that his fifth amendment right had been violated. The Decision in that case was the same, Judges deciding on the technicality that Mr. Adamsosn's fifth amendment may have been violated, and this would have held in federal Court, but this privileged did not extend to the State courts on the grounds of the due process clause of the fourteenth amendment, which prohibits the arbitrary deprivation of life, liberty, or property, by government except as authorized by law. Justice Hugo Black argued that dissented with a poignant opinion stating essentially that the ruling was unconstitutional. Moral to the Story: Very interesting the United States of America that whether or not one is penalized for his committing a crime depends on his and his counsel's clever ability to defend oneself against the allegations; as the rule is "innocent until proven guilty beyond reasonable doubt." Of course there be multiple factors to consider; among them; evidence, eye witness, jury, judge, character witnesses, experts, forensics, and all the other tools and toys that come with proving and deciding important cases. The point I'm trying to make is, does this system truly uphold justice if one who has committed a crime can get off easy, or one who has not committed anything can be criminally penalized due to their lack of savvy or cleverness. I guess one must study for themselves, to show themselves approved, needing not being ashamed, but the point is Sometimes or Most times mercy is necessary in the face of guilt. The motive to the crime or reason why, if it is just, does this mitigate a sentence or acquit, if it is a righteous and just motive. Or is a crime a crime; and judgment sure. This to think about.

This next case deals with another theme that we have dealt with before, and that is a man being convicted under the pretenses of speech that declared violent overthrow of the government. In the case of Dennis v. United States (1951). Mr. E. Dennis, Secretary of the Communist party, was denied the right of free speech, publication, and assembly, because he was plotting to overthrow the government. The Court's decision was mainly based on the fact that the Communist Party USA's document was the "The Communist Manifesto" by Karl Marx which advocated Socialism and the violent overthrow of governments. Interestingly enough, later this decision was modified or overturned by *Brandenburg v. Ohio (1969)* which stated that "the government could not punish inflammatory speech unless that speech is directed to inciting or producing imminent lawless action and is likely to incite or produce such action" Moral to the Story: Our beloved country and countrymen who limits and yet gives leeway to so many American Citizens, immigrants, refugees, and those seeking asylum; Truly the Land of the Free, and Home of the Brave, besides the cliché rhetoric. Yet truly we must care and be careful that our leniency or laissez-faire and de facto sensibilities, lead us not into chaos nor destruction.

## Chapter 80:

## Justice Stanley Forman Reed (1884-1965)

Justice Stanely Reed was born native to Kentucky, was an Army Veteran of WWI and attended Law school but did not graduate. N He served as a councilmen to the Kentucky House of Representatives and was nominated by President Franklin D. Roosevelt to the US Supreme Court as Associate Justice. In terms of undergraduate career, Justice Reed attended Kentucky Wesleyan College for his first B.A., then went on to Yale University for his second B.A. He took on the pursuit of Law degree from two different Law Schools; Columbia University, and the University of Virginia, yet as aforementioned, did not finish. Nevertheless, this did not stop him from opening his own practice and carrying on the business of being admitted to the Bar and establishing a successful Law practice. In terms of Jurisprudence and philosophical pennings, Justice Reed was known as a moderate, yet he was also considered an economically forward thinking, advocate for desegregation, civil liberties, economic regulation, trade union right, Notwithstanding, on basic issues such as National Security, Free Speech, and Social issues, Justice Reed was mainly considered conservative.

One case in which Justice Reed was known to have a dissenting opinion was that of *McCollum v. Board of Education (1948).* In this case, we have the public school system being challenged by an Atheist Mother who is upset because she felt her son being ostracized from other classmates because of his refusal to attend optional religious classes. The details of the case reveal that this was a test of separation of church and state with respect to education; and the fact that these were tax funded programs receiving federal aide to do religious instruction. Apparently, Ms. McCollum raised legal challenge against the school board on the grounds that the Establishment Clause of the First Amendment had been violated under the Separation of Church and State principle stated in the Constitution. Moreover, Ms. McCollum argued that the religious instructional classes went against the Equal Protection Clause of the fourteenth amendment. Thus, the State court ruled against McCollum, upon which she sought a US Supreme Court review, which stated that the classes were in fact unconstitutional. Moral to the Story: The practicing of one's faith or the option of taking a Religious Studies should be available to public schools. Seems that it would be just the same as a History, Government or Philosophy elective. To band, or disallow it completely seems a bit inhibiting, as we are a nation of freedoms and according to Justice Reed's dissent, it was the interpretation of the Establishment clause that he disagreed with, stating that "an incidental support of religion should have been permissible with a more narrow reading of the First Amendment."

In this next section we will discuss another case dealing with the Espionage Act of 1917 and its regulations. Two men, Mr M. Gorin, a Soviet Intelligence Officer and Mr. H. Salich a United States Naval Employee. Salich sold personal information and documents on Japanese activity in the US to Gorin. Salich's reasoning and justification for doing such activity wasbeing that Japan was a common enemy at the time; in addition, it did not help that Mr. Salich was short on cash at the time due to an aggressive gambling problem. The way Mr. Salich was pinched is with some humor, apparently there was a spy note with dollars wrapped inside a jacket pocket taken to the dry cleaners. The manager at the dry cleaners' shop checked the pockets and found the note and money and immediately reported to the local police precinct, which was reported to the FBI. Investigation proceeded after this, in which confession was obtaineby Mr. Hafis Salich. The charges were enough to sentence the two to approximately 10 years collectively, individually 4 and 6 years. Moral the Story: Crime doesn't pay, especially when your trying to betray your own country, or leak confidential government secrets, irregardless of motive. Of course there's always the philosophical caveat; for example what about in cases where the American public should be informed of something about their government; Whistleblowers and Wikileaks people... What about Edward Snowden. Is he Hero or Trader? These tight quagmires of situations if you will present opportunity for if not community, national and global discussions that can lead to Solutions. Notwithstanding, anyone who has the audacity to steal from their government and rely to the public or international allies or enemies abroad had to have considered the risk.

## Chapter 81:

## Justice Felix Frankfurter

Justice Felix Frankfurter was a Jewish son, born in Vienna, who immigrated to the States with his family. His new home being New York, he end up attending City College of New York, graduating on to Harvard Law. He showed off his stellar abilities by becoming editor of the Harvard Law Review. As an adolescent he read voraciously and attended public lectures on political topics such as trade unionism, socialism, and communism. Ultimately he would become a Lawyer, Harvard Professor, and Associate Justice of the US Supreme Court. He held other State Department positions such as, Judge Advocate General during WWI, and a sort of companion and advisor to then President Franklin D, Roosevelt. In terms of his philosophical leanings with respect to the Courts power and authority, he believed in judicial restraint and the Courts not interpreting the constitution in a way that would "limit authority of the legislative and executive branches". He authored just under some 250 opinions, we will consider a few of such cases.

This first case deals with public schools having the right to compel students to pledge allegiance to the American flag. It was later overturned in some three years. The particular case is *Minersville School District v. Gbitis (1940)* and involved the US Supreme Court ruling in favor of the public school district in mandating Johovah's Witness Students to solute the Flag as well as recite the pledge of Allegiance. Sources report that in the aftermath of the case, Jehovah's Witnesses were persecuted because of the decision. As previously mentioned, the case was overturned by *Virginia State Board of Education v. Barnette (1943).* A little history and background on the case, the impetus behind mandatory pledge allegiance was to galvanize patriotims in the states during wartime. The pledges were first made mandatory during WWI and the Spanish-American war. Relevant to this case, J.F. Rutherford, who was the President of the Watch Tower Society in 1935 stated that pledging allegiance to a flag ascribed salvation to it and unfaithfulness to God, therefore many Witnesses decided to follow his leadership. Walter Gobitas, the defendant in this case, wanted to take a stand and endure persecution for the Faith, and thus challenged the system. Moral to the Story: Today our civil liberties are such that an individual can burn an American Flag without prosecution as a exercise of their first amendment right and freedom of expression, let alone skip out on the pledge of allegiance. Have we developed into a nation that holds freedom and self-expression in such high regard to the point that lack of respect for our nation's history and pride is celebrated? I'm not suggesting that we all be blind little lemmings without any knowledge to the weight of blood, tears, sweat, and sacrifice that our nation has shed, even at he sleight of other people's and nations; nevertheless, it is our heritage, and the nation that we built as a people from all parts of the world. Whether we are ashamed or proud of our history, it is ours, and our in my very personal opinion, I believe we should celebrate the history, and the values that built our country; that good and bad, for it only makes us stronger. When we decide to let hatred rule to the point of self-destruction from within, then we are in perilous times. For we were called to be, One Nation, Under God, Indivisible, with Liberty and Justice for All. May sound like rhetoric, but the power of it's implementation and the ringing in the heart of our youth, makes us strong, connected, and powerful. One would think that such patriotism needed in light of the coming winds of Communism; where governments beat and harass their citizens with literal batons and fear tactics and the people are limited in their choice, liberty and individuality. Or what about the sleeping idea of a world ruled by Islam; a theocracy of violence that does not tolerate any different form of religious practice or worship. If these are the alternatives to our Great Republic, then truly we should continue to instill in our children the great principles of our Democratic Republic.

This next case deals with murder and maham and the alleged murderer who supposedly confessed to the crime and was imprisoned and soon escaped, only to be re-apprehended and appeal his case to the highest court in the land was a man by the name of Irvin. More specifically, in the case of *Irvin v. Dowd (1959),* the murders were committed in Indiana, and the local Police Precinct once they had Leslie Irwin detained, notified the public that Irvin had made a confession to the crimes incriminating himself. The jury was said to be extremely bias having predetermined his guilt beforehand, his Fate, so to speak, was sealed. He was given a guilty verdict from the judge, sentenced to death and some how managed to escape, leaving behind letters prescribing his innocence. Once the court hit the Supreme Court document, the judgement was no different, and the judges had to consider the weight of his escape form Prison, which denied his writ of habeas corpus. Although the court was slightly divided. Some judges opposed the prejudge mental jurist in his State trial. And others like Justice Frankfurter who upheld judicial restraint were opposed to federal courts interfering with State matters and granting the writ of habeas corpus. In the Finality, the case was sent back to the State Courts and in two years wound right back up at the US Supreme Court level. Habeaus Corpus denied, Moral to the Story: Also in the finality, the importance of an impartial jury was deemed necessary in order for the criminally accused to be tried fairly. We'll never know the full story behind how those murders were committed in Indiana, but we do know one man was caught, presumed to have confessed, and ever before his day in court, fought to escape, succeeded, and was re-captured and tried twice. Did he do it? Looking back, with our superior forensics, and blood sampling DNA tests, I wonder what the outcome would be?

## Chapter 82:

## Justice Frank Murphy (1890-1949)

Justice Frank Murphy was a WWI veteran who attended Michigan Law school beforehand. He was born to Irish parents who immigrated from across the pond. He held a number of federal positions; Attorney, Judge and Mayor of Detroit. Ultimately he was appointed by President Franklin D. Roosevelt to the U.S. Supreme Court, serving on the court nine years up until his death in 1949. Justice Murphey's Jurisprudence was considered to the side of the liberal leanings. His philosophy caused him to distinguish himself from certain conservative thinking on topics pertaining to ethnic minorities, illegal immigrants, criminals, and dissenters. His notions and sentiment will be seen through a few of the cases we will herein discuss. Although we already spoke of *Korematsu v United States*, it must be noted that he dissented in that decision.

The first case up for discussion is one that was that of a financial nature; *Securities and Exchange Commission v. W.J. Howey Co., (1946).* It dealt with the U.S. Supreme court determining a certain companies land contracts, financial instruments in actuality and in violation of the rules and laws of the Securities Act of 1933; more specifically with respect to the mailing system being used and interstate commerce. Because of this, a Howey Test was given to determine whether or not a profit could be made and the contracts could be considered of the Investment type if marketed by a third party. Justice Murphey ruled that in a four prong test this company was in violation of all of them, and that the security like investment was not registered. The law stipulated the unlawful issuance and sale of unregistered securities was in fact not permitted. Moral to the Story: When it comes to financial instruments with respect to land, securities, options, derivatives, loans, commodities, and now and eventually Bitcoin and crypto-currency; the government usually finds a way to introduce taxes and regulation. This goes back to the inception of our nation with respect to banking and international trading and the introduction of tariffs and eve interstate taxes. Our Big Brother, and Uncle Sam Government makes sure to get a cut of all these types of transactions, it's just the way things are; Capital Gains Tax on investment instruments, State and international taxes on trade and commerce.

In this next case, *Falbo v. United States (1944),* is a matter in ambiguity and classification of a Jehovah's Witness. Either conscientious objector or minister of religion, it was the time of 1940 when America was at war and deploying the strategy of "All Hands on Deck, "at home. Essentially All divisions and realms were requited to report for assignment as to how they would be participating in national service. When Falbo failed to report to be trained , and adamantly refused the board's order, he was classified as a conscientious objector. The consequence to being classified as such, was a Federal indictment and after his very firm refusal to report to personnel duty, so to speak; he was sentenced to five years in prison. His defense was that the Court might have reconsidered their determination on the basis that there might have been some bias against him, from the local board in their "pre-judgmental mindset." No such evidence was submitted to groove these theories, thus Falbo's sentence stood fast. Moral to the Story: If the country is in a state of War and requests all hands on deck for national service, for God and for Country; conscience objectors, I believe, should be indicted and jailed for their refusal to serve, fight, administrative, or otherwise give their talents and skills so freely developed in our land of liberty. In a sense, it is a type of ungratefulness, betrayal, and lack of heart—cowardliness.

## Chapter 83:

## Justice Harlan Fiske Stone (1872-1946)

See Chapter 75

## Chapter 84:

## Justice James Francis Byrnes

In the case of Justice James Byrnes, he was a native of South Carolina with great democratic leanings as we will see. He served as an Attorney, House Representative, Senator, Secretary of State, and United States Supreme Court Justice. In terms of early years, Justice Byrnes attended Catholic School and dismissed himself at the tender age of 14 to work in a law office. From there he would eventually clerk for a Federal Judge, study the Law, and hold a number of State Department positions. His Jurisprudencial philosophical fortitude led him to support President Roosevelt's New Deal, as well as maintain an adversarial position against the Nazi Regime in Germany and Imperial Japan. Of course, today, both Germany and Japan be our allies, and it is now China, Russia, and North Korea who pose threat with their Communist Regimes. Interestingly enough, although Justice Byrnes was opposed by the Ku Klux Klan on certain campaigns, he actually in one of his opinions on a case leaned toward resisting anti-lyching laws, and asserted that these practices along with "Rape" were responsible and necessary to keep the Negro in check. These types of beliefs allows one to understand on some level what was the impetus behind certain behaviors. And mainly, some of the hateful acts conducted by peoples and sometimes even government, were strong arm strategic tactics of leadership; some my call it tyranny, and although the reasons, in my personal opinion, do not justify the means; it does at least give explanation as the question of, Why? That answer being, to keep the Negroes in check, as they have the tendency to get, "too big for their britches," (parenthesis my addition). Historically, Justice Byrenes was the second to last Supreme Court Justice to sit on the Court without having attended Law School, but on have admitted to studying the Law. He served on the US Supreme Court approximately 15 months.

In the following case, we have *Lisenba v. California (1941)* which is a matter dealing with a capital punishment sentence for then said Major Raymond Lisenba, who allegedly murdered his wife, and confessed to this crime when questioned, or in his testimony, aggressively coerced by authorities. His defense was that his due process rights' of the Fourteenth Amendment of the US Constitution were were violated. Apparently, as sources report the details of the case, Major Lisenba purchased an insurance policy on his wife, classic red flag, and in a few months she untimely was found dead, by drowning. Prior to this, Major Lisenba had purchased more than a few rattlesnakes with the intent or motive of murdering his wive, and more evidence was disclosed to the court that Major Lisenba was previously married multiple times, and one of his wives were found dead under relatively similar same case scenario as his current diseased wife. The judgment was sure in spite of the alleged coercing of testimony from Lisenba, for the very reason that the precinct had received a full testimony from an alleged accomplice to the crime just before the interrogation. Moral to the Story: Crime doesn't pay in the long run; especially when committed stupidly by sloppy, have witted criminals. Not to glorify the murderers, thieves, and clever criminally minded individuals who get off or go on undetected, but the point is, when faced with the consequence of heavy heartily committed crime such as murder, mass murder, rape, child rape, child sexual abuse, terrorism, war crimes, crimes against humanity, and genocide, and not to mention, treason, espionage, sedition, piracy and aircraft hijacking, drug trafficking, drug dealing, and drug possession. The question becomes, when faced with the consequences of committing such crime, how much time or severity of punishment is necessary for that particular level of crime and at what passion, premeditation, or hate was it committed with. I think the death penalty is necessary on some level, otherwise, those bent on doing the severe acts of evil in society will face no consequence, but to permanently better themselves in prison. I'll leave it to the legal Leaders of the Judicial and Legislative branches of government give point to the details of what such crimes truly require death penalty sentencing, but to do away the death penalty completely I believe points us in the direction of judicial weakness and possibly a more lawless society that breeds Anarchy.

In this next case, we have a law in California during the early 1940's that stipulated that no California resident could bring an indigent person back to the state. In the case of Edwards, v. California (1941), Edward brought his indigent causing from Texas to California. Apparently, Edward's causing, Frank Duncan was unemployed, had only a few possessions, and thus Edward was tried and sentenced to six months in jail, his deference and appeal to the US Supreme Court on the grounds that this law was unconstitutional and was a violation of the Commerce Cause of the 14$^{th}$ Amendment. The US Supreme Court overturned the indignant law in California, overruling it, and deeming it as unconstitutional. Moral to the Story: California was such a "rich" state, that legally you couldn't even enter into the territory without having a job lined up, or some kind of holdings or proof of wealth. Not sure if this law was effective and for how long, but it would definitely motivate individuals to succeed in order to enter a land of success. Yet so many stories we here of California being a Mini America so to speak or land of opportunity. What about all the starving and broke artist that bummed around until they made it. Of course, this rush was probably after the law was struck down. Furthermore, what about all the Mexican immigrants, how were they affected by this law? History paints broadly upon the Canvas of the present, but the details of the original sketch only the Creator and a few watchers may know.

## Chapter 85:

## Justice Robert Hougwout Jackson (1892-1954)

Justice Robert Jackson was born native to the state of Pennsylvania, although his parents raised him in cold state of New York. He graduated form high school and began to develop a proclivity toward writing. Thereafter was a guided tour of personal study and development, more specifically, a study of the law under the tutelage of his Uncle Frank who was an Attorney and allowed him to partner with his firm. In addition to this on the job training and apprenticeship, Justice Jackson also attended Albany Law School choosing an available option in their two year program to test out of the first two years receiving this certificate. From this launching point, it was back to private practice, where he developed a successful Law practice and became known in New York for such. He sat and weighed in on some historical cases, such as *Korematsu v. United States*, as well as, *Brown v. Board of Education*, and was even around for the *International Military Tribunal, (1945-46).*

In this first case that we will consider; a case where Justice Robert Jackson sat on the bench, bu did not necessarily give the majority opinion, is the case of *Chaplinsky v. New Hampshire (1942).* In these proceedings the extent of "fighting words" and their protection or lack thereof is examined in light of New Hampshire law in 1941 that prohibited "intentionally offensive speech directed at others in public places." So, the story goes, Mr. Walter Chaplinsky was doing "God's" bidding by doing some Moning Street preaching as he belonged to the Jehovah' Witness Sect. This was downtown Rochester and his overriding theme that morning was calling organized religion a Racket. Well, a crowd began to gather and soon the authorities also took notice as the crowd began to block the street. As a cop approached Mr. Chaplinsky for his disturbance, Mr. Chaplinsky hailed the approaching cop a "Racket," or more accurately to the point, a "God-damned Racket," and "a damned Fascist." Mr. Chaplinsky was apprehended by the officer and taken down to the precinct and to court where he was booked and arraigned by the Judge. Ultimately, as Chaplinsky's defense was that his first and fourteenth amendments were violated; however, the US Supreme court ruled in upholding the arrest; Justice Murphy essentially using the language scripts taken from the first and fourteeth amendments: "narrowly limited classes of speech" that protected by the constitution and "lewd, obscene, profane and libelous" directed at people to incite hate, animosity and have no social value, unprotected by the constitution. Moral to the Story: People breath, say, whisper, and shout out loud fighting phrases and words on a moment by moment, daily basis, in public spaces, work places, schools and Universities, the public square and market, and even the most "sacred and consecrated" temples. People get offended when words toward them condescend, and degrade instead of inspire and enlighten. Such to the point that certain states had laws prohibiting fighting words or what might today be consdered "Hate Speech." How often was this case used as precedent, or were these Stately statutes inforced, I'm not sure, or the matter is ambiguous, the the fact that libel exist today on a global level, and even for sport and laughs on news media, talk shows, and in every facet of society we have people talking offensively, purposely, as to not seem weak, seems that we, as a global community will have to deal with the matter and not be so sensitive. Though people's aggression at times be annoying and even abrasive, it seems more so a personality and character issue as opposed to a criminally prosecutable offense; unless this speech of Hate incites and leads to violence, in my personal opinion.

In this next case we will embark upon a discussion about the Oklahoma laws that permitted compulsory laws that essentially nurtured criminals, both male and female in an ongoing rolled out process called "compulsory sterilization." The backdrop of Skinner v. Oklahoma (1842). The statute was enforceable when criminals were int trouble with the law having more than three or more convictions. The other thing worth mentioning was that these laws only applied

of offenses which were distinctly other than "white collar crimes," and were thus felonies that were immoral. And yet morality is relative depending on who you ask and what their value system is, but the line is drawn at federal offenses that are distinctly violent, abusive, and overly aggressive in nature. Such instances are: armed robbery, theft (just not on the securities level), aggravated assault, rape, kidnap, murder and the like. Such persons who committed such federal offenses and were convicted three or more times fell victim to having a vasectomy or salpingectomy part of the penal levy weighed against them. Although in Skinners case; stealing chickens was his first offense, and the second two were armed robbery, his council appealed his case to the Supreme Court. The ruling that came down suggested a discrepancy in the Act because white collar crimes such as embezzlement were judged differently and therefore because of this distinction of jurisdiction of crime, the law violated the equal protection clause of the fourteenth amendment. Moral to the story: Once again, crime is crime, yet there be various stratified and divided levels of criminal offenses. The devastation of being made surgically steril by the State is severely harsh to say the least, if released and found to be incapable of reproduction, but then, does the punishment fit the crime is the question? Secondly, it must be noted that these types of practices were also done to the mentally ill or "feeble minded," sometimes to their unawares.

## Chapter 86:

## Justice Wiley Blount Rutledge (1894-1949)

Justice Wiley Rutledge was born native to Kentucky and went on to accomplish his bachelors degree at the University of Wisconsin. From this point in life, Justice Rutledge went on to Law School to earn a Bachelors in Law. Launching from this point into private practice for approximately two years, and then it was a number of Associate Professorship positions and various American Law Universities: University of Colorado, Washington University School of Law, and University of Iowa College where he also served as Dean. In terms of his Jurisprudence and philosophical leanings, it seems that he was one to give even the worst of the nations enemies right to a fair trial, or their due process, being considered a liberal. Such a position he held when the Japanese General Tomoyuki Yamashita was being issued due process. We will consider a few of his cases herein.

In this first case we will discuss, it deals with a German born man by the name of Anthony Cramer who was allegedly accused of treason; guilty by association. Apparently, there were two German men sent to the States on a sabotage mission—Operation Pastorius which ultimately failed. In the aftermath, these two men; Werner Thierl, and Edward Kerling, were apprehended along with Mr. Cramer due to his close affiliation with these subverters. His original sentence given by Judge Henry W. Goddard a prison term of 45 years. In Mr. Cramer's appeal to the higher Court, that is the US Supreme Court; he was granted a certiorari, which was essentially a Supreme Court Review of the case, in which they overturned Judge Goddard's decision. The reasoning behind such ruling was the upholding of the Constitution which strictly defined treason as waging war, and/or aiding, that is giving material assistance to an enemy. Apparently, there was no such evidence of this type of behavior by Mr. Cramer, only a loose association, and it is said by some sources, that Mr, Cramer had not even "paid for drinks" of his two German associates, thus the Court reversed the decision on these grounds. Moral of the Story: We are all familiar of the cliché saying, "Birds of a feather flock together," Well, I guess in this case we have to consider the other saying which says, "which one of these is not like the others." Honestly, I would think that it would be horrible to be convicted for only being associated with someone who was committing grave crimes who you had no knowledge of, but because of your association you were taken to trial along with. So many people, know of others, or have associates that they only know to do their own business in their own manner, and we have no full knowledge of the extent of their deeds, but wouldn't it be a travesty to be tried along with them if those certain individuals were criminal in their behavior. Of course, this case speaks to a different time, this was 1945, just at the conclusion of WWII, a time of uneasiness, and German intelligence had still waged full out war against the United States recruiting their countrymen and patriots to do their misdeeds at any costs. Much like the Taliban, Al Queda, and Terrorist networks that may be operating in the States and abroad today. Not to mention the more recent espionage attacks by China and Russia.

In this next case we will cover, the range of free speech was tested, unjustly censored by an inferior State Court, and duely reinstated by the ruling of the US Supreme Court. In the matter of *Terminiello v. City of Chicago (1949)*, we have a situation where essentially the laws on free speech set by the city of Chicago were more stringent than the Constitution allowed for. The City of Chicago prohibited speech which, "stirs the public to anger, invites disputes, brings about a condition of unrest, or creates a disturbance." Apparently a suspended Catholic Priest was giving a speech to some 800 people with over 1,000 outside the auditorium in protest. The speech contained inflammatory, provocative comments toward the various racial groups present according to sources which were offensive. The Chicago precinct was failed at keeping the order and thus Mr. Terminology was issued a fine of $100.00 for violating the speech ordinance. Of course he appealed to the various State courts, but did not receive his vindication until the US Supreme Court heard his case. It was the Justice William O. Douglas who authored the majority opinion stating that in freedom of speech in fact is suppose was suppose to "invite dispute and even go as far as inciting anger; and provocative, and inflammatory speech could be seen as potentially positive." The limits of free speech are fighting words and of course all out hate speech. Moral to the Story: Hmm. Free speech, well, this particular case delt with a suspended Priest preaching a semen, Maybe he was a little disgruntled, Who knows? Not even sure what the speech was about, but think of how good Preaching or Motivational Speaking and the like does tend to challenge the listeners with the intention of provoking them to action. This type of speaking albeit in many cases needs to be provocative and maybe a bit inflammatory to potently carry the point. Nevertheless, those ho have obtained mastery in the craft of Oratory can also move the crowd to action through their gifts of persuasion. It happens on Sundays in Protestant churches, Monday's in Executive Boardroom meetings, and all throughout the globe in various languages, from the battlefield to the highest court, and the head of State's Staff meeting men verbally and sometimes aggressively spar with one another. As the scriptures say, "Iron sharpens Iron."

## Chapter 87:

## Justice Harold Hitz Burton (1888 -1964)

Justice Harold Burton had a very active life; from his graduate studies at Harvard Law, to his time in France and Belgium serving in the United States Army during WWI, and his position as the Mayor of Cleveland, Ohio, in addition to his time serving in the Senate; although he was born native to Massachusetts. Justice Burton was considered "technical and procedural" rather than ruling on cases solely on constitutional grounds. Sources also report that he was a sort of "mediator" personality when heated tensions rose in the Court. Aside from his State service, Justice Burton also opened a private practice in Cleveland, Ohio where he worked for a time and then an opportunity opened up to work for his wife's Uncle in Utah, for a Power and Light Company and he decided to leave. Major forks in the road to decide, and I'd imagine he probably thought back on his decision and wondered how'd things would have turned out or been different if he stayed working for himself, growing his own practice. Nevertheless, another fork in the road came when he committed himself to the Fight of WWI. Such were the trials of American Men during that time, just before the 1920's. Some of the cases Justice Burton was on the Court for ran the gamut of topics; Cold war, loyalty oath, and subversive rulings, Church and State, Criminal Procedures, Antitrust, Racial segregation/Desegregation and the like. Some of the specific cases in which he gave opinion on we will herein; J*oint Anti-Fascist Refugee Committe v. McGrath (1951)*, and *Lorain Journal Co. v. United States (1951)*.

In this first case we are considering, *Joint Anti-Fascist Refugee Committee v. McGrath* (1951) , we have a backdrop history of warfare and there were certain laws and groups that sprung up that got certain scrutiny because of the nature of their creeds and ethos operating stateside on American soil sometimes with subversive agenda's and sabotage in mind Some of these organizations were; Totalitarian, Communistic, Subversive, or Fascist in nature, and the Anti-Fascist Refugee Group even though originally given tax-exempt status and considered a relief organization was grouped along with these others, and put on the Attorney General's List of Subversive Organizations under the auspices of President Harry Truman's administration.

They immediately lost their tax exempt status and were thrown into a whirlwind of rejection as they asked the State to reconsider their case as to their defense they were being denied due process and the First Amendment. Sources report that their arguments went unacknowledged until the case reached the level of the US Supreme Court and were given an official certiorari. Upon review it was Justice Burton who co-authored the joint majority opinion that the group was indeed an "bona fide charitable organization" and issued a remand for the District Courts to order investigation to determine if indeed the organization was communistic. It is unclear to the writer what perused after this ruling. Moral to the Story: America had to keep a watchful eye, not only abroud but at home. Even today these still exist organizations who committ melign activities and have subversive agenda's. I am not sure if the modern day Antifa group gets their roots from this first Anti-Fascist Refugee Committee organization, but their indoctrination and methods of operation are sophisticated, organized, and destructive according to author and journalist Andy Ngo.

This next case has to deal with an advertising company strong arming techniques toward another advertiser's clients and the Sherman Act. More specifically, in the case of *Lorain Journal Co. v. United States (1951),* we have a major corporate publishing agency called the Journal that has a monopoly on reaching the community through radio, and once it sensed competition from potential break out radio stations who also advertised, it mandated that all of its clients maintain a relationship of exclusivity with the Journal when it came to advertising or be canceled. So, for example, a company could not advertise with WEOL and keep it's contract with Lorain. In the Supreme Court ruling, Justice Burton said that essentially Loraine was denying other clients and companies access ti essential facilities considering Loraine had maintained a firm monopoly reaching the city of Lorain from 1933-1948. Thus the station was necessary in order to effectively reach the population. Moral to the Story: My question is, Is it the fact that Lorain desired exclusivity, or the fact that they had a monopoly on advertisement that put them their legal dilemma? Reason being, because many of company today play the same game or strategy as to lock in exclusivity with their clients and I don't think they get taken to federal courts on that basis, of violation of the Sherman Act. But Some of he major Social Media platforms have gone through Anti-Trust Lawsuits, but this of course was mainly due to their magnitude that weighed in on the market as opposed to contracting exclusivity with clients. Targeted advertisement by algorithms and artificial intelligence are other issues that arose to the forefront in the more recent years and in my opinion this in itself seems ideal, only that people be intelligent surfers/researchers on the web and be active in their searching, not just passive. One does not have to accept everything they are offered and can intelligently retrain their algorithm to be interest they prefer. Now, Big Data and the use or selling of it to and by third party companies is a whole other realm of privacy concerns.

## Chapter 88:

## Justice Fred Moore Vinson (1890-1953)

Justice Fred Vinson was born native of Kentucky and went on to aim at the law degree in order to practice as an Attorney. He end up joining the US Army during WWI and after his discharge, he went on to get involved in politics; more specifically the U.S. House of Representatives. Later it was the Senate, where he oversaw the Anglo-American Loan, handled business with the International Bank for Reconstruction and development and the International Monetary Fund. Young "Fred" Vinson as they called him worked in his home which was the county jail, helping his father with the prisoners. After high school graduation he went on to attend Law School at the State Central University and then on to his own private practice. He had no idea that he would one day serve as Chief Justice of the US supreme Court, or maybe he was clairvoyant and he did; nevertheless, it was in this position that he tackled a number of cases and authored sweeping majority opinions that changed the landscape of society. Decision such as on topics such as segregation, unions, communism, and loyalty oaths. Justice Vinson was nominated by President Harry Truman to the Chief Justice position.

The first case we will discuss where Justice Vinson actually sat as Chief Justice is *Youngstown Sheet & Tube Co. v. Sawyer (1952).* In this case, we have a land grap by the sitting President Harry Truman and the legal question at hand is; did he have the authority to seize the land of the steel production facilities because the workers went on strike, demanding wage increase. As this occurrence was during the Korean War, President moved in his executive office along with his administration to confiscate the land of the Steele meals in and place them under federal control as not to be effected by the upcoming and ongoing strikes by the United steel Workers of America. Apparently the Steele workers were congruent with this decision to be considered federal employees, but the Steele companies pushed back questioning the constitutionality or the Authority exercised by the President. As it goes, the President needed Congressional approval to make such a move, and so ruled the US Supreme Court under this decision; Chief Justice Vinson in dissent. Moral to the Story: It has been my understanding that, the role of the Commander and Chief is to act with the Nation's interest in mind and handle matters of foreign policy as well as issue domestic policies measures to aide and govern the country. It this case, it seems that the effort to seize the steel mills was almost a matter of National Security because of the Korean War and the need for continued Steel Production products. W heather constitutional or not, I'll leave for the lawyers, but in my opinion, it seems that President Truman was doing the necessary thing to preserve the supply line for defense contracts. On the other side of things, this type of action on a greater scale, that is government taking over businesses could be very problematic considering we live in a free State where private companies are suppose to flourish and prosper. Where would be be if Big Government took over all industries in the name of National Security or National Interest?

This next case deals with racial segregation as the subject had been delt with in prior cases most noteworthy; *Plessy v. Ferguson (1896)* , and *Brown v. Board of Education(1954).* In this specific case, we have a situation where a Black man wants entrance into the Law program at the University of Texas, School of Law. At the time Texas State law mandated that integrated education would be not allowed. Because of this rule, Heman Marion Sweatt was denied entrance into the graduate school and program and decided to take this matter to a higher authority to get it resolved. The Strategies and Answer of the State District Court in Texas was to continue the case for six months, enough time to build a "Negro" Law School, that was anything but equal the University of Texas; although they had fewer Professors, inferior facilities, a smaller law library; they were still a Law School. Still, the State Supreme Court made no changes in the District Court Division; while a mandamus could have been issued; that is an immediate mandate of action from the University of Texas, none was issued. Ultimately it was the US Supreme Court that ruled in favor of Mr. Sweatt and said essentially that the graduate experience must be of "substantially equality," and at that point and in me, the newly created Thurgood Marshall School of Law, at Texas Southern University was not. Moral to the Story: There was a time when segregation of all industrial, educational, and social institutions in America was de facto, as in, that's just the way things were. Today, even after segregation laws have been now many years passed, there still remain segregated schools of higher learning that receive federal and state funds, but that are open to all. The point is, American graduates should have options just as professional adults should have options as to what type of environment they want to work and grow in. If one prefers to be in an institution or setting where the majority of persons look like them, they can so choose, the only thing, if those institutions be federally or state funded, they can not legally keep others out. Likewise, if other persons seek to be in a more diverse and cultural friendly environment; they should also have that option, knowing that this Micro setting may or may not be the future of Corporate or professional life, but on a global scale, depending on the industry, may very well be. American graduates should have options, and no matter what they choose, be in environments where their dignity is preserved.

## Chapter 89:

## Justice Thomas Campbell Clark (1899-1977)

Justice Thomas Clark was born native a native Texan but went on to attend the Virginia Military Institute for approximately one year but had to come home due to lack of finances. He then volunteered to get into the fight of WWI with the National Guard as an infantryman. He was too small at the time to join the Army, which was is first branch of choice. After the War was over, he went on to continue his career and education by attending the University of Texas at Austin for his Bachelors, and then there were graduate studies at the University of Texas

School of Law. It was President Harry Truman who nominated Justice Clark to the US Supreme Court as an Associate Justice. He also had previously served as US Attorney General. Sources say that it is unclear as to tell where his jurisprudence convictions lie due to his varied authored opinions which did not quite classify him as conservative or liberal. Notwithstanding, sources also report that he voted with Justice Earl Warren on numerous occasion. We do know that we stood for racial integration in graduate and law schools and also supported *Brown v. Board of Education(1954).* I will herein discuss a few other of his cases.

In the case of Hernandez v. Texas (1954), we have a situation where a Mexican American is convicted of murder without a jury of his peers and is convicted. The case gets picked up by Mexican American Council who appear before the US Supreme Court for the first time in appeal, winning the unanimous ruling that Mexican American's and all other racial groups have equal protection under 14th amendment. More details on the prior case, Peter Hernandez worked in the agriculture industry and it was at a bar when he shot a man by the name of Joe Espinoza. Further details as to reasons or motive behind the incident are unclear, except that Joe Espinoza was his employer. The arguments made in the US Supreme Court Case by the Council of Gustavo C. Garcia were that there was a systematic exclusion of Mexican American Jurist" which played a key element in them first being denied by the State of Texas as they sought protection under the 14th amendment which was primarily used for African-Americans in Civil Rights. Apparently the ruling initially came down as Mexican American's where white and could not benefit from the protection of the 14th amendment. Of course, this was later overturned in the US Supreme Court case unanimously. Moral to the Story: Although we have the great Rule of Law and Government given and instructed by the US Constitution; unfortunately within the cracks of the Judicial System there were racial discrimination engineered within the framework of certain laws and practices of the system and institution itself. For whatever reasons are not as important as to the repair of these fissures in our justice system, yet quiet obviously traces of white supremacy and dominance is what ruled in some state laws and permeated throughout the country. The pertinent and relevant question I feel for today is how is our present Justice System doing? Is Mercy and Justice given to all, or only a select few. Does meritocracy, nepotism, class, and race play vital parts in deciding weather those sitting trial are released, given lighter sentencing or judged more harshly; or does it depend solely the circumstances of the case and the skilled arguments presented by Prosecutor and the Defense. Philosophically speaking, is the whole process of determining innocence or guilt a Science or an Art; are cases really objectively determined, or does more subjectivity weigh in the mind and decisions or jurors and Justices. Shall we not rejoice without complaint at the freedoms we enjoy? Or shall coming generations revolt at what was done either on their behalf or to their disadvantage depending on the color of their skin.

In the case of *Burton V. Wilmington Parking Authority (1961),* we have a situation where there is a symbiotic relationship between a private business and government and because of this relationship, that business becomes classified as a "state actor" qualified to receive the benefit of the Equal Protection Clause. This allows for any individual to receive the full protection of the law and to not be discriminated against. In the details of this particular case, Wilmington Parking Authority was a government agency run parking garage attached to a coffee house in which several Black men attempted to desegregate the shop by staging a sit-in. They were arrested for trespassing, after which a local attorney went about things another way, strategizing by having the local Councilman go and park at the garage and then be refused service because he was African-American. This led to Justices deciding in a US Supreme Court case that this was "state action participating in discrimination which was contrary to the Equal Protection Clause." Moral to the Story: This is an interesting case, along with an interesting history of the Civil Rights Movement. Makes one think of the various methods that disenfranchised, or victimized and discriminated against persons, namely African-American, used to fight against segregation, discrimination, racial hatred, and other unjust state laws. Taking nothing away from all the Marches and non-violent protests that helped give visibility to the cause and exposed much of the negative racial behavior that was going on during that time, similar to body cams on certain law enforcement agencies today; Notwithstanding, I can't help but think, what if everyone just did their best to study for themselves and go to law school and strategize and fight the system from within, within the rule of law to make change. Would less have been brutally bitten by police dogs, and trampled by horses, and beaten with batons in the name of civil unrest, police control, and civil disobedience. Who knows, maybe both fronts are needed and work in key "symbiotic relationship;" nevertheless, less injuries, more professionals, better understanding and economic mobility if there was a massive push for the study of the law, fundraisers to send promising candidates to Law Schools to prepare to negotiate the wiles of socially engineered systems that were rigged to challenged the African-American and keep their behaviors in check. On the contrary, once one achieves the mastery of how to "go in and come out," or in other words, go to court and make their case or petition known, I would imagine progress could be and was made. Not only that, but once certain aptitudes are realized and law degrees and Ph.d's obtained, for those with a proclivity toward government, they can at least qualify to be considered for certain key positions where they can influence and be gatekeepers, or leaders, judges, and legislators of future benevolent and just laws, policies, and statutes that can benefit our society and civilization as a whole.

## Chapter 90:

## Justice Sherman Minton (1890-1965)

Justice Sherman Minton was borne native to the state of Indiana, and started off attending grade school all the way up to the completion of his middle school years in a 2 room school house. He was considered athletic and a prankster in High School and then it was off to college at Indiana University Bloomington where he participated in sports, debate, and political clubs. Next it was Law School at Indiana University Maurer where he also maintained the position of fullback for the Indiana University Football Team. Considered well rounded, he would launch his legal career. Shortly after practicing privately, working with other partners and doing some traveling, the World War I had began and he enlisted to become an officer by taking a course at Fort Benjamin Harrison. The Commission for Officer was not granted right away, but after he took leave, got married and returned to repeat the course he was commissioned as a Captain. Serving in the 84$^{th}$ division of the Expeditionary Forces, he protected supply lines in Belgium and aided scouting, and transporting men and supplies to the front line. After the War was over Justice Minton decided to remain in Paris to further his education. He studied Roman Law, International Law, Civil Law, and Jurisprudence at the University of Paris according to online sources. After he returned to the States and went on with his legal career it was later that his friend and then President Harry Truman nominated him for the US Supreme Court Associate Justice position. Justice Minton's Judicial philosophy can be described as attempting to uphold the original intent of legislation. He authored a few opinions and dissents in which we will cover herein.

In this first case we will consider; a case in which Chief Justice Fred Vinson authored the majority opinion that dealt with States Secrets privilege. The title of the case is, United States v. Reynolds (1953), and further details illuminate the facts that there was a major accident to the measure of a plain crash. There were three employees and one military government contractor who was flying the plane, when according to previously classified documents stated that there was a fire that broke out in the engine, which essentially was the source of the problem. The pilot could not recover. The legal matters started when the widows of the deceased brought suit against the Federal Government on the grounds of the Federal Tort Claims Act seeking damages for the lost of their loved ones. These widows demanded accident reports from the crash and the Air force responded that this was an impossibility due to the national security interests at hand. Suddenly, there were court proceedings and Appeals, that ultimately led to a US Supreme Court decision for the Government to compensate the widow's $170,000.00 for release of liability as well as a disclosure of the documents. In Justice Vinson's majority opinion, he stated in so many words, and I paraphrases, that, " due to the power of the Federal Torts claim Acts, the federal government has to release documents, that it would have otherwise kept classified. And because these documents hold the government liable, then the ruling is in the Respondents (plaintiffs) Favor. Moral to the Story: Some cases against the United States, one might feel that they are always vicious, and dangerous in nature and stemming from an angel of hatted. On the contrary, this is not always the case, because plenty of Federal Court cases that include the United States were initiated essentially as a means to an end to get some decision in their favor that would have otherwise been lost. In this particular case the widows did son and were worded collectively up to the tune of half a quarter million.

In the next case we will discuss, we have a situation where a man with dual citizenship with the US and Japan was convicted of Treason for his behavior's toward American POW's in

Japan during World War II. His name was Tomoya Kawakita and it is the case of Kawakita v. United States (1952), and in this case Kawakita's argument toward his defense was that he lost his US citizenship when he was in Japan; but all courts disagreed, and maintained that he kept his dual citizenship and he was almost sentenced to death, but was instead given Life in Prison. Eventually; eventually he would be released by President Kennedy to be extradited back to Japan, though he was born to Japanese parents in California, and never to return to the United States of America. Justice Minton sided with those of the majority option of the court. Moral to the Story: This is an interesting case. I think that whether or not Mr. Kawakita maintained or lost his dual American/Japanese citizenship is irrelevant to the point, but the major concern is that if he was once an America citizen, agreeing to our creeds, and then traveled to Japan and mistreated American POW's during the War with the audacity to come back to the States and live in peace, seems his guilty verdict was just. Of course, this is only my humble opinion.

## Chapter 91:

## Justice Earl Warren (1891-1974)

Justice Earl Warren was born native to California and accomplished mean feats in his lifetime. After High School graduation, he enrolled himself at The University of California, Berkeley where he majored in Political Science. After he completed his Bachelors degree, it was off to Law School at what is now UC Berkeley School of Law. After graduating from Law School, Justice Warren went to work for a major oil company for a short time but didn't really like the ethos so got on with another private firm. Right around that time WWI was underway and Justice Warren decided to volunteer for an Officer Training Camp, he went through some difficulties but got back in and even stayed part of the Army Reserves eventually obtaining the rank of Captain. It was President Dwight Eisenhower who nominated Justice Earl Warren to Chief Justice of the US Supreme Court after all, he had 17 years in public law. He had served as the governor of California as well as the Attorney General. Sources report that Justice Warren's judicial philosophy was one that held high the US Constitution as embodying the quintessence of American values. Furthermore, he held on to simple things such as: motherhood, marriage, family, flag, and principles. Herein, we will consider a few of his cases.

The first case we will consider is *Trop v. Dulles (1958)*. In this case, we have the US Supreme Court ruling that it goes against the constitution for the Courts to revoke a individual's citizenship as punishment for a crime. Grounds for this argument come from the "evolving standards of decency" clause in the Eighth Amendment. In the details of the prior cases that led up to the US Supreme Court decision, we have a situation where a man, Alan Tropp who was a homegrown, native, American Citizen who enlisted in the US. Army circa 1944. This was around the time of WWII, and German Occupation in Europe posed threat to Great Britain and Russia, our allies in the War. Ironically, Trop was stationed in Morocco, and went awall, later self-surrendering to an officer, where he was transported back to base and immediately Court-Martialed, declared guilty, sentenced to 3 years hard labor, stripped of pay, and dishonorably discharged from the the military. District and State courts agreed upon this decision revoking Trops application for a passport under the Nationality Act of 1944. Moral to the Story: I guess the heart of the issue is courage and weather or not courage or lack there of should be judged for good or bad in the Court of law. Should one be judged harshly for lack of courage, for deserting there post in the Armed forces. The dissenting opinion said the hard labor sentence was the alternative to "death" On the surface this seems like a good deal, but in depth, it is just treating people with lack of heart, more harshly. This in itself is not necessarily wrong, because that individual did desert, but I think the inner question would be should that person be stripped of everything including citizenship because they refuse to fight. I can hear many saying yes, because in reality when we don't assert or at times passively or aggressively forward our petition, whatever it may be, we loose. Nevertheless, the US Supreme Court ruled that men should retain their citizenship even in light of their lack of courage and abandonment of any oaths that they took to protect and serve against enemies foreign and domestic. Sometimes we know not what we sign up for, and possibly these men got in over their heads and didn't realize they were innately ill equipped to do the job of soldiering. Should they be punished for this inadequacy, desire for war, or inability. Who knows? But I think it would be wrong and a disservice to set or create a precedence that completely overlooked and did not penalize those persons who desert their post or position or fail to fulfill their signed contract with the military for unexcused reasons, lack of courage, and just lack of motivation to execute what one started. I write these things not as an ex-military veteran, but as one who wanted to join, was methodically unsuccessful, and yet went through a number of convoluted circumstances that taught me to Think before committing actions and yet understand how Courage be necessary for Survival, and the use of Cowardliness the reality sometimes to Live. A Hurtful Reality, but nevertheless, many times the Truth.

In this following case Miranda v. Arizona (1966), we will consider, an individual's Miranda rights and their right to not incriminate themselves at the point of arrest or being interrogated in Police Custody. According to the US Supreme Court Ruling detained persons cannot self-incriminate under the fifth amendment of the Constitution unless they have been properly notified of the right to council with a lawyer before police questioning, and that individual not only has understood their rights but properly waived them. In the specific details of the first case that went to trial, Ernesto Miranda was apprehended by Phoenix Police

Department in 1963 on circumstantial evidence associating him with the kidnap and rape of an 18 year old. After a few hours of interrogation he gave a statement of confession without being informed of his right to an attorney. Mr. Miranda also included in his report that he was not coerced but gave his confession voluntarily. In the US Supreme court ruling which overturned the State Court's decision, the majority opinion written by Chief Justice Earl Warren state in so many words, that because it was not disclosed to Mr. Miranda his right to receive council from a lawyer and furthermore that whatever he said could be used against him in court, his case was overturned. Moral to the Story: Every American citizen is entitled to be read their Miranda's right, but on the contrary; if there are eye witnesses to that particular crime and even the Officers see what the perpetrator has done, is it still necessary for the defendant to be read their Miranda rights? And I would venture to say yes, because that person is still entitled to a lawyer, unless the crime is deemed a Terror Threat, then different rules apply and from what I understand even their due process can be taken away.

## Chapter 92:

## Justice John Marshall Harlan II (1899-1971)

Justice John Harlan II was kind of an international student, as he studied abroad during is graduate years of Law School at Balliol College, Oxford. He also attended a few different colleges to complete his undergraduate degree, among them, the prestigious Princeton University where he graduated. One position before his seat as Associate Justice on the US Supreme Court was Attorney for the Southern District of New York. During WWII, Justice John Harlan II Volunteered for Military Service, and was ranked in the position of Colonel in the United States Army Air Force. In terms of Judicial philosophy after Justice Harlan II received his nomination to the US Supreme Court by President Dwight Eisenhower. He was one who held high the position of keeping precedence as opposed to being a textualist, when it came to the Constitution and Constitutional Law. He thought that the Judicial branch of government should allow for the political process to discover and resolve most issues and that the branch of government in which he served should play a "limited role" according to certain sources. We will consider his positions in a few cases discussed herein.

In this first case of discussion we will venture into the details of Leary v. United States (1969). Apparently at one point in American history, before these recent post legislation legalization of the use and sale of Cannabis, there was an act that collected tax on Marijuana 1937, and legal usage of the Cannabis drug was done in the states as early as 1906. I'm not a smoker, but I found this pretty interesting. It was the a case of interstate commerce and mix up between one State outlawing possession of marijuana, Texas, and another state requiring proof of tax being paid on the purchase, New York. Leary was traveling through Texas and was stopped by a High Way Patrol officer who found Marijuana seeds on the floor and on some of the persons in the vehicle. It is a bit ambiguous as to his direct charge, but ultimately his conviction was overturned by the US Supreme Court, and the ruling, majority opinion authored by Justice Harlan II ironically declared the Marijuana Tax Act unconstitutional. Moral to the Story. Interestingly enough, Congress later implemented a Controlled Substance Act which regulated not only the use but the manufacturing, importation, possession use and distribution of certain drugs. Upon reading this, I thought this was extremely liberal legislation for that time although it be around 1970, my original thought was that this act it permitted scheduled drugs to enter the States just in a more regulated matter. We all know of the reputation of the 70's and 80's for high drug usage and "Rock 'n Roll." Notwithstanding, upon second glance, it seems that it was more to rehabilitate drug abusers and those fighting dependency and to reinforce federal police authorities in their combating the field of drug abuse. Who knows? More specifically to this case of Leary v. Marijuana, seems that he was just caught in the wrong state that had different tax and possession laws than the state which he purchased.

In the next case we will consider, we deal in the matter of privacy in lieu of the fourth amendment and the modifying of "search" and "seizure" protocol. In the case of Katz v. United States (1967), at the Supreme Court level we have Justices overturning a conviction given by State level courts to a gambling man who was eavesdropped on by the FBI. Apparently the Federal Borough of Investigations placed a listening device on the phone booth where Kantz conducted his "illegal" business of placing bets and placing handicaps. The FBI's maneuver of argument was that the device was actually placed outside of the booth, and therefore no warrant was necessary, but Kantz defence pointed to the fourth amendment which wasn't enough for the US District Court for Southern District of California, nor did it fly in the 9$^{th}$ circuit Court of Appeals. But at the US Supreme court level, Katz was vindicated, and Hon. Justice Harlan II wrote a concuring opinion as well as devised a two part solution suggesting that what man says in his home should be protected by privacy and what one says, "objects, activities, or statemtens in plain view" are not protected. Moral to the Story: What do we do in a day and age where people desire privacy, but we also desire to be free from the threat of terrorism, cyber attack and constant government scrutiny. Well, maybe foreign online threats are real and people do get hacked, but government scrutiny may not be as intense or as bad as we have in our mind from our New World Order reading and Big Brother Cities with Cameras everywhere. Or maybe it's worst depending your perspective. No one really wants to be placed under the microscope and dissected, audited, determined a cheat, immoral, socially unacceptable, and privately perverse in their conversation and behavior. On the other hand, do these strange and awkward compromises somehow "fit in" with the ongoing and slippery moral decay of society. I guess it depends on what were talking about, how we feel that day, and the moment to moment decisions we choose to make that build or tear down our character and value system. Building Character is tough, and so is keeping our morals. Maybe for some it's harder or easier than it is for others. Some have maintained their inner philosophical and/or religious,scientific, economic, political principles firmly for a long time and have benefited a life from reaping the reward of sewing to the good nature of self, life, and humanity. Others of us, have backslid on our values, ignored inner and outward contradictions, doubted our beliefs, and subtly refused to remedy these major imperfections in our lives that can ultimately become hugely problematic. Nevertheless, don't we all have some good in US, along with some bad, and seek to get along in life, obtain the best future we can live and see, hoping that The God of The Earth and The Heavens will Grace our paths with Mercy and Truth of Understanding and that we find rich abundance in our way. I think, such would be the prayer of the common man or women, or even maybe those above and below, yet how do we get to the point of where we all need to be individually, collectively, nationally and inevitably globally.

## Chapter 93:

## Justice William J. Brennan Jr. (1906-1997)

Justice William Brennan was born native to New Jersey and utilized the public school system to indoctrinate himself with the fundamentals of education and go on to the Wharton school of the University of Pennsylvania where he graduated with distinction in economics. Next it was Law school at Harvard right around the 1930's. He would graduate and then start a private practice in addition to serving in the US Army during WWII. Later in life he served on the Supreme Court of New Jersey and was ultimately appointed to the US Supreme Court by President Dwight D. Eisenhower. Today we would call him a liberal progressive Jurist, known to be gregarious in his opinions and views, opposed the death penalty, supported abortion rights and we will discuss few of his cases here within. It must be mentioned that he is thought to be known as one of the most influential jurist of the 20$^{th}$ century as reported by sources for his ability to help guide the other jurist into a favored vote for a decision on hard cases.

One of the cases and issues that Justice Brennan felt was essential was that of *Goldberg v. Kelly (1970)*. In this ruling a certain judgment was made that would not permit government benefits or entitlements to be taken away from individuals without the due process of a court hearing either federal or state. Apparently this case arose from alleged fraudulent activity of some 20 welfare recipients in New York that hurt the budget. Moral to the Story: I do think that it is important and necessary that the government steps in to help and give aide to those individuals who may need assistance and that such programs encourage independence and self-sufficiency helping those individuals to help themselves by either going to school, taking up a new business, learning a vocation, or joining the military. How long should such benefits be available and how they should be cut off is controversial, yet I would carefully say, until that individual has proven self-sufficiency for a specified time as well as an effort to do so. In cases of the mentally ill and disabled, that time may or may not ever come, but those individuals can still be encouraged to do productive work and programs to contribute to their quality of life and society. Sometimes we as people need rest and relaxation for a time and life gets tough and hard, and it's nice to have the government as a safety net, but if people can work, and need to, in my humble opinion, we should do something for ourselves, weather it be working as self-employed persons or even for certain non-profit and charitable organizations just to stay active continue learning in this quest we call Life.

The next case we will discuss considers the death penalty and it efficacy as well as its cruel nature from Justice Brennan's perspective. In this particular case, Furman v. Georgia (1972) which was in many ways similar to two other federal cases that invalidated the death penalty for rape, considered the eighth amendment and the US constitution. Under these statutes the death penalty could be considered cruel and unusual punishment and in the details of this specific case a man was in the heat of a burglary and as he attempted to escape gave two different stories of how his gun mysteriously fired and shot the victim. The felony murder was originally given the death penalty yet he punishment was never performed. Somewhere, Justice Brenan is quoted speaking on the electric chair and calls it a modern burning individuals at the stake. Moral to the Story: There are many crimes that one could commit that one would consider deserving of death. Notwithstanding, when one takes a thought about it, life in prison is really a worst sentence. It may weigh more on the economy and the prison food, laundry, and canteen inventory, but who wants to be locked up in closed custody for 25 years, and then after that still have to live out their years in old age, behind bars, the gate, the wall, or in a cell. I say Nobody, they probably as well desire to be put out of their misery, yet I don't mean to be flippant in this matter. But seriously, I think that any brave criminal facing the death penalty or a life sentence would probably, obliviously want to live, but in the end facing no chance of release, might at this point, want to die. Who knows?

## Chapter 94
## Justice Charles Evans Whittaker (1901-1973)

Not many people, let alone a US Supreme Justices can say that they went to college with a future President of the United States. Ironically Justice Whittaker was one of those such persons, borne native to Kansas, he came up "the rough side of the mountain" so to speak, he did not necessarily come from wealth, although his Father was a Farmer, and he would do this job in high school when he dropped out early on high school when his mother died. He would still daily read the news paper and glean information on criminal trials as he realized early that he had a proclivity for the law. It was during his time at the University of Missouri-Kansas City School of Law that earned him his Bachelor of Laws an shortly thereafter it was off to take the Bar. He and young future President Harry Truman were friends and colleges on campus. Apparently Justice Evans never established a constant judicial philosophy and vacillated often between opinions, and even openly regretted some of his decisions. Herein we will discuss a few of his cases.

The first case we will discuss is actually one that was controversial as holding the line between a political and a judicial affair as Justice Whittaker would resign himself from deciding on this case. On the surface, with hindsight, it doesn't seem like that big of a deal, but perhaps there are some underlining factors no obvious to the contemporary observer. B*aker v. Carr (1962)* was a case that dealt with the issue of redistricting and all the geographical factors that went into determining if elected representatives would be chosen for either State legislature or the Federal House of Representatives. Ultimately this case did not have a huge effect on electoral districts but precipitated two other cases; *Wesberry v. Sanders* and *Reynolds v. Sims*, which established districts of "one person, one vote". Moral to the Story: Usually we hear of zoning and redlining of districts being discriminatory because of certain housing, urban planning and how and who decides what areas will receive the benefit from federal and state tax monies. In more instances than not, it is the Suburban areas that traditionally benefited from such politics. But what was making the tension tense in this issue was the politicization of the Judicial Court. The Judicial Branch of government is suppose to be nonpartisan and ambiguous to the politics of both the executive and legislative branches in theory. I believe this is what made Justice Whittaker recuse himself from deciding on this case, which spoke to his ethos although he was considered an judge who was not firm in his philosophical leanings.

In this next case we will discuss the matter of entrapment as addressed in the case *Sherman v. United States (1958).* Apparently there was a man, last name Sherman, who was in recovery and duped by a fellow recovering addict, Kalchinian, into scoring more drugs for him and relapsing back into addiction. Kalchinian reported these instances back to the Federal Bureau of Narcotics whom he had been informant to in hopes of lightening his sentence from former drug charges. As it goes, Sherman was convicted by lower courts but his defense argued for his case on the grounds of "entrapment" and Kalchinian himself confessed to inducing Shermen to obtain the narcotics as well as return to his habbit. It took a Supreme Court ruling to overturn the conviction. Moral to the Story: This is interesting, and I learned something new. On one hand, everyone is responsible for their own actions and decisions, weather tricked, trapped, insane, mentally ill or not. And on the other had, man, that sure is some ethically shady criminal or "smart" police work to get your buddy, family member, or trusted "crony" to turn against you to lesson their own conviction. I guess it comes down to what's important and whats a priority, with the ultimate goal of cleaning up the streets, but then again there are principles, rules, and street rules and justice that certain people live by, and some folks are just going to do whatever the "F^*!" they want anyway. Good cop, bad cop has been a game and role we all have seen played on various television series and syndicated movies all of our lives as American "boob tubers" or movie goers. I can recall a few fun ones, probably dating myself, *Beverly Hill's Cop Series*, *Lethal Weapon Series*, and *Tango and Cash*. The point is, usually the informant brought in, from what I can remember, is considered a "slime" of a character. More thoughts come to mind, and I think of other examples where the "double agents" are in fact directly working for the Bureau or government agency such as in *True Lies*, the more recent *The Departed*, which was a cluster F^*!, and one of my all time favorites, *Catch me if you can*. So, this isn't intended to be a movie review, but to the main point, what a problem for the criminal to have or anyone for that matter, when they can't trust close friends, family and associates because of their success, failures, behavior or actions, or pure jealousy and resent from their peers. And really, what is "Trust" anyway? The fact that someone would be loyal and would not betray your secrets. On one level, sure, but what else?

## Chapter 95

## Justice Potter Stewart (1915-1985)

Justice Potter Stewart was known for being a brave scholar. Native to Michigan, Justice Stewart attended a special magnet school for high school by the name of Hotchkiss which was a preparatory School in Lakeville, Connecticut affiliated with the Ten Schools Admissions Organization. After his graduation, it was off to Yale where he again graduated with High Honors and went abroad to The Cambridge School of Law in England for an intensity in International Law for one year before coming back state-side to finish up his Law Degree at the Yale Law School. Somewhere, Justice Stewart found time to serve during World War II in the

U.S. Naval Reserve, it is unclear, but he may have had a skill as a Tank Mechanic, working on oil tankers. Later it was President Dwight D. Eisenhower who gave him a recess appointment to the Supreme Court. In between two factions warring with one another on the court, Justice Stewart arrived at a time where he was considered the swing vote. Justice Stewart's judicial philosophy can be put as one commentator suggested, "particularistic, intuitive, and pragmatic," after hearing his ruling on an obscenity case which we will later herein consider. Ironically, the thoughtful Justice Stewart mentioned only one thing from his years of judicial service that he would have maybe said differently; and that was what he said in his judgments on "hard-core pornography,' which were, "I'll know it when I see it," thus protecting the, Louis Malles's movie, *The Lovers* against complete censor. To be candid, I'm not sure weather he said this comment with all seriousness and gravity, or if it was said and written with a light heart and him being facetious.

In the first case we will consider, *Irvin v. Dowd (1959),* we find that even within the ranks of the Supreme decision room, that sometimes politics play a role in how judgments are made. Not that bipartisan politics so to speak, but maybe there are rifts between liberal and conservative, and sometimes these vote together and at other times certain principles matter more to some than others, and friendships and ties are broken. According to sources, such was the case in the matter of the The Warren Court; which as aforementioned was divided into two factions; liberal and conservative; and at one point in time, apparently those on the court during this time use to vote together. In this particular case, we have a mane who escaped from prison after his initial sentence for allegedly murdering a number of individuals in time between 1954-55. The local precinct got a confession from Mr. Irvin, and his lawyers on the case went through the process of moving the trial to deter local bias in the jury according to what was written about the case. To the point, the main issue or legal question was, did Irvin's escape dispel any chances of him appealing for an appeal in his sentencing and case in general. Obviously he wanted to be release d under the writ of habeas madate, but was denied this privileged by the US Supreme Court. Moral to the Story: Maybe it doesn't really matter what I think about any of these cases personally, but nevertheless, seems common sense that if one would have the ability and the fired determination to escape from jail or prison after they have been federally sentenced, they are essentially throwing all care to the wind, and giving up further rights to a formal appeal, in hopes of escaping and never to be found to face charges again. Seems that maybe the person being charged has made this decision themselves. Yet and still, Mr. Irvin did leave a letter pleading his innocence, and although I still do not know the granular details of this case, such as the murders themselves, and the situational evidence involved, seems that it was enough in the court of law to gain a murder conviction. Who knows what it would have been if the forensic investigation techniques along with camera surveillance we have today were available to perform back then, along with DNA sampling and analysis, to either further confirm Mr. Irvin's guilt or prove his innocence. Makes one go back to the question of privacy and protection and philosophically wonder if they are dichotomous, synonymous, or juxtaposed civil virtues.

In this second case, ***Jacobellis v. Ohio*** (1964), the main issue of obscenity comes up with regards to the film genre medium, as well as the other two conjoining issues of censorship and the first amendment. In this particular case, the state of Ohio, through Local, appellate and State Superior Court ruled that the romantic film, by Louis Malle, entitled The Lovers was indeed obscene" Later during the US Supreme Court appeal, Justices divided over these issues but came out deciding that the film was not obscene, and Justice Stewart in particular, and I'm paraphrasing, but he wrote that he knows hard-core porn when he sees it, of which this material certainly was not. Moral to the Story: I think every young man, and now days possibly even women at some point in their lives sense the urge to view elicit videos of a sexual content. Today's is a lot different from that of the past, and yet quite the same in many ways. It would be a fallacy to make generally broad and sweeping dogmatic statements putting them as fact, but I think for the most part, at some point, whether it be out of curiosity, desire, or research, people watch others make coitus. And for others this is not the extent of it, and for some it is. In the specifics of this case, Justice Stewart's ruling suggested that he himself at one time or the other had seen for lack of a cleaner euphemism, some good ol' porn, and this film was not it. Such was the case in this matter; criminal charges, and fines, dropped or overturned...against the Movie Theater defendant. Let it be said, that I have not seen this "Lover's" film, although I have read my fair share of desperate Romance and inserted pornographic novels...And I call myself a Christian. Henry Miller's stuff was a personal favorite.

## Chapter 96:

## Justice Byron Raymond White

Justice Byron was the all around scholar, and athlete, who also happened to serve in World War II as an intelligence officer. Born in Colorado, and graduating from a high school class of six, it was off to the University of Colorado in Boulder and where he played football and majored in economics. He studied abroad at the University of Oxford in England and a was closely acquainted with a few of the Kennedy brothers, as their father Joseph was U.S. Ambassador to London. It was WWII that brought Justice White home to Stateside, where he served in the department of intelligence as an officer for the US Navy. After his stint in the service it was back to Law school Law school at Yale where he first earned top grades and graduated form Yale with the idea of one day practicing privately as he did as a transaction attorney in Denver. Before this he clerked for Chief Justice Fred M. Vinson. In terms of jurisprudence and judicial philosophy, Justice White was for the expansion of big government and its powers and adamantly opposed to the creation of constitutional restrictions of the police departments and those that served in the field. His angle was that aggressive police actually invigorated and enhanced the individual right of law abiding citizens. An interesting discussion that would be in today's current affairs. Justice White sat on cases dealing with a range of issues from due process doctrine and capital punishment to abortion and civil liberties. Herein we will discuss a few of these topics in selected cases.

In this first case that we will discuss we have a routine stop by an officer of the law who comes across an individual with heroine tracks in their arm from rapid drug use. Apparently Robinson allegedly confessed to narcotic use but later denied this confession. At the time of this Case mandated that it was against the law to be addicted to drug use. Robinson was sent to trial and convicted of 90 days imprisonment. More details of the California Health and Safety code dictate that no one should be under addiction of narcotic unless under the direction of health care agent license with the State. So, at the US Supreme Court level, justices had to toss around the decision and philosophical idea as to whether or not it was fair and just to punish someone because of their "addiction," "condition," or "disease," and because drug addiction was defined as a disease, to punish one for this habit would be considered cruel and unusual punishment. Thus the US Supreme court reversed the decision; the majority opinion being written by Justice Stewart, joined by Justice Warren, Black and Brennan. It was Justice White who dissented, being tough on crime and drug addiction ousting the other Justices suggesting that they were reinterpreting the constitution and state legislatures laws making themselves out to know more about how to handle the drug addiction that it's own state representatives. Moral to the Story: Even today in my own state of residence drugs, narcotics and pills are a major problem. Especially with the homeless; it's almost frightening to see such a great epidemic of perkeset use amongst this population, often referred to on the street as, "blues." Many of the addicted individuals need serious treatment because of the chemical dependency they face, but don't really want the help telling themselves they use the narcotic for pain management. I personally feel that because of the mental state, health risk, and behavior this particular drug causes some to exhibit, that if and when these persons are caught and apprehended by authorities that they should face a sentence of drug treatment or recovery centers to help them rehabilitate their life. Otherwise they stay stagnant and in a declining position in life with no opportunity of real success unless they beat their habit. Many addicts loose their homes, marriages, children, burn bridges with family and friends, and also may have it rough on the streets when even their own friends or fellow addicts steal from them when they sleep at night. It's definitely not the ideal lifestyle and I know this from my time in Case Management as well as recent research and real life investigation that I have done.

The next case has to deal with the 8$^{th}$ amendments cruel and usual punishment clause and the principle of proportionality. In this case of Harmelin v. Michigan (1991), we have one who was convicted and sentenced to life without parole because of a possession of 672 grams of cocaine. The justices could not decide in a common vein to flow in but upheld the sentence, Justice Scalia giving a historical argument taking the 8$^{th}$ amendment back to being an English Bill of Rights of 1698 derivative and identifying such horrors as disemboweling, drowning, quartering, and beheading as examples of cruel and "illegal" punishment of that day. Justice Kennedy argued on the principle of proportionality; which simply tries to fit the time to the crime; and not give excessive weight to small or minor offenses. Justice White ironically dissented all together and felt that the sentencing was excessive. Moral to the Story: Serving life in prison is more than a notion. Actually, any time in a confined space with no privilege of freedom, a concrete bed and cement walls to look at I guess can livable for some and cruel and usual to others. And that's not even the extent of it. The point is, the life without parole sentence was not overturned by the justices for this man's possession of excessive amounts of a controlled substance; in this case Cocaine. A substance that in today's economy and liberal Social system may one day in fact be made legal just the way Marijuana was. I myself am no consumer, but it must be noted that there is this notion or ideal out there that people should be allowed to do what they want as long as they are not harming others. Personally, I feel that it should still be considered a illegal substance and those who sale, use and posses should face some type of recovery, treatment, training or deterrence education program. Obviously, those with the intent to sale and distribute should bear the heavier judgments, as in a way directly or indirectly causing users to harm themselves, or even harm others depending on their reactions and behaviors to the narcotic. I in no way presume to write case law just my humble thoughts and observations.

## Chapter 97:

## Justice Arthur Goldberg (1908 -1990)

Justice Goldberg was a prominent scholar and agent of change for the nation and in government. Born in Chicago and offspring of a Jewish Father who immigrated from the Russian Empire. Justice Goldberg did well for himself by attending Northwestern University School of Law, serving in the US Army during WWII were he also served in an espionage group pre-CIA—The Office of Strategic Services (OSS), where he was responsible for developing European contacts and networks within the grassroots labor movement during the War, to resist Nazi Germany. It was later in life that he was nominated to the US Supreme Court by President John F. Kennedy, in which after some years he resigned his position to fill an appointment by President Lyndon B. Johnson as the Ambassador to the United Nations. He was considered a liberal Supreme Court Justice, his judicial philosophy grounded in the fundamental rights of individuals to liberty and justice. In this position he condemned capital punishment, appeasing to the International community suggesting that it also considered the death penalty "cruel and unusual punishment" in direct violation of the eighth amendment.

In the case of *Griswold v. Connecticut (1965),* the judgment came forth that married couples shall not be prevented the use of contraceptive to prevent child birth by the State, laws, or any other local authorities. This was substantial legal change, because originally there was a law in Connecticut, "Comstock law" that prohibited any person from using "any drug medicinal or instrumental to prevent conception." The underlining issue is one of privacy which is not directly mentioned in the Bill of Rights, but instances of intrusive search and seizures were mentioned by one judge as instances of inappropriateness by any law enforcement agency. Not that search and seizures are wrong when necessary according to the rule of law, but hypothetically would be inappropriate to search an Officer of the law's marital bedroom for contraceptive. Ultimately the ruling came down to one of "marital privacy." Moral to the Story: This doesn't seem very relevant today, because it would seem so absurd for such a law to exist. I mean, we live in a nation where freedom and liberty does exist and if a marital or an otherwise couple choose to prevent childbirth by the use of contraceptive, so be it. Maybe if national circumstances dictated such behavior was harming the population and continued existence of of a race or nation, then could see banding contraceptives, but as normal life continues and society functions there's no need for such a law in my humble opinion.

In the case of Berger v. New York (1967), a case in which Justice Goldburg had nor opinion nor dissent but was tried during his time on the court. In this case the US Supreme Courts moved to invalidate certain New York law under the fourteenth amendment disallowing electronic eavesdropping without required procedural safeguards. This case developed because of a certain attorney caught on surveillance for attempting to bribe a public official. Subsequent other detials, the surveillance went on for approximately a total of four months; enough evidence acquired in that time. Nevertheless, there was no warrant, jurisdiction limits, nor protection measures. Thus the ruling from the courts. Moral to the Story: Privacy and Protection have come up a number of times during this series. As well as the idea of global, national and local surveillance in one of my previous books. But here, when there is verifiable crime being committed or suspicion of conspiracy, I guess the formal question lies in, is a warrant to survey necessary to obtain? Perhaps not after 9/11 and the Patriot Act. And how easy it is now days for government agencies to get cell phone records from cell phone companies or how ever many other methods there are to gain access to the wireless communication happening all over the globe. The point is, maybe someones is always listening, and maybe nobody cares, but warning to the high crimes criminal who wants to communicate over the phone; and all the other message and media technologies that exist; we live in a era of transparency and cloaked IP, VPN software, as well as block chain technology that people believe can't be traced by federal agencies. Well, George Orwell's, *1984* to the future, *Big Brother still A Watch'in*!

## Chapter 98:

## Justice Abraham Fortas (1910-1982)

Native to Tennessee, Justice Fortas had a number key responsibilities as he traversed through his political life and legal career. Studying in his undergraduate year as what is now know as Rhodes College, he majored in English and Political Science, earning high marks and receiving the option of attending Harvard or Yale on full Academic Scholarship. He chose Yale Law School, and finished his professional degree only to move into the area of the US Securities Exchange Commission where he worked. Holding responsibilities and positions under three different American Presidents. It was under President Franklin D. Roosevelt's that he was selected to Committees that assisted in organizing the United Nations right around 1948. It was President Lyndon B. Johnson who nominated him to the US Supreme Court, and even for the Senior position of Chief Justice which was filibustered in the Senate. In therms of his judicial philosophy and Jurisprudence, he wrote a book entitled, , Concerning Dissent and Civil Disobedience. Which I assume says something about his moral code and societal ethics. Upon further research it actually is a work that explains and defines the limits and scope of permissible dissent and civil disobedience. So it would seem that he was one who because of his strong belief in the constitution and American Civil liberties would be comfortable enough in his own skin, to allow someone who believed and thought different then himself to stand and enjoy the same liberties, as long as they were abiding by the law.

This first case we will consider deals with the fourth amendments protection against warrentless searches, as well as that of the fifth amendment which covers n protection against self-incrimination and searches that intrude the body. Until the case of Schemer v. California (1966) it was quite ambiguous as to weather or not warrants needed to be obtained to perform the necessary duties to gain access to a blood sample. Science and logic would prove that in certain cases time is of the essence and the bodies metabolic turnover time puts police precincts at risk of loosing evidence if not performed in a timely matter. One instance would be in the case of collecting blood alcohol levels. I myself have been pulled over at times and given breathalyzer and even made to extract blood sample to test against the claim as to weather I was drunk driving or not. Fortunately, these test always came back negative, and the culprit was always sleepy driving, or driving without my prescription glasses. Nevertheless, back to the case at hand, Around the 1950' s, certain police officers broke into the home of a suspected narcotic dealer and before apprehending him he put two small objects onto his mouth. This action by the suspect precipitated the Officers involved to take him to the hospital and have his stomach pumped to determine the actual chemical nature of what the nature ingested. At the time the Court rule that the involuntary stomach pump was invasive, brutal and violated the substantive due process clause. Future cases have danced around the issue as to weather collecting necessary samples are legal with or without warrant, but I think the point is if one has nothing to hide, then giving a sample, much like a simple urine test, mouth swap, and all the above tests, it easy to cooperate to prove ones innocence. Moral to the Story: The question of is a warrant necessary to obtain bodily fluids and evidence was obviously answered by the US Supreme Court of the 1950's with a resounding yes. Later trials would determine differently dependent upon the exact circumstance. Notwithstanding, the main issue is the individual civilians rights being protected to the full with the fourth and fifth amendments not being violated. That is illegal seizures and the right to consent to evidence being taken. I suspect all these rights are privileges for those law abiding and for suspects in the heat of heavy crime can expect those boundaries to be pushed by high authoritarian government law enforcement agencies.

In this next case, Afroyim v. Rusk (1967), deals with the fact that it is virtually impossible for an American Citizen to loose their citizenship unless they denounce it. In this specific case, we have an Poland man who was a naturalized U.S. Citizen and decided to still vote in a Israeli election after his confirming his American Citizenship. Federal courts decided that Bey Afroyim maintain keeping his citizenship under the Citizenship Claus of the fourteenth amendment, although there was also a federal law that mandated citizens loose their citizenship when voting in foreign elections; this law was struck down. This was also just before but opened wide the door to the Carter Administration allowing dual and multiple citizenship. Moral to the Story: Though I be not deeply versed in Citizenship law and the fourteenth amendment, it seems the High Federal Courts have determined that there be no conflict of interest for American citizens to have duel and multi-national citizenship I'm assuming to the point of voting in multiple elections. The only controversy arises in my mind is when duel citizens are from countries of our adversaries instead of our allies. So, does that hypothetically mean one could be a citizen here in the States and also of let's say Iran, China, North Korea, and Russia; and vote in our election and theirs. On the surface this seems ok, I guess, but then again what type of commitment does an American Citizen of dual nature have to US, voting in a foreign election. Then again, maybe it's all a matter of perspective, because possibly they could vote our interest. Who knows, all above my head, but such matters should be monitored in my personal opinion.

## Chapter 99:

## Justice Thurgood Marshall

Justice Thurgood Marshall was born in Maryland, Baltimore to be exact. He attended Frederick Douglass High School and finished early to go off and attend the Historically Black College; Lincoln Univresity. Although his father was without formal education young Justice Marshall felt as though his father trained him to become a lawyer by taking him to court and inciting debates about the process an decisions after the cases were over. The ambitious Justice Marshall wanted to attend the predominantly white University of Maryland School of Law after his undergraduate career at Lincoln, but ultimately decided not to apply because of the school's segregation policy in place at the time. He end up going to Howard University School of Law, where he excelled and graduated first in his class in 1933, *magna cum laude*. After graduation, Justice Marshall went back home to Baltimore, Maryland to start his own outfit, private law practice. He also would initiate his affiliation with the National Association for the Advancement of Colored People (NAACP) during this time by representing the group in a law school discrimination lawsuit, *Murray v. Pearson*. It also must be noted that Justice Thurgood Marshal pledged Alpha Phi Alpha Fraternity, Inc. during his undergraduate years at Lincoln University. His private work with the NAACP also earned him a position of Chief Council and he even rubbed shoulders with J. Edgar Hoover, then director of the Federal Bureau of Investigation (FBI). It was President Lyndon B. Johnson who nominated Justice Marshall to the United States Supreme Court and his legal philosophy could be considered classified more so liberal than conservative, as he is quoted saying, "You do what you think is right and the law catch up." Most famously known for his champion work on *Brown v. Board of Education of Topeka(1954)* as a lawyer, to end segregation of schools in the public school system; as a Justice he was quietly known as a judicial activist. Serving on the court for some 24 years he heard and wrote opinions on cases dealing with individual rights, especially those of those criminally indicted. Abortion rights, death penalty, civil rights, criminal procedure, Labor Unions, Securities law, and Representation were some of the range of cases he sat on. Herein we will discuss a select few.

In this first case, we have the equal protection clause of the fourteenth amendment allegedly being violated by a women who argued that the law stating that hiring preferences should go to veterans over non-veterans is unconstitutional because there are or were fewer women veterans. Such was the matter in the case of Personnel Administrator of Massachusetts v. Feeney (1979). The Gritty details of this case speak to the massive impact that such law had in Massachusetts during this time. Hiring preferences going to veterans substantially decreased opportunities for women to find jobs. Or in Justice Marshall's dissent piece for this case, this law purposely discriminated against women and limited them to inferior positions or those of less responsibility and pay such as Secretaries and Secretary assistants. Moral to the Story: This case was just four short years after the Vietnam War was announced over by President Gerald Ford at Tulane University in 1975. So there must have been all kind of Vietnam Veterans in need of employment in order to support their families. I don't oppose to women working as well as women's rights, and voting, and holding key positions of responsibility in government, business, sports, and the rest; nevertheless, at this point in history I personally fell it was necessary for Vietnam veterans to have a leg up in obtaining jobs of substance and given a means to provide for their wives and children over women who could be provided for by their husbands working. Of course this was not the 50's era, but I thing some American tradition and the nuclear family still played a major role in the way society functioned. Thus, I would have to humbly disagree with my good ole' Fraternal Brother Justice Thurgood Marshall on this point. I respect the fact that he obviously had more insight into the case, the law, as well as the economic and political situation of that day, but from my perspective, seems that women could let the men lead in this area and not be offended that their War Heroes needed solid work when they got back from serving their country, and legislation aided them in obtaining it. The funny thing is, today the dynamics of this case might have changed because there are many more women veterans who serve. So maybe this case would be moot. Who knows?

In this next case, we delved into the world of mergers and acquisitions, shareholders, board members, shareholder voting, and the question of "materiality." In this particular case of TSC Industries, Inc. v. Northway, Inc. (1976), we have the financial capable National Industries, Inc. purchasing 34% of the company TSC's voting stock from the corporation founder. . At this point, five National nominees were placed on the TSC's Board of Trustees. Some time there after a meeting is held in TSC 's offices and there is a motion on the table to sale the rest of the assets of TSC to National. One condition on the table was that the merger be a type of exchange of common and preferred in TSC for that of National. The board made of the two companies came together and issued a joint statement to it's shareholders for a vote of confidence and approval of the official merger of the two companies. The conflict of this case lies in the fact that the company Northway was a shareholder who received the proxy report from the conjoined board and thus after review stated that the report was in fact misleading because it did not openly disclose how much actual power the company National, Inc. had over TSC, Inc, and if in fact the motion to sale and if the merger was an actual good decision or in the best interest of TSC, Inc and their shareholders. Turns out that the District and Appeals court did nothing for the plaintiff, Northway, Inc., but it was Justice Marshall who redefined the term "materiality" which is the significance of facts that are within a report., and remanded the case. In this case the question was that there was not enough *material* in the report to make a proper and informed decision or that certain necessary facts were omitted from the report, and this also violated the Securities Exchange Act of 1934. Moral to the Story: Shareholders, Voters, Board members, and those who make up the representative constituency should be fully informed on the issues when presented with issues that they have opportunity to vote on. Or perhaps, to be fully informed on every issue would require the transfer of reams of legalese and documentation unnecessary for a vote, but that the constituency or shareholders in business be given pertinent and necessary facts as recommend by Justice Thurgood Marshall in his majority opinion, to place an educated vote. And surely no malicious disinformation or omission of significant material facts should be practiced by companies, boards, and governments in good ethical standing.

## Chapter 100:

## Justice Warren E. Burger (1907-1995)

Justice Warren Burger was born in the state of Minnesota. He attended John A. Johnson High School and got into politics early, serving as President of the Student council. Well rounded as a scholar and athlete, he played a number of sports as well as wrote articles for local news papers. Young Justice Burger was accepted into Princeton University on partial scholarship but declined to attend to do financial hardship. He took a job that summer working on the Mississippi River Bridge. Justice Burger took on part time work while he attended extension classes at the University of Minnesota for two years. His day job was selling insurance for Mutual Life. After he completed this program, he went on to St. Paul College of Law, today Mitchell Hamlin School of Law, and earned his Bachelor of Laws, graduating top of his class. From there he took a job at St. Paul law firm and got involved in leadership. He wanted to serve active duty in the military during WWII , like his grandfather had served in the Union Army during the Civil War, but was held back due to a spinal injury, and did his part by serving with the Governor of Minnesota to help the fight of desegregation and also improve police relations between city police and minority communicates. Justice Burger was nominated by President Nixon to the United States Supreme Court, but this is after he was nominated to the US Court of Appeals for the District of Columbia Circuit by President Dwight D. Eisenhower. Justice Burger participated in a number of rulings as a US Supreme Court Associate Justice such as abortion, capital punishment, religious establishment, and school desegregation. Ironically he was considered primarily a conservative Justice, although he also wrote some liberal majority opinions on the aforementioned cases. In one particular case where an individual was sentenced to life imprisonment for writing a false check, he considered the judgment cruel and unusual punishment.

In this first case we will consider we will look at integration of the public schools by way of the busing system. The High Courts of the land had rule that busing was indeed an acceptable way to cure the racial imbalance within the public school system. This case in particular, *Swann v. Charlott-Mecklenburg Board of Education (1970)* of course came some 15 years after *Brown v. Board*, and was the North Carolina response to put into practice the new idea of integration. It also must be said, that there were other legal battles and skirmishes that tried to split hairs and say that *Brown v. Board* ended segregation, but did not in fact order integration. The details of the case tell a story of Board meetings, demographics, zoning, inclusion, car bombing, and a mixed emotional body of people trying to make things right. Moral to the Story: Racial Integration was key, monumental, and instrumental in the further development and economic-political, and social well being and upward mobility for Black-Americans during that time and forever moving forward. Not to say that Blacks did not have their own "second-class" educational institutions with less government funding, and all the potential talent creative and natural ability that just needed to be trained, educated, taught and refined with the centuries old skill and Wisdom from Ancient of day and Antiquity as well as the modern technologies that would build the black infrastructure and community up to a point of mentionable and notable competition in the free market place of ideas and trade. But this is a case of integration and not segregation, and I can remember after I graduated from high school with a 4.167 GPA, having attended a very diverse high school in Southern California, and ranked only 20 in my class of some 800 students I had applied to both Historically Black Colleges and Primarily White Research Universities. I remember vividly the choice that was upon me as to what world I wanted to be in or how I wanted to spend the next four years of my life. When I saw myself at a black college like Morehouse, Xavier, or Tennessee State University, all I could think about was all the time I would probably waste chasing women. I had to be honest with myself; I didn't think I would be able to focus at a black school. When I saw myself at a primarily White institution, I saw myself more focused, and dealing with the realities of real life, so I made my choice. And The University of California, San Diego it was. Now, I still chased my fair share of young women, had my fun, attended parties, participated in clubs, and somehow still managed to pledge a black fraternity on campus, but the overall experience of attending a major University, I would not trade, and I think every youth deserves this experience or opportunity for social development. Now, the rest of the story is that I did not finish up at UCSD even after four and some years, but relocated to Arizona where I would complete a different undergraduate and graduate degree other than my previous years of study at Grand Canyon University. Not to mention my major schizophrenic breakdown, attempt to join the military, and Time in between...but that's another book.

In this next case, we will revisit a case briefly mentioned in the intro/bio of this chapter, that is the case of *Solem v. Helm (1983).* In this case we have one who was convicted of fraudulent check writing and sentenced in the State of South Dakota to the maximum sentence of life imprison at the State Penitenury. Mr. Solem was in dire straights for his minor offense of criminal behavior until the Court overturned his sentence, Justice Burger writing, “Suppose several states punish severely a crime that the court views as trivial or petty? I can see no limiting principle in the Courts holding?” This leaning of though was said to flow in his constructionist judicial philosophical bent, which interprets the law directly from the exact wording of the law. And in this case, Justice Burger's sentiments were that this punishment fir saud crime was brutal and exceedingly excessive. Not to say that writing false checks isn't wrong, but to be made to endure a lifetime of incarcerated drudgery, just because one is down on their luck, or feeling slightly clever, I think also is little much. There was later a three part rubric, or legend if you will, on how to in the future to judge weather or not sentences were fair. Those safeguards were to first examine if the punishment or penalty was equal to the nature, severity or gravity of the crime or offense committed. Secondly, that the sentence be compared to other sentences committed for same or similar offenses within that jurisdiction and then in other jurisdictions. Moral to the Story: Harsh sentencing can be extremely painful to watch and I'm sure to endure. Possibly it will deter others or the general population for ever committing such major or minor offenses, but the point is that it takes mature and experienced, clear eyed Justices and Judges to be able to look at the mal or mis action- whatever the case may be, and the law, for what it is and make hopefully merciful rulings when fitting.

## Chapter 101:

## Justice: Harry Andrew Blackmun

Justice Harry Blackmun was born in the ole state of Illinois where he grew up in a working middle class neighborhood and went to the specialized school of Mechanics Art High School. Graduating in the top one percent of his class, he originally thought that he would attend the University of Minnesota, but was offered a full academic scholarship to the prestigious Harvard University. After he completed his Bachelors in Mathematics from Harvard, it was of to Harvard Law. From there, he stepped into the world of private practice, in which he offered council, clerked for a bit, served as adjunct faculty, and specialized in the areas of trusts and estates, taxation, and civil litigation. In terms of Judicial philosophy and jurisprudence; although Justice Blackmun was expected to be conservative, as that is the way he voted at the inception of his Supreme Court career; notwithstanding, over time, he became more liberal in his opinions and rulings; instrumental in Roe v. Wade, and dissenting in *Rizzo v. Goode (1976)*, in which herein we will discuss.

In this first case we will discuss, the case of Rizzo v. Goode *(1976)*, we have the US Supreme Court coming in and overruling in a State prophylactic injunction placed on a police department to come up with a comprehensive plan to essentially handle grievances from the public citizenry. Furthermore, it was the State Court of Appeals that granted this ruling for the plaintiffs in the case who asserted systematic mistreatment of certain citizens from officers. Again, US Supreme court ruled against this decision stating that the inferior courts exceeded their jurisdiction, among a number of other points, such as the statistical evidence did not add up to the reportedly said amount of Police offenses to the public, and finally, there was no unconstitutional actions found in the ranks of those responsible authorities. Thus "the court created a limit on federal injunctive power in matters of state agency internal affairs." (wikipedia). Moral to the Story: Interestingly enough, this is sort of relevant given the community wide anger toward some precints throughout the nation in which there are petitions to defund the police. I personally feel this is a naive, and quite frankly "stupid" idea. Who want's lawlessness in their streets, communities and neighborhoods, where there is no check whatsoever against drug dealers, addict homeless, rampid domestic violence issues, crime, robbery, and whatsoever else the common criminal can think of to get away with without the consequence of being stopped by an official authority of the law. Sure people can police their own neighborhoods, and there are private security agencies and mercenary organizations, but I think these replacing State departments with leads to more violence, unprofessionalism, and possible corruption.

In this next case, we have a situation where an Attorney fresh out of law school starts a private practice and finds out he will need some extra advertisement in order to put his legal business where it needs to be in order to make a profit as well as maintain the overhead expenses of running a law office. There was some legal conflict because the State Bar of Arizona prohibited lawyers from advertising their services in the State. Well in the case of Bates v. State Bar of Arizona (1977), he bit the bullet and went for it anyway and is still in practice to this very day. US Supreme Court ruled that it Bate's right to advertise was upheld by the commercial speech clause of the First Amendment. Moral to the Story: Many times, ambitious youth, including myself at one time or the other think of what we want to be in life and think of how much money we would like or see ourselves making, but don't have the experience to consider all the minor cost and possible legal and logistical hiccups. This is not true for all professions. Some come out of college and do extremely well with their first job; professions like engineering and computer software or science engineering, and a few other degrees. But sometimes, there is a training or biding in the water period where those of us in other professions or majors have to wait and work harder to get the salary, pay, or profit we desire. I am an author and this being my sixth book, and long time graduate, but being one to seek self-employment rather than work directly for some other company or organization, it has taken me a few years to gather my marbles and find out what I really want and am going to do to make a substantial profit. I think I've secretly found it, and look forward finally to some fatter calf years, the good Lord willing

## Chapter 102:

## Justice Lewis Franklin Powell Jr. (1907-1998)

Justice Lewis Powell, was one of the more cerebral Justices who sat upon the bench as an Associate Justice. Born native to Virginia and attending Washington and Lee University for undergrad, he ultimately ended up earning two law degrees, a bachelors from Washington and Lee University School of Law and a Master of Laws from Harvard Law; writing his thesis on "*Relations between Virgin Court of Appeals and the State Corporation Commission*." Early involvement in politics and leadership as he was elected the Student Body President and took on the position as managing editor of the University Newspaper. After graduation from law school, it was not off to practice right away per say, but it he first attempted to join the US Navy but was turned away due to poor eyesight. He landed in the U.S. Army Air force working in the area of Intelligence and wound up doing some intelligence missions in North Africa, Europe, England, and the Mediterranean Front. After his discharge in 1945, Justice Lewis went on to practice with a Law Firm out of Richmond, Virginia where he specialized in Corporate law as well as mergers and acquisitions; mainly dealing in the area of Rail Roads. After doing this for some time he was noticed and appointed by President Richard Nixon to the US Supreme Court after some convincing from the President asking a second time along with the Attorney General. Justice Powell had a would have to make a number of adjustments along with having a few concerns about his background in mainly corporate law, he was not absolutely sure he would be able to effectively influence his Justice colleague on all the nations issues that would arise, not to mention the hit to his maga corporate lawyer salary. In terms of Judicial philosophy and leanings, seems that he mainly voted or wrote leaning toward the liberal side, as he was pro-choice, lenient toward a rapist-murderer in setting aside the death penalty, and gave affirmative action a shot, just to point out a few of his major decisions. Herein we will discuss.

In the first case we will discuss, we have a convicted felon on charges of rape, kidnapping, first degree murder, and aggravated assault , who escapes from prison and essentially repeats the same charges by raping the victim in her home and then stealing the family vehicle. This is the matter of *Coker v. Georgia (1977).* Upon assessing the decisions that came down, the state of Georgia originally assigned the death penalty, notwithstanding, it was Justice Powell who asserted the opinion that "the injuries sustained were not serious and lasting and thus not beyond repair." Of course this ruling came in 1977 and maybe men's views on the inner and emotional damage that can beset a rape victim were not fully realized, nevertheless, Justice Powell, although he acknowledged the women's rape and her pain, did not fell it dictated the death of the assailant. Moral to the Story: To the point, Rape is wrong, the death penalty sucks. What is one to do in this scenario, because life in prison sucks as well, and quite frankly, it is unclear as to what sentence Mr. Coker end up getting for committing this crime. Although, it must be acknowledged that there was a three strike law being being or that had been legislated by Congress that I'm not sure if applied to this case.

In this next and final case for this chapter, we have the fiasco of the *Regents of the University of California v. Bakke (1978).* In this scenario we have a Vietnam Marine vet who applies to a few medical school all across the nation and concentrates his attention to California where noticed some minority students who had lower grades and test scores got in above him. He grades and scores were above average, not to mention his military service and work at NASA, but he was 33 and some medical boards called him too old. He fought against the qoata system in Davis which allowed 16 out of 100 seats to be reserved for students of Color, or African-Americans. He ended up winning his case and his seat, destroying the quota system at UC Davis, and I would imagine turning out to be a successful physician. It must be said that there is a distinction between the affirmative action law that was in place that allowed Universities to consider race as a factor in determining admissions and a flat out quota system, like practiced at UC Davis Medical School. Moral to the Story: Well, I can see Bakke's point, but at the same time I can also see the quota system as a sort of reparations to the African-American community for past years of pain and suffering due to slavery, oppression, Jim Crow, racism and and all other matter of other evils committed by cruel and bigoted Americans to a whole race of people. And I am a patriot mind you. It would be like taking away federal monies and land won by the Native American Tribes because this was somehow "reverse discrimination." So, Although I can understand Marine Bakke's complaint, that someone with lower test scores and grades got in above him, I would argue that those seats were reserved for students of color for specific reasons, to help rebuild a community, provide positive examples and role models to Black youth and show them what was possible and necessary to lift themselves out of poverty. Justice Powell ruled in dissent of the Bakke win, that constitutionally we could get away with such programs.

## Chapter 103

## Justice William Hubbs Rehnquist

Justice William Rehnquist grew into a young man in the state of Wisconsin and attended Shorewood High School. After Shorewood it was off to Kenyon College in Ohio for a short time then off to the US Army Airforce. He specialized in pre-meterology and was assigned at first to Denison University, but the program shut down. So, he traveled all over the States attending different training programs with the Army Air force; Oklahoma City, New Mexico, Texas, Illinois, New Jersey and ultimately after gaining the skill of weather repair and maintenance of instruments, he was sent to North Africa as a weather observer. After his discharge from the service, Justice Rehnquist used his GI bill to pay his tuition at Stanford University where he obtained a Bachelors and Masters Degree in Political Science. Next, it was off to Harvard University where he earned his 2$^{nd}$ Master's Degree in Government. Then it was Stanford Law School where the Justice Sandra Day O'Connor was a fellow colleague and classmate of his, of whom he would also eventually serve with on the US Supreme Court. Unfortunately, Justice Rehnquist was against desegregation and wrote an opinion piece on the matter as a young law clerk, as he clerked for Justice Robert H Jackson on the US Supreme Court. This of course was before his ascension to the US Supreme court himself as an Associate Justice, nevertheless, some of his judicial sentiment and philosophy could be understood. Justice Rehnquist was nominated to the court by President Ronald Reagan. Justice Rehnquest was not only an Associate Justice but served as a Chief Justice implementing rules and regulations for his Justice colleges to be more productive in discussion over cases. It was thought that Justice Rehnquist would have massive conservative influence over the Supreme Court as Chief Justice and push the Federalism doctrine, that is Federal or Congressional powers being limited over the States; notwithstanding, it was not as big of and impact as one may think, as reported by select Reporters.

In the first case, majority opinion written by Chief Justice Rehnquist, we will consider the aforementioned idea of federal limitations over the states; specifically with respect to interstate commerce, wage standards, and labor hour limitations. In the details, the case of *National League of Cities v. Usery, (1976),* the US Supreme Court decided that the Fair Labor Standards Act could not constitutionally be applied to state government. This case was later overruled some twenty years later in the case of Garcia v. San Antonio Metropolitan Transit Authority. Essentially *National League of Cities* spelled out and removed certain exemptions for employees of state institutions. Moreover, the act would have also enforced policy upon public employers minimum wage standards and work hour limitations, that had been in the past only restricted to business and individuals engaged in interstate comerse. Moral to the Story: Seems that Chief Justice Rehnquist wanted to limit and regulate state to state inter commerse as private and individual business were regulated. I do not necessarily see the fundamental problem with there being minimum wage standards or work hour limits, even thoughit seems the case was later overturned, it seems the underlining issue of conflict was that Congress can not inhibit State legislature ability to manager their affairs. It is not that Congress does not have "affirmative authority", but that for matters such as wage regulation and limitation of hours worked, not. Nevertheless, given today's minimum wage increase to $15.00/hr that came down from the executive branch, and I'm not abreast of current work hour limitations, but it seems that whatever is functionally best for the people stands against technical bureaucratic red tape, but not the constitution. The question is, what measures will be in place to monitor or enforce states to uphold national minimum wage policies, and secondly, do these wage increases contribute to inflation, or ultimately help build a greater economy.

In this second case we have what on the surface seems to be an issue of the 2nd amendment and gun right laws, but once uncovered we see that in the case of *United States v. Alfonso D. Lopez, Jr., (1995)*, the issue was more so dealing with the commerse clause in which the Supreme Court decided that Congress had exceeded it's power under the Commerse Clause. In the details of this case, we have a young man that brought a .38 caliber revolver to the school with five unloaded cartridges to sale for a profit of $44.00. Someone made a tip that got to the on campus officers and young Alfonso was apprehended and charged with not illegal possession of a firearm,, but Gun-Free School Zones Act of 1990. Apparently, and I assuming that Alfonso was under the age of 18, it was ok that he had the firearm, but not ok that he had it to sale on school grounds. Mr. Lopez's legal strategy was to try to get the indictment dismissed on the grounds that federal powers of the Congress had no such a power to legislate under Congress Clause. This argument won in the Appels Court and the United States kicked it up the the US Supreme Court which upheld the Court of Appeals decision. Moral to the Story: I don't think this would fly today because of the massive school shootings and violence that has taken place over the years in our public school system due to adolescent and teenage gun violence. I believe that most of campuses have these zero tolerance policies, that is no guns, knives, or weapons of any kind on campus. Regardless of how the regulation comes down, I personally think that it is necessary to preserve safety and innocent lives. Too many violent video games that paint war and violent images in our youth that can perhaps influence unhappy young souls to imitate what the see and play if given the opportunity to freely carry, buy and sale, or distribute guns on campus. Not to mention schools that have trouble with gang violence, race riots, hate speech and bullying where free gun use would only escalate some already problematic scenarios.

## Chapter 104:

## Justice John Paul Stevens(1920-1919)

Justice John Stevens was born to a well to do family in the state of Illinois. He attended a special predatory school by the name of the University of Chicago Laboratory Schools and then it was off to complete his undergraduate studies at the University of Chicago. After earning a Bachelors in English, it was off to join the Navy, coincidentally one day before the Japanese attack on Pearl Harbor. He would serve as an intelligence Officer in the Pacific Theater. Specializing in Code Breaking, it was Justice John Stevens work along with his team that assisted in bringing down the high ranking Admiral Isoroku Yamamoto's, Japaneses commander in Chief of a whole fleet during WWII. After his discharge from the Navy, he used his GI bill to pay for and attend Law school at Northwestern University School of Law; he graduated Top of his Class. Considered a conservative moderate in terms of his voting record, Justice Stevens actually aided in the re-reinstatement of capital punishment, opposed race-based admissions, yet and still he also had a liberal bent; voting with liberal justices on abortion, gay rights, and federalism. It was President Gerald Ford who nominated Justice Stevens to the US Supreme Court

In this first case that we will discuss, it is one of where the court made a judgment, and this is a mouthful, but basically, "that judges under the sixth amendment, when the right to jury trial, along with the fourteenth amendment prevented enhanced criminal sentences beyond statutory maxima based on facts other than decided by the jury beyond a reasonable doubt"(wikipedia). This essentially means that Judges were not suppose to add extra sentencing or cross the statutory maxima based on evidence not evaluated, and assessed by jury. An interesting case that this rule sort of applied to, in the gory details of Apprendi v. New Jersey (2000), we have a basic hate crime. A black family moves into a predominantly white neighborhood, and Mr. Apprendi takes it upon himself to shoot their house up, pumping .22 caliber bullets into their new home. Once apprehended, Mr. Apprendi confesses to the cops that he committed the crime because his new neighbors where black and he didn't want them in his neighborhood. After his arraignment, Mr. Apprendi was facing 5-10 years on weapons possession charges and as part of his plea bargain, the Prosecution by law, reserved the right to seek enhanced sentencing on the basis that the crime was committed with prejudice. Mr. Apprendi took measures to appeal his case and it kicked up to the US Supreme court, and the US Supreme Court actually sent it back to the Court of Appeals. The case is a bit ambiguous, but in the end, it appears that Mr. Apprendi end up getting 12 years for his asinine hate crime, in which he later argued was not a hate crime, but that he was intoxicated. Moral to the Story: It's very interesting that this type of behavior still exist in the in the 21st Century in America, and not only that, but some arguments can be made that some hate crimes have even been escalated. You know, that black family could have moved to a poor neighborhood in the ghetto, or less economically favored community and one might think there would be a higher chances of something like that happening do to gang violence or a robbery if it was a terrible neighborhood, but the reality its, it probably would not have happened. Go figure, a well to do black family moves to a higher economic community and deals with essentially gang violence and bullying. But that was not the main thrust of the case. The main issue was the actual sentencing of Mr. Apprendi. After what I thought was a pretty tough but fair sentence for aimlessly shooting at someone's house, there was deliberation over the enhanced two years. Seems that the extra two year stuck, but the whole deliberation over the enhanced sentencing was that evidence that determined such had to be heard by jury and ruled as such beyond reasonable doubt, not just by a judge during a bench hearing, was my clumsy understanding and assessment. Main point, shooting in peoples houses is wrong, do the Crime, beware, the Time.

In this next case, it is the matter of Kelo v. City of New London (2005), and basically it deals with the utility of an "eminent domain to transfer land from one private owner to another for the purposes of economic development." The whole case surrounded around the issue of a condemned property being used by another private company for redevelopment; the judgement allowed he company to proceed with plans, but they were unable to obtain funding, and left off trying. It was Mrs. Kelo who sued the city of New London for the misuse of eminent domain power arguing that any property taken for public use was those owners were to receive just compensation, but such was not the case in this instance. Moral to the Story: I can remember toward a freeway being built that would cross my High School's parking lot and part of the neighborhood on the Main Street that my High School was on. These residents had to leave the property that they had mortgaged, owned and rented because the city, state, or local government, not sure what agency, was building a freeway. Now, I did hear that these residents received compensation for their property and for having to move although given a deadline. But the main point is, it happens. This scenario is not the exact mirror of the Kelo v. New London case, but it speaks to eminent domain and just compensation.

## Chapter 105:

## Justice Sandra Day O'Connor

Justice Sandra Day O'Connor was born and grew up on a large ranch in El Paso, Texas, where she carried a .22 caliber rifle of her own, shooting Coyotes and jackrabbits. She later Co-authored a book with here brother, *"Lazy B: Growing up on a Cattle Ranch in the American West (2002)."* She attended a private school for girls, Radford; and graduated Austin High school early, 6th in her class. At 16 years of age, she began attending Stanford University, as she would major in economics and finish at the top of her class, then it was off to Stanford Law where she served on the Stanford Law Review. According to sources, Justice O'Connor would turn down a written marriage proposal from her classmate and future colleague Justice Rehnquist. After law school, Justice O'Connor faced the reality of a tough job market for women as she had chose to marry John Jay O' Connor III who was eventually drafted and Justice O'Connor followed her husband to Germany where they both worked, she as a attorney for the Army's Quartermaster Corps. She would stay there doing her job for three years before their relocation back to the States; more specifically, Maricopa County, Arizona. She served as the assistant to the Attorney General and became involved in politics serving as Arizona' s Majority Leader. It was the President Ronald Reagan who nominated Justice O'Connor to the US Supreme Court as she would serve as an Associate Justice writing many concurring, and a few significant majority opinions. She mainly leaned conservative but was considered the swing vote when she first came to the Court. In her time, publications positioned her as the

"Most Powerful Women in the World," and she was awarded the Presidential Medal of Freedom by President Barack Obama in 2009.

This first case shows Justice Sandra O'Connor's more liberal side, even though she was considered a more so conservative Justice or as aforementioned, swing vote to the court. In the case of *Grutter v. Bollinger (2003),* the court ruled in favor of a type of affirmative action that favored underrepresented minorities; that this did not go against the constitution, specifically the fourteenth amendments Equal Protection Clause, and these evaluation points are acceptable so long as other constant variables are used for all other candidates. In short, race can be used, as long as all other factors for admissions considered for every applicant. In the gory details of the case, we have a what seemingly is a perfect female candidate for the University of Michigan Law school. Mrs.Gutter held a 3.8 GPA, along with a LSAT score of 161 and still was not granted admissions to her school of choice. She filed suit for her grievance, complaining that it was because of the schools race policy that prevented her from receiving admissions. Ultimately, it was Justice Sandra O'Connor who wrote the majority opinion in this case where she reasoned that, " the United States Constitution does not prohibit the law school's narrowly tailored use of race in admissions decision s to further a compelling interest in obtaining educational benefits that flow from a diverse student body." Furthermore, she indicated in so many words that this was a sort of temporary solution, that is that in the next 25 years, affirmative action would be unnecessary to promote diversity. Moral to the Story: I think that the affirmative action programs that existed in the past were excellent tools necessary to help build up minority and ultimately the overall community with providing a gate or bridge for underrepresented students to pull themselves up and create a social standard that economically, and politically for that matter benefits society as a whole. It is unclear to me as to weather or not these type and kind of programs exist on the same level or to what scale today, but one would think significant progress was made and continual strides may have to come from more of a merit based system, given all things equal. Notwithstanding, on the contrary, philosophically speaking, life is not always fair, and even though we live in a egalitarian society where opportunities are in theory and applied practice made available to all, this does not mean that the student who has come from the well to do family with advance training as a youth gets denied because of their privileged; it simply means that the underprivileged student will have to work and study a bit harder, making themselves a stronger candidate. This is not inherently unfair, just a simple reality of life. It seems often times now days people make great complaints for what seemingly are life's "unjust" realities, instead of doing the necessary work to effectively create the opportunities and society necessary that coincide with such ideals.

In this next case, we see a case that would make a good heart wince, it is the case of *Lockyer v. Andrade (2003).* This case ruled that Mr. Andrade, a nine year Army Veteran, would have to serve 50 years to life, for stealing on a number of occasions children's videotapes from department stores. Apparenlty he had priors since 1982, and in and out of federal prison; for petty theft, residential burglary, and transportation of marijuana, but under the California three strike law, this 50 year to Life sentence was given. Further stated in the sentence, there would be no relief of habeas corpus which can be argued went against the eighth amendment's cruel and unusual punishment clause. The courts dismissed the idea of lessening Mr. Andrade's two petty theft charges to misdemeanors and he was sentenced to two consecutive terms of 25-years-to life in prison. In short, Mr. Andrade's argued his case before a few courts, Court of Appeal, District, and Circuit; a review was denied from the California Supreme Court; ultimately the review came from the US Supreme Court by request from the Ninth Circuit. This matter was a legal cluster fuck, for a number of reasons, but one given that in the Majority opinion three separate prior holdings or relavant precedents were given that could be identified as slightly ambigous to say the least, simply put, not really an exact match to Mr. Andrade's case. We won't go into them here; *Rummel v. Estelle, Solem, V. Helm, and Harmelin v. Michgan;* but in Mr. Andrade's case, it was determined that because of the case of Rummel, it was even if remotely possible for Andrade to obtain parole, but that the sentence was not a matter of disproportinality or "unreasonably" applied. Moral to the Story; Be a good citizen, don't rob people and steel things, because it can come bite you hard, that is in California back in 2003 anyway. I think about this case and because I wasn't there and there are a lot of unknown's from my perspective, I wonder why Mr. Andrede didn't get kicked to Military Court being an nine year Army Vet. Furthermore, what was this guy doing burglarizing people; maybe he had a case of PTSD, was the victim an enemy, and sounds like the guy was mentally ill. Not sure, has his parole come up yet, not sure....But all of the crimes seem petty besides the residential burglary and in my personal layman's opinion do not deserve a double 25 year to life sentence, unless he was some type of local terrorist really hurting and harming people. Like I said, hard to understand all the factors and variables that were at play here from my perspective, but lesson from this case is to stay out of trouble, especially if you live in the land of three strike your out California.

## Chapter 106:

## Justice Antonin Gregory Scalia (1936-2016)

Justice Antonin Scalia was an intellectual and maybe that had just a little to do with his father being an Italian Immigrant and Professor of Romantic languages. Born in New Jersey, on his own merit, young Justice Scalia earned a Academic scholarship to the prestigious Xavier

High School, which was a type of boarding/Jesuit military school where he excelled. After graduating as the valedictorian, it was off to Georgetown University where he earned a undergraduate degree in history. After this, it was non other than Harvard Law to become an Attorney. It was the city of Cleveland, Ohio where Justice Antonin Scalia first began to practice; he actually worked at a law firm. Next, it was off to the University of Virginia where he stood and taught as a Law Professor. Then it was work for the State Department under the Nixon and Ford Administrations, and landing the post as Assistant Attorney General. On more Professor job during President Carter's administration, and then he was appointed by President Ronald Reagan to the US Court of Appeals for the District of Columbia Circuit. Finally it was from this position that he was again promoted and appointed by President Reagan to the United States Supreme Court. Mostly considered a strong Conservative, his voting record and philosophical leanings speaking consistent with what he stood for as a Catholic judge who worked tremendously hard to get to where he was. He felt that the death penalty was constitutional and on the contrary that affirmative-action, abortion, and same-sex marriage were not. Herein we will discuss a few of his decisions.

In this first case of discussion, it presents an interesting concept, that is evidence classified as hearsay admitted into court. More specifically, under the Confrontation Clause of the sixth amendment, in the case of *Crawford v. Washington(2004)*, the US Supreme Court decided to reformulate the standard for determining when the admission of hearsay statements in criminal cases is permitted. It was determined that cross examination must be performed to admit prior statements of witness who may no longer be available. In this case, Mr. Crawford heard that his wife Mrs. Crawford was threatened by a Mr. Lee with rape. Mr. Crawford went to confront Mr. Lee, to defend his wife's honor and stabbed Mr. Lee. Later in custody Mr. Crawford said it was in self defence and that he thought Mr. Lee had a weapon. Mrs. Crawford, when giving her testimony having not been there said she didn't think the stabbing was in self defense and that she did not think Mr. Lee had a weapon. Due to the nature of the testimony and all the factors that would make the her testimony consistent with her husbands, it was admitted. Moral to the Story: I think it's ok to defend your wife, daughter, or loved one's honor, but beware of the consequences for whatever action you plan to take and count the cost. Not to mention, be sure that your loved one wants you to do such a thing and you guys have your story straight. Because seems like one act of vengeance can come back to bite you. Know one really wants to accept it. Nevertheless, the bible records, "Vengeance is Mine, sayeth the LORD, I will repay (Rom. 12:19)."

In this next case to be discussed we have an overzealous schizophrenic man who feels compelled to confess a murder he has admittedly committed after waiving his Miranda rights after being repeatedly prompted by officers on duty to hear his Miranda rights instead of being coerced into a confession. After waiving council, in the case of Colorado v. Connolly (1986), Mr. Connolly confessed in gruesome detail his murder and was determined incompetent to stand trial and received therapy for six months before standing trial. During the hearing, Mr. Connolly's Psychiatrist reported that Mr. Connely relayed that he felt God told him to either confess or commit suicide. Because of Mr. Connely's SMI status, his confession was suppressed in the Colorado Supreme Court under the due process clause of the fourteenth amendment. The US Supreme court came back and using *Miranda v. Arizona* declared that the testimony should not be suppressed because it was not coerced by manipulative government interrogation. Moral to the Story: Murder is a serious crime, and by first hand, I know that mental illness, especially schizophrenia is a serious illness. It's like when the first onslaught of auditorium and visual hallucinations happens, one feels as though there is another world superimposed on this world breaking through our out or the line or barrier or interface between the natural and the supernatural is being made transposeable, so that with ones mind's eye or even natural eye, they can see and hear things on the other side. Sometimes in the sky, sometimes on the wall, or one's person. I have personally even felt the attack of the supernatural on my physical body. Well, when this world comes to the uninformed or one without insight into their illness, and a voice of authority tells them to do something, one automatically feels it is a voice or voices of a higher realm, or of intelligence and for the mere curiosity or stupidity, or bad judgment most often than not carries it out. This why schizophrenia is such a scary and dangerous disease. I have lived with it for over 18 years now, having an advanced break maybe 13 years ago. I can say now that it is easier to manage my symptoms of auditory hallucinations, and they daily and hourly be with me. Medication management does help with some suppression and quieting down the voices, but their always there. I have also experienced the split mind scenario, racing thoughts, word salad, memory loss; all these as best as my articulation can describe it happened when it feels as though there is some external or even internal force driving the the mind, splitting the mind, and even shutting down the mind. On the contrary though, I do believe that such illness can be quieted with medication along with and if one can bring themselves to concentrate during the quite times with reading, meditation, painting, or whatever activity focuses and sharpens that persons mind for them...I believe that overtime with insight into one's illness along with, understanding, progress can be made, and this does not have to be a degenerative disease in every case.

## Chapter 107:

## Justice Anthony McLeod Kennedy

Justice Anthony Kennedy was born in Northern California, and was exposed to the political scene at an early age, getting involved in local activities as a youth, and even working as an errand runner for the California State Senate. He graduated near the top of his class from C.K. McClatchy High School with honors. Right out of High School, it was off to Stanford University where he began to thirst for the Law, more specifically Constitutional Law. He studied abroud his Senior year at the London School of Economics and end up completing his undergraduate degree with a bachelors in Political Science; next it was Harvard Law School where he finished up. After Law school, Justice Kennedy twice fortunate enough to start working on his own private practice in San Francisco, California, and also pick up a few more clients in Sacramento, California after his father whom had a firm in that location died. He Professor-ed for a while and also did some work with the California Army National Guard. Justice Kennedy was nominated and appointed by two different Presidents, to two different federal posts. The first being President Gerald Ford, who appointed him to the United States Court of Appeals for the ninth circuit; and the second being by President Ronald Reagan as an associate Justice, to the US Supreme Court. Justice Kennedy was mostly considered a swing voter on the court, similar to Justice O'Connor and authored a few majority opinion cases, some of which we will consider.

In this first case we will look at it covers the pressing matter of habeas corpous, a constitutional right for most criminals, in this case the right was originally raised because the persons involved were originally considered "enemy combatants" rounded up by order of President Bush after the herrendous event of 9/11. This right was waved specifically by the Military Commission s Act of 2006, which Justice Kennedy found in a 5-4 majority ruling that this commission that denied enemy combatants detained in military facilities the right to file for habeaus corpus, unconstitutional. These maters are in the case of *Boumedien . Bush* (2008) and in it found that overall the United Sates exercised de facto sovereignty in this court case, although it was located on leased property in Cuba, that is the Guantanamo detention camps of Guantanamo Bay, where US Supreme court held ultimate jurisdiction. Furthermore, although this Military Commmission Act of 2006 was created to take away privileged from detained enemy combatants, it had no superior authority to challenge. Moral to the Story: These transactions happen under President Bush's, "Global War on Terror," and originally because of the location of the Guantanamo Naval Base, the US holding an ongoing lease in Cuba to the base; war criminals had no protection under the US Constitution not the American Justice System. Such a set up, gave US soldiers, government officials, and black-op team specialist freedom to conduct their internal interrogations and investigations as they saw fit. In short, sucked to be a war criminal or even an allegedly accused suspect of such high crimes. Also we that Federal Judicial powers overrule any Military C omission Acts established by any other entity besides the Judicial Branch of government.

This next case we will herein discuss deals with the US constitutional authority to establish a US Sentencing Commission. Apparently, the court ruled that the Sentencing Commission represented a Constitutional delegation of powers. More specifically, in the case of *Mistretta v. United States (1989).* Mr. Mistretta was criminally indicted for the sale of cocaine. Upon his awaiting trail Mr. Mistretta tried to maneuver by motioning to have the States Federal Sentencing Guidelines; attempting to prevent an excessive sentencing, He was ultimately given 2 years in federal prison. Appealing to the eight circuit court. Moral to the Story: Just a note, seems that smart criminals, if that is a real thing, or oxymoron, seem to always be appealing to another court, constantly trying to get a better ruling or judgment.

## Chapter 108:

## Justice David Hackett Souter (born 1939)

Justice David Souter was born in Massachusetts, and graduated from a public school; Concord High. Next it was off to Harvard University with an undergraduate degree in philosophy. He continued along with Harvard and attended law school there, graduating in 1966 two years before the assassination of leaders, Martin Luther King Jr, and President Robert F. Kennedy. Like many new lawyers fresh out law school, Justice Souter tried his hand at private practice and found that he did not enjoy it, and steered his career in the direction of public service, being slotted into a position of Assistant Attorney General for New Hampshire, and eventually became the Attorney General where he prosecuted criminal cases. Later it was his nomination for the US Supreme Court Justice by President George H.W. Bush. Before this he served on the New Hampshire Supreme Court as well as the US Court of Appeals, first

Circuit. In terms of judicial philosophy, most thought him to be a strict conservative, but he classified himself as a moderate and one who was opposed to radical change and cared for upholding precedence. Herein we will discuss a few of his cases.

In this next case we will deal with the US Supreme Court intervention in dealing with those declared not guilty by reason of insanity. In Foucha v. Louisiana (1992), we have an individual who remained involuntarily confined on the reason of his potential threat and danger to himself or society, although he no longer suffered from attack of the mental illness, which was the initial reason of his intake. In the gritty details of this case, we have Mr. Foucha who performed an armed burglary and then subsequently fired an firearm in the direction of law enforcement officers. After his apprehension and detainment, he was declared incompetent because he clearly demonstrated no evidence of understanding the difference from right and wrong. He was committed to East Feliciana State Hospital on the traditional grounds of danger to self and others. State Louisiana law stipulates that those committed to psychiatric hospital under criminal charges or otherwise and held until recommendations of discharge or release by special review committee. Mr. Foucha was continual committed originally for a drug induced psychosis and the later diagnosed with antisocial personality disorder which at the time was not considered a treatable disorder. In terms of the US Supreme court ruling on the matter, they decided that an individual could not be kept in the Mental Hospital solely because they were classified as dangerous. Just because of an defendant's plea of insanity they should serve their term within the Psych Facility and then be released considered upon final evaluation. Moral to the Story: Apparently, it is not illegal be dangerous per say, but illegal to commit crime and act on ones danger potential. The metaphorical act of translating potential energy or power into kinetic energy or power, that is resting Energy, to active, or energy in motion. So we see that the Supreme court stepped in and ruled in favor of the criminally mentally ill by releasing them from an indefinite Psychiatric hospital stay or sped up future discharge review

In this next case we will consider what the courts ultimately ruled as cruel and unusual punishment of certain inmates, whereas others in the dissent felt that such treatment may have been immoral, tortuous, criminal and even remediable; but ultimately not cruel and unusual. In the case of, *Hudson v. McMillian (1992)* the excessive beating from prison guards on a petitioner Mr. Hudson reported that he received minor bruises, facial swelling, loosened teeth, a cracked dental plate. This type of treatment may in some ways be expected for some prisoners who have certain “off putting” charges, but in an ethical scheme of things, is never right or appropriate. This is a certain street justices or simply criminal behavior that seeps into the justice system to punish certain individuals, or perhaps there are certain political reasons these things happen or they may even be racial. The question as to weather or not a good “beating” from the prison guards are cruel and unusual as oppose to just criminal and mean, I guess would fall under what were the inmates charges, what prison rule or regulation did inmate break that demanded repercussions, and how bad were the injuries. In Mr. Hudson's case, he had a broken dental plate and loosened teeth, and the said report does not give reason or motive. I think this was excessive, criminal, and if one had to go through this on a daily basis, could be considered cruel and unusual. Moral to the Story: Stay out of prison if you can help it.

## Chapter 109:

## Justice Clarence Thomas

Justice Clarence Thomas was born in the state of Georgia. He revered his grandfather who taught him hard work and self reliance and left him with meany wise words and teachings; one of which stuck, "Never let the sun catch you in bed." Justice Thomas grew up Catholic and attended a black perish as well as a Catholic High school. He would go on to attend Seminary, on the path to become a great spiritual and effective leader when the assassination of Dr. Martin Luther King influenced his decision to choose another path to progress, saying to himself that, "the church did not do enough to combat racism." Ultimately, Justice Thomas would attend College of the Holy Cross where he majored in English, and then it was Yale Law School in which he earned his Juris Doctorate. Justice Thomas noted of his experience that law firms after he graduated showed less appreciation for his Yale Law degree thinking that he only got there due to affirmative action. He is considered a conservative Justice on the court, but some of his literary and film interest may expose him to having “some very strong libertarian leanings.” Conservative on economic issues, and liberal on personal liberties. Justice Thomas has had one other federal appointment before his nomination to the US Supreme Court, although he also served with the Reagan administration in the US Department of Education. He also served on the First Circuit Court of Appeals before his ultimate position as Associate Justice on the US Supreme Court.

This first case we will herein consider, we take a look at the US Supreme Court's value of giving counsel to defendants who can not afford such representation. More specifically, in the case of Gideon v. Wainwright (1963), we find that under the sixth amendment of the US Constitution a unanimous decision ruled that all criminal cases must receive counsel in the event that they cannot afford under the constitution of the United States, highlighting specifically the fifth and sixth amendments. In the gory details of the state case, essentially there was a burglary that was committed in the state of Florida and apparently there was an eye witness that came forward reporting that he saw a man in name of Mr. Gideon. Mr. Gideon was quickly apprehended and sent to trial, he judge stating that at the time Florida State law prevented the judge from assigning him counsel, and thus he was sentenced promptly on the allegation that he was seen present before or after the said robbery. The US Supreme Court came back and appointed Mr. Gedeon to counsel that was top rate, a third year law student from Yale Law School. Ultimately the US Supreme Court case ruled in favor of Gideon, with him being released from prison, and it also resulted in the release of some 2,000 other said persons being “freed” as a result of the Gideon case. Moral to the Story: If ever in legal trouble, falsely accused, or without representation in a serious affair, seek counsel, because it is your federal and constitutional right whether one is innocent or guilty of the matter at hand. I think this gives an extra check and balance to our Court Trial Justice System, although public defenders or essentially State employees in most cases it is comforting for the alleged criminal or defendant to haves some type of support in an ordeal that to say the least can be extremely stressful and overwhelming for the individual not familiar with the law or it's proceedings. The anticipating of sentencing, the anticipation of a judgment, the mental fuckery of setting in jail or prison awaiting trial, the confusion and unfamiliarity of all the legal jargon, terminology and language, the confusion of deciding weather or not to accept a plea bargain as opposed to staying incarcerated longer to fight a trial that may or may not go the defendants way. It's all quite debilitating and can be extremely humiliating, bringing the strongest of men to long hours of mental, emotional, physical and spiritual introspection and tears of sorrow all the while laughing at this strange new freedom that they will forever possess.

In this next case we will consider a specific case dealing with gun rights in the state of Chicago. A certain man, Mr. McDonald, noticed the decline of his neighborhood. Such that it was being overrun by gang members and drug dealers. Also, his property and garage were burglarized several times. At some point he became fed up, seeing his front lawn full of Babbage tossed from careless pedestrians; this perturbed him in particular given the fact that he was a retired maintenance engineer. Also a skillful hunter having multiple shotguns in his possession, he knew what he could do to protect himself and his property, but felt the shot guns were a little too unwieldy so went to purchase a handgun for his self defense and herein lies the legal conflict. The state of Chicago required the registration of all handguns but no registrations were granted since the year of 1982, if I am understanding this case properly. The Court of Appeals at first upheld the Chicago ordinance with regards to certain other cases as precedence. Nevertheless, the US Supreme Court wrote in favor of "keeping and bearing arms," using the 2nd amendment backed by the due process clause of the Fourteenth amendment that an individuals right to life, liberty and the pursuit of happiness shall not be arbitrarily infringed upon or taken away. Moral to the Story: Seems that Mr. McDonald was feeling a bit run over by his community and situation. I would too, all those years working in maintenance to come home and have my place robbed and trashed by thugs and neighborhood punks. Not sure if McDonald was a veteran or had a military background; the source saus he was a hunter who kept shot-guns in the house. He probably thought to himself what he would do if he caught

# Chapter 110:

## Justice Ruth Bader Ginsburg (1933-2020)

Justice Ruth Bader was born in New York City from with a Jewish heritage. As a youth she and her family attended a conservative synagogue and she was taught and became familiar with the Hebrew Language and culture. She participated in extracurricular activities as a youth such as summer camp and even became a camp counselor. She would eventually graduate from James Madison High school and go on to attend Cornell University in Ithaca, New York. It was there that she majored in government and graduated having had Vladimir Nabokov as mentor and later reported that he was a major impression upon her, and heavily influenced her writings. I always simply thought him a Russian author and read his "*Lolit*a" account some time ago. Shortly after graduating from Cornell University, Justice Ginsburg would marry her husband Mr. Martin D. Ginsburg and as they relocated to Oklahoma where he took a Army Reserve post, Justice Ginsburg applied herself to assisting the government in the department of Social Security Administration. After some time, Justice Ginsburg decided on Harvard Law School and due to another move, would have transfer her 3rd year to finish up at Columbia Law School. She graduated with high honors and tied as the top student of her class. Justice Ginsburg would write a book on civil procedure later in her career after law school, she also clerked for a few Justices. She also was a strong advocate for Women's Rights working with the American Civil Liberties Union. She held one other federal appointment besides her nomination to the US Supreme Court by President Bill Clinton, and that was her time a judge on the DC circuit Court of Appeals, appointed to that position by President Jimmy Carter. Her Judicial philosophy includes a strong belief in constitutional privacy and as well as gender equality; she was mostly considered a moderate consensus-builder on the Court.

The first case we will consider, deals with women's rights, as Justice Ginsburg was a strong advocate on this front. More specifically how in the case of the United States v. Virginia (1996); the court overturned the standard quo of male only admission policy at the Virginia Military Institute; allowing for women to have equal access to this educational experience, knowledge, and facilities. Justice Ginsburg was at the helm of the court decision writing the majority opinion stated that VMI had no reason or quite simply failed to show " exceedingly persuasive justification" for it's *discriminatory* or sex based admission policies. (Wikipedia). The grounds for this litigation was based upon the constitutional fourteenth amendment and it' s Equal protection clause. Thus a program that ran along side VMI's all male process was proposed by the executive leadership Virginia Military Institute. It would be located at the Mary Baldwin College; one of those Heavy on the Humanities, private liberal arts college for women. Moral to the Story: In hindsight, when thinking of the whole matter, how ironic that the program that supposedly opened the door for access for women to attend Virginia Military Institute, is restricted or put in place at the Women's Liberal Arts College. Perhaps, I'm looking at this the wrong way, but it seems that the program should have either been on VMI's campus, and if not enough room, additional zoning and construction for more facility space should have been added. The logistics and realistic budget for this, I'm not sure what the costs would have been back in 1996, but it certainly seems that it would have been feasible, plus; I'm sure this would have livened things up for the boy's and beautified the campus. After all, this was the whole point of striking down the Virginian statute, that is making the campus coed.

The next case we will consider deals with equal pay on the job for both male and female. It seems that way anyway, but the underlining issue is that there is a case where a women filled suite because she felt that her pay was discriminatory against her gender status of being women because it was not equal to even the lowest paid man at the job, but significantly less. In the case of Ledbetter v. Goodyear Tire and Rubber Co. (2007). Mrs. Ledbetter who worked for Goodyear Tire and Rubber Co. figured out that her check, even though she began with the same pay as her male counter parts, but toward the end of her career, she was bringing home around $3,727.00/month, while the lowest paid male worker was raking in around $4,286.00/month. The courts ruled in favor of Goodyear on the grounds that Employers could not be sued on the decisions of pay discrimination based on race or gender 180 days ago or more under Title VII of the Civil Rights Act of 1964. So, essentially the matter was one of technicality and statute of limitations. There were other laws that Mrs. Ledbetter could have sued under, but the "paycheck accrual rule" was not one of them. Laws such as Equal Pay Act would have been a bustier hit with a longer statue of limitations for race and gender discrimination claims. Moral to the Story: Ordinary Citizens when going to court for civil, corporate, family, or even criminal matters need to either know the law or laws their fighting for or against to make a good case or have a good, experienced and knowledgeable lawyer who will argue in the best way asserting the best precedent cases. Of course, there is always justice, and I guess in this case I can see both sides. I mean, in the back story it was stated that Mrs. Ledbetter's performance evaluations were not up to par with the men, so that played a factor. Also, did she have a family or kids and take time off for pregnancies. This may be unfair, but also something Employers I think back then looked at and perhaps considered a liability. Today, this line of thinking may be considered to come from non other that a male chauvinist pig, but in many ways facts are facts, and yet we must be considerate of the day's sensitivities.

## Chapter 110:

## Justice Stephen Gerald Breyer (born in 1938):

Justice Stephen Breyer was born in the state where I grew up, only he was in the northern part of California, San Francisco that is; and I was in San Diego, but obviously not in 1938. Enough about me, Justice Breyer, according to sources grew up as a middle-class Jewish family and had a proclivity toward debating as a youth. He obtained the rank of Eagle Scout in the Boy Scouts, graduating from Lowell High School, and participated in multiple live debate tournaments, being a key member of his High School's Lowell Forensic Society. After graduation, it was off to Stanford where he took up Philosophy as his major. He quickly graduated and obtained a scholarship that sent him abroad to England, where he took up philosophy, politics, and economics at the Magdalene College, Oxford to earn a second Bachelor of Arts. After that, it was back stateside where he enrolled in Harvard Law School to earn his Law degree. He graduated with High Honors and also dutifully spending eight years in the Army Reserves; and 6 months active duty as an Army Strategic Intelligence Specialist, ranking Corporal Officer at his honorable discharge in 1965. A family man, with a Psychologist for a wife and three children, one being an Episcopal priest and author. Justice Breyer was an author himself, expert in administrative law, writing two books; after graduation from Law school, he would return to Harvard to Professor. He took several leaves to work for the State Department, namely two years in the Department of Justices Antitrust Department, as well as special assistant to the Attorney General. His Judicial philosophy and leanings as we will briefly herein discuss were that of a complex and yet practical approach to law interpretation as well as judgeship, writing an additional work on the matte entitled; *Making or Democracy work: A Judges View.* Complex, because he often uses several factors when interpreting, observing and considering the: text, history, tradition, precedent, purpose of the statute, and consequences of competing interpretations. Practical because he deems these tools useful and he is mostly considered a "conservative emissary to the Courts right wing," by fellow Court Clerks. Justice was nominated to the First Circuit, US Court of Appeals by then President Jimmy Carter, and in later years appointed by former President Bill Clinton to the United States Supreme Court as Associate Justice. In his tenure, he has written notable opinions on Abortion, Census, Copyright, Death Penalty, Environment, Health care, Partisan Gerrymandering, and Voting Rights. Herein we will consider only two such topics discussed in the cases below.

In this first case, dealing with the controversial issue of abortion, we see it in some ways forwarded and benefited from a different angle, that is in the case of *June Medical Services, LLC v. Russo (2020)*, the US Supreme Court ruled that standing Louisiana state law that placed hospital-admission tests in fact was unconstitutional. This is a different way of looking at abortion considering usually abortion cases deals with a women's right to perform one or when a embryo is considered viable and things of this matter. But this case actually deals with the "zoning" or regulation per say and requirements that prevent or allow certain doctors to perform the procedure. Apparently, the original intent for these statutes which originated in Texas were to eventually close down abortion clinics by granting abortion Doctors admission to perform procedures in hospitals within a 30 mile radius of their office. As briefly aforementioned, the politics and controversy behind weather or not the procedures were ethical, humane, or a women's right to choose, were not the emphasis of this particular case, however the pressing matter was more so the fact that because of such rules and regulation in the state of Louisiana, there was only one qualified doctor for the whole state, which mirrored it's bill from Texas. This presumed to be problematic, and thus US Supreme Courts weighed in on the situation and deemed the law unconstitutional. This was just in 2020, while Texas state law was struck down in 2016. Moral to the Story: Not sure if I fully understand or grasp the logic or reasoning behind the bills that originated in Texas that I assume made it more difficult for abortion doctors to perform their procedures. Yet, on the other hand, from my laymen's perspective, it also gave the doctor's more access to more clients in a more official setting. The hospital also was suppose to be a backup to the clinic's in case something went wrong. Maybe this was simply a nonpartisan law, and one of usage as it is difficult to see how it would benefit either liberal or conservative social agenda;' or maybe that is only difficult to the untrained eye. Either way, it was considered unconstitutional by the Highest Court in the land.

The next case that we will consider deals with the copyrightability of computer code, more specifically put, The software company that wrote or owned the the source code for application programming interfaces(API's) that are encompassed with in Java's programming language was a key factor in the original Android operating system put out by Google. This source code was owned by Oracle, stemming from Sun Micro systems; and after two Circuit court hearings that went in favor of Oracle, The ruling ultimately went to Google, stating that the application usage of Oracle's Java API's fell under fair usage and thus it was lawful for Google to license and sale its Android products. This of course reversed two Federal Circuit court decisions. Moral to the Story: Try to patent and copyright any and all creative and intellectual material that you feel will be profitable in the future and that other people may use without your permission. At the same time, have a generous attitude toward humanity, and if you can create something for the benefit of society that is used for the ultimate progress and betterment of the world at large, then understand that that in itself is a huge profit and contribution. On the contrary, it seems that in many cases persistence wins the fight. Google faced two Federal Circuit court defeats and petitioned all the way the Supreme Court to gain clearance and beat a 8.8 million dollar lawsuit filed by Oracle for Google's "infringement" and damages. I thought of putting myself in Oracle's position, and I would be pissed off if someone used 11,000 lines of my source code, and I got no credit or monetary compensation for it.. And yet and still, I think I would also upset if there was no regulation on such matters and I used a source code to further develop my one Operating System and got sued for damages and infringement for doing something common to the programming community. Go Figure.

## Chapter 112:

## Justice John Glover Roberts (born in 1955)

Justice John Roberts was born in New York, and attended Norte Dame Elementary school as a youth; his father was an Electrical Engineer. Next it was La Lumiere School which helped give him a strong academic foundation, which was a small wealthy, but academically vigorous Roman Catholic Boarding School in the state of Indiana. He was his class's valedictorian, and also excelled in Athletics, as he won the regional championship in wrestling, and made captain of the football team. Next it was off to Harvard, entering with sophomore status and making the decisive decision to major in History. He wrote some provocative and philosophical material himself; "Marxism and Bolshevism: Theory and Practice." which won a prize for the most outstanding sophomore writing at Harvard. His senior paper was entitled, "The Utopian Conservative: A study of continuity and change in the Thought of Daniel Webster." Having not read Justice Robert's work, but remembering the book *Utopia*, I'm wondering if he included thoughts or an analysis of ideas from Thomas More. Irregardless of the fact, contemporary sources say that Justice Roberts thought of per suing a Ph.D. In history, but ended up at Harvard Law, where he also edited the Harvard Law Review, graduating with Top Honors and a solid J.D. After Law school, it was clerk work for a few Justices, then government work in President Ronald Reagan's administration. He also served under President's George H. W. Bush, whom appointed him to the US Supreme Court. Among other accomplishments, practiced corporate law at a private law firm in Washington, DC and held a Adjunct professor position at Georgetown University Law Center. Ironically, Justice Roberts gave no particular jursprudential philosophy but likened himself unto a baseball umpire stating in so many words that, "It is my job to call balls and strikes, not to bat or to pitch." Herein we will briefly review a few of the cases that he wrote an opinion on.

In this first case, *Gonzales v. Oregon, (2006)*, we consider the matter of, for lack of a better euphemism, physician assisted suicide in the state of Oregon. This practice was permitted by the US Supreme court in the state of Organ, which affirmed a law that Oregon passed for competent and terminally ill patients whom were six months within death to take a cocktail of medications given by certified physicians to end their life. This act was voted upon in Oregon as the, "Death with Dignity Act" and passed with a 51.3% to 48. 7% margin. Although the law passed in the state, it faced opposition from the a US district judge, issuing an injunction which was to prevent the state from enforcing or practicing the law, declaring the event unconstitutional under the equal protection clause. This of course was rejected and dismissed by the Higher US Supreme Court. But this was not all the fire that the law and practice took. Next, certain members of Congress attempted to prosecute the physicians who practice this event under the Controlled Substance Act; nevertheless, it was the Attorney General Janet Reno who opposed this interpretation, asserting that the federal government had no authority over physicians submitting to Oregon state laws. Moral to the Story: I can remember a high school teacher bringing up the issue of Physician Assistant suicide as a point of discussion for the class and at first hearing the practice it seemed nothing less than barbaric. But after some discussion and explanation, it was revealed to me that it was indeed what the what the patients wanted, and not something that they were coerced into doing. Secondly, one way to look at it is such that the patients are receiving services from the hospital and physicians and this (PAS) is a sort of customer service provision that they are requesting or opting to do. Not to be insensitive, but in business terms, "the customer is always right." Of course there are other factors that come into play, such as disgruntled and opposing family members, who may feel that there loved one is leaving to early. Yet and still, on the other hand, such practice can keep down medical bills, and gives credit to the hospital administrative staff that there is no financial motive for practicing the event, because would it not be more financially profitable to keep the patients on life support for as long as possible gouging insurance claims? Go Figure.

In this second case we will consider, the matter seems to be one of a domestic family issue, but turns out to be one of procedure and search and seizure laws and practice. In the case of *Georgia v. Randolf (2006),* we have a matter where the US Supreme court ruled that without search warrant, if one consenting adult permits the police to search the residence but their co-occupant disagrees to the event, then legally the police have no grounds or authority to search the house of residence without a search warrant unless the co-occupant is absent. Both occupant parties must consent to the procedure. In the gory details of this case, we have a family experiencing a separation and breaking marriage and the wife Mrs. Randolph takes off to Canada with the couples in common child. She eventually returns, and one day petitions the police that after an argument her husband had take the child somewhere to her unawares. When the officers arrive on scene, she relays that her husband is a drug user as well as abuses alcohol and that they are free to search the premises. Mr. Randolph arrives shortly thereafter and does not consent to the search. He also explains that he did not want his wife to take off to Canada again with their son. Long story short, the police begin the search under the wife's initial consent and discovered evidence of cocaine. The officer went to get an evidence bag and made call to the district attorney whom advised him to stop search and apply for a warrant. Both occupants were detained; it also must be noted that Mrs. Randolph changed her consent to a refusal. After obtaining warrant, officers returned to apprehend the evidence for which Mr. Randolph was indicted for possession. In the aftermath, Mr. Randolph moved to suppress evidence on the grounds that the search was illegal, but the motion was denied declaring that the wife had "common authority" to consent to the search. Moral to the Story: Of course, I am only onlooking from afar, but at first thought, it almost smells of a set up or some form of entrapment. I am not making an accusatory statement here or do I in any way attempt to slander anyone's character, but academically looking at the case for a point of discussion it seems as if the wife had motive to plant the drugs and tell the cops to go find it, in attempt to put blame or accusation on the husband. I could be wrong, very wrong, but on reading the case's summary, that's what it smells like. Secondly, although both parties were detained, I did not read if the wife was charged with anything, although according to husband's statement, she was also or the illicit drug user in the family. Of course this becomes a matter of he said, she said, and a domestic issue for the local precinct and court, but because of the federal search warrant became a US Supreme Court case. Second Moral to the Story, and I'm trying to put myself in the husband's position, if I am ambushed at my house by my wife making a drug plant and the police at my door, I guess the only maneuver is to be completely honest and allow the officers to search the place and consent to a drug test, encouraging them to do any forensics necessary; such as finger printing, blood samples, the whole gambit to prove innocence. But man, such a frame, would indeed suck.

## Chapter 113:

## Justice Samuel Anthony Alito (born in 1950)

Justice Samuel Alito was born in New Jersey and grew up in the suburbs. He graduated high school at the top of his class and went on to pursue his undergraduate career at Princeton University at the Woodrow Wilson School of International Affairs. His senior thesis was entitled, "*An Introduction to the Italian Constitutional Court.*" and after graduation he went on to attend Yale Law School. At Yale, he was involved in student government and fought on side of privacy in the midst of domestic intelligence gathering in the midst of national security surveillance. Being alive in the era of Selective Service, Justice Alito joined the ROTC program on campus and completed a 6-week boot camp program. Ultimately he would be commissioned as a second lieutenant in the U.S. Army Signal Corps and be assigned to the United States Army Reserve. He received his honorable discharge in the year I was born, 1980. Justice Alito, held a number of federal positions with the State Department before he was nominated and appointed to the US Supreme Court. He was chief of the appeals division Assistant U.S. Attorney. He was Assistant to U.S Solicitor General Rex E. Lee, and also Deputy Assistant Attorney General. Finally, two other positions were the United States Attorney for the District of New Jersey and an adjunct professor at Seton Hall University School of Law teaching constitutional law, material on terrorism an civil liberties. Justice Alito was first nominated to Federal Judgeship by President George H. W. Bush to the United States Court of Appeals for the Third Circuit. President George W. Bush nominated Justice Alito to the US Supreme Court during a time when two seats where made available by way of one Justice retiring and another one dieing. We will from this point two cases in which he wrote; one opinion and one dissent. Many times Justice Alito voted on cases in what one might consider a conservative bent, but could not be fully considered a conservative.

Holmes v. South Carolina was Justice Alto's first written opinion as newly sitting Associate Justice on the US Supreme Court. In this cases gritty details, we find that it deals with the right for criminal defendants to present third party evidence to aide them in their case and plea for evidence. In this particular case, Mr. Holmes right to do so was denied, apparently on the strength of the Prosecution's evidence, which had forensics such as: DNA evidence, blood spatters, finger prints, and eye witnesses who claimed to see the defendant at the scene of the crime shortly before it was committed. On the surface, this type of evidence does seem overwhelming, but even common sense doe hear the other party out, just to hear what they will say; and our constitution does give one the right to defend themselves in trail. This reasoning, in so many words, was the ruling of the Supreme Court under the "Compulsory Process Clause of the Sixth Amendment and the Due Process Clause of the Fourteenth Amendment" (Wikipedia). Apparently this case went to the State Supreme Court where the defendant's presentation of evidence was again denied. Alright, so going deeper into the case, a women in her 80's was raped, assaulted , and suffered lasting injuries that ultimately led to her early death, so to speak, her being eighty. Nevertheless, the State took up the case and prosecuted Mr. Holmes with the full extent of the law finding the aforementioned evidence at the scene of the crime and on Mr. Holmes's person. On the contrary, when we take time to listen to Mr. Holmes statement, a black man; he asserts that he was "framed" and that a white man, Mr. White was going around bragging about the crime and that he was also seen by witnesses at the scene by eye-witnesses provided by Mr. Holmes. Of course, sadly enough, this evidence was not permitted to be heard in court in the good old state of South Carolina in 2006, and thus the the conviction of rape and murder were upheld until the US Supreme Court stepped in and "vacated the rape and murder conviction on the grounds that evidence was denied the opportunity to be presented. Moral to the Story: What do you do, when the very powers that you are supposed to be able to turn to for help and justice seem to be set up against you, so much so that you are being "framed" and systematically placed into dire straits. Mr. Holmes, if his evidence and testimony were true, was being framed by the local law enforcement's forensic's department, as well as unfairly judged by the Court system that refused to hear his defense. It would be like if God and his Holy Angels were evil and after being taught all your life that God was good and that his Angels helped the weak, though they be just in judgment, had some warped and evil intent to send every man, women, and child to torment and hell. This may be a little hyperbole, but I say, what a feeling and a sense of hopelessness to be fought by the very power and people in which you are suppose to ultimately Trust in. It's certainly an Mind Fuck. Fortunately, in this case, Mr. Holmes did not give up, and the US Supreme court stepped in and found the injustice in the trial and overturned the ruling. Weather or not the case was retried with the new or additional evidence, I am unaware, as well as to the prosecution of Mr. White, I know not.

In this next case, in which there was great controversy; and I think even Hollywood got a hold of it and made a movie that I happened to see this year at the drive-in with my wife. I'll say this, when my wife asked me my reaction to the film, I was sort of unresponsive and didn't want to speak because there were few things I didn't understand. I must say, I was I bit confused. Upon reading the some of the summarized court documentation, and a getting somewhat of a background, if this is the same guy and case, I could be wrong, it seems that this case comes down to a matter of jurisdiction, international and constitutional law, and due process; in my layman's judgment. I will give my reasoning, but in the gritty details, and we will only get so gritty, but apparently during the Second Bush Administration a man, Mr. Hamdan, was captured by militia forces and handed over to the US Military. His position was bodyguard and chauffeur for Osama bin Laden. In President' Bushes judgment, he wanted and did establish a military commission to try those detainees in at Guantanamo Bay. Apparently, this commission was unable to legally proceed because of Uniform Code of Military Justice (UCMJ) as well as Geneva Conventions. Therefore, the US Supreme Court ruling in this case, stopped the proceedings, stating that this military commissioned court, or tribunal if you will, was in violation of such aforementioned (UCMJ) codes and international Geneva treaties. Justice Samual Alito dissented in this case. I'm sure there are quite a few details that I am overlooking consider this was a matter sensitive to national security, Department of Defense, Pentagon, and Central of Intelligence Agencies all involved. But, from my understanding, President Bush would have had to have gotten approval from Congress to uphold such a court. And, then there were additional matters of, did the US Supreme Court hold the far reaching power and address issues on the Naval Military base in Cuba at Guantanamo Bay. Moral to the Story: Don't be a Terrorist, you might save yourself some headache and litigation. And yet, for those who work for clandestine services and other private or government agencies that may operate in foreign territories, beware of the great possibility and threat of danger, capture, torture, or even death.

## Chapter 114:

## Justice Sonia Maria Sotomayor (born 1955)

Justice Sonia Sotomayor hailed from the Bronx, New York City and was born to become the first Latina Associate Justice to the United States Supreme Court. She was valedictorian

of her high school class, and chose to go to Princeton for her undergraduate career, where she was awarded full scholarships for her academic performance in high school, although affirmative action was present at the time. She was involved on campus, where she first started as a shy freshmen, being one of the few women, and fewer women of color. She blossomed and after graduating with high honors decided to attend another Ivy Legue Institution, Yale that is, for Law School. She soon finished her studies , earning her Juris Doctorate and her first job was the Assistant District Attorney in New York. She did this work for the State for around four years and then it was off to private practice. In her private practice years she sat and wielded power on a number of boards of directors. Puerto Rican Legal Defense and Education fund, the State of New York Mortgage Agency, and the New York City Campaign Finance Board (wikipedia). Her next step was being nominated by President Bill Clinton to the US Court of Appeals 2$^{nd}$ Circuit wheres she heard over some 3000 cases and wrote just under some 400 opinions. It was the President Barack Obama who nominated Justice Sonia Sotomayor to US Supreme Court as Associate Justice. She was classified as being advocate to the rights of the defendants and has vigorously made impact on issues of race gender, and ethnic identity among other things. We will discover two such cases herein and see if we can't detect a bit of her judicial philosophy.

In this next case we will discuss the matter of *Schuette v. Coalition to Defend Affirmative Action*. In this case, The United States Supreme court ruled that in the state of Michigan, the fourteenth Amendment's Equal Protection clause did not prohibit States from putting in place bans against affirmative action. It was actually the Michigan voters who came together to approve a Michigan Civil Rights Initiative that would change or add to the state constitution declaring affirmative action that would cause legal discrimination based on race and sex in education and the work place illegal. The background of this case goes back to President John F. Kennedy enacting an executive order creating the federal act of affirmative action which called for all projects receiving government funding to require in their hiring no discrimination or employing where racial bias existed. Then came along the Civil Rights Act of 1964, in which discrimination on the basis of race, color, religion, sex or national origin was prohibited. There are a slew of cases that consider this act and make precedence with regards to University admissions incorporating race into their admissions policies. One of which we have previously discussed, that is, Regents of the University of California v. Bakke (1978), Irregardless of the fact, Justice Sotomayor dissented in this case on the grounds of the long history in which in which racial minority rights were "stymied"and how they were kept from the political process. She asserted that such a law was a direct hit against minorities and provided other ways in which voters could have lobbied University board or suggested the University change it's policies, but this hit changed the political process. She also hinted or included that she herself attributed her acceptance and entrance into her Universities of choice were due to affirmative action, and calls herself an affirmative action baby, suggesting that she might not have gotten to where she was had it not been for such programs. I would add, that Justice Sotomayor was a stellar student, according to sources, valedictorian in High School, Ivy League educated with full scholarship, graduating with High Honors from Princeton, and a Yale school of Law stand out. In my opinion, she needed no program, but achieved on her own merit, even if the program did assist her.

In this next case, we have a situation where the acting President made an executive order that entailed a travel band from these following countries due to there heavy Muslim population. It was done as a matter of National Interest and National Security by President Donald Trump, but fought in the courts as motivated by "anti-Muslim animus." President Trump issued travel band on the countries of: Iran, Iraq, Libya, Somalia, Sudan, Syria, and Yemen. It was the the US district court that first gave opposition to the executive order stating that the ordinance was out of compliance with the Establishment Clause of the First Amendment to the United States Constitution, not to mention was far reaching when it came to Immigration and Nationality Act (INA) which had been enacted by past President Lyndon B. Johnson which ended the discrimination against the immigration of certain Southern and Eastern Europeans, Asians, and non-Northwestern European peoples. This is essentially the case of, *Trump v. Hawaii (2018).* Justice Sotomayor wrote the majority opinion in this case giving the precedence of Korematsu stating in so many words that America was on the same dangerous and illogical road as when we established the Japanese concentration camps during WWII, and "replaces one gravely wrong decision with another" (wikipedia). Moral to the Story: Personally, I could see the past President's logic in creating the Travel Band on these named countries. I think the error is what the courts found, that there could be more scrutiny applied to making sure we were allowing the right people to come in, but an all out blanket disapproval of certain persons because of race, or religion would be standing against certain constitutional principles. On the contrary, as an American, one can see how our Leader in charge of Foreign Policy didn't want a completely open door policy in allowing any and all peoples to diffuse through our porous boarders without any regulatory checks that would ensure only safe aliens enter our matrix. Such danger, from terrorist disguised as refugees, or spies with the motivation of sabotage, or any other any enemy combatants, if gone undetected, like a cloaked virus or bacteria to a cell, could infect the solution of our population, destroy the infrastructure and mechanics that help us operate, and change the make up of our country, with the ultimate possibility, if these events continue and rise to their full potential, of transforming or converting our very nation to a cancerous cell, like the others. I mean, that is the overall goal and end of Muslim Theology; a politics that is ruled by it's Theology, or Sharia Law. This same level of thinking can also be appropriated to those Communist states that seek to rule in our Free Thinking Society.

## Chapter 115:

## Justice Elena Kagan (born 1960)

Justice Elena Kagan was born in New York City and attended an advanced High School at which her mother was faculty. She needed no form of nepotism to assert herself though, getting involved in student government, elected as her class President and continued her persuites on to Princeton University after graduation, where she completed her Bachelor's degree with High Honors. She did complete a tasty Senior thesis, which I have not read, but it was entitled; *To the Final Conflict: Socialism in New York City*. In her own words, it was a study of Socialism, not an endorsement; although we will find later her college counterparts were hard pressed to get political viewpoints from her and themselves classified her as somewhat liberal, democratic, and progressive in "Lower Case Letters"(Wikipedia). She was the beneficiary of an academic scholarship that allowed her to study abroad at Worcester College, Oxford after graduation from college. Using this time to author another thesis on the *Exclusionary Rule and Judicial Method*, as part of her Ivy League graduating requirement, sent her off with a mind for Law School having earned a Master in Philosophy in Politics. Expected to excel, coming from a Top Tier background, Justice Elena actually unperformed her first semester at Harvard Law, but greatly recovered earning 17 A's of the 21 courses that she took in her Law School Career. Justice Kegan worked in several law offices during her time as Graduate Law student. It was during her assistant professorship at the University of Chicago Law School that she seemed to receive what seemed to be cosmic connections and that would later facilitate her being advanced into her future current role; meeting both President Joe Biden and President Barack Obama who both would later in life have high appointments for her. She did some time serving with the State Department and then came back to the private world as a Professor at Harvard Law, and eventually made Dean of the whole program. Under her leadership the program increased greatly; more funding, larger staff and faculty, and making bold moves to even support bans on military recruiters from Harvard's campus. Federal ruling went all the way to even prevent The Pentagon from continuing to disburse funds. When Justice Kegan, then Dean of Harvard Law understood that this was leverage, she banned the military, that is military recruiters from the school's campus. Herein we will discuss her jurisprudence on a few supreme court cases that she authored opinion on.

The first case we will consider was her first case authored as a new Associate Justice of the US Supreme Court. It was a case dealing with discretionary finances and debt obligation verses living expenses and how all that was officially calculated and determined in bankruptcy; the case entitled, *Ransom v. FIA Card Services, N.A. (2011).* The official language deals with a means test being added to the US Bankruptcy code, implemented by the Bankruptcy Abuse Prevention and Consumer Protection Act of 2005. This *Means Test* is a type of formula used to determine how much money debtors have obligated to creditors and also allows for a certain "shielding"of some income that can used by for personal living expenses as determined by a matrix created and provided by the Internal Revenue Service. In this particular case, although seem to be a minor civil bankruptcy issue, was about the IRS permitting a car payment allowance as long as it was a loan or lease payment. Nevertheless, the judgment was interesting to say the least considering that it was a split circuit decision between the 9th circuit and three other who allowed for the car allowance even for held the title in ownership for their vehicles with no loan or lease payment. In Justice Kegan's written opinion, she thus clarified that debtors may claim such expenses that are "applicable" to the budget. That is, those expenses that incur costs, according to the IRS table provided for budget standards. Moral to the Story: Personally, I would have to side with the dissent on this case, in that Justice Scalia asserted in so many words that one should be given the car allowance irregardless of the fact of if they were making loan or lease payment. Costs add up, and why should the one who sacrificed to purchase a used car in full or pay of a new car overtime be penalized and not get the full car allowance benefit. Were they not they the wise; though both parties be in debt, one chose to cut expenses and the other chose to incur more debt with taking on a new loan or lease payment. In my humble opinion, either reward both, or deny both, but to choose to reward the party who made the more fiscal risky or careless decision seems to be rewarding the behavior of excessive spending while overlooking those more frugal or who have been more diligent to pay off their auto creditors.

In this next case, we deal with patent and royalty rights in the case of *Kimble v. Marvel Entertainment, LLC. (2015)*. It actually is a case that the Supreme Court used a precedent case *Brulotte v. Thys Co. (1964)*, to help in the final decision or ruling. As we know, US Supreme Court decisions out weigh and overrule all State and Circuit Courts. So, that is important in this case because it was the Supreme Court's decision to uphold a prior ruling in the realm of patent royalties, that they were unnecessary to pay after the patent passed it's expiration date. More specifically in the actual details of this case Mr. Kimble, and obvious creative and man of oportunity, came up with an idea to market a product so that kids and anyone could imitate the Marvel Comic Spider-man by spraying web from the palm of their hand. In Mr. Kimble's idea, it the web was pressurized foam string....or *silly string*. He did not just sit on his palms, pun intended, but took action steps to get the idea patented and moved forward with negotiation meetings with the President of Marvel with an intention of selling his patent. Coincidentally, Marvel comes out with a similar toy product shortly thereafter, the "Web Blaster" that mimics Mr. Kimble's idea. Not pleased, Mr. Kimble takes Marvel Entertainment, LLC to court for patent infringement or breach of contract, and Marvel settles to buy the patent from Mr. Kimble for around $500,000 and a indefinite 3% royalty. The idea was that Marvel would continue to pay the royalty from as long as the product sold, but upon discovering new knowledge that they were not subject to pay after the patent expired under the aforementioned, *Brulotte v. Thys Co. (1964),* the reneged on the deal and chose to no longer pay a royalty fee. There was another suit from Mr. Kimble and a counter suit from Marvel and ultimately US Supreme Court ruled in favor of Marvel under the technicality of Brulotte v. Thys Co. (1964), Justice Kagan stating in so many words that there has the patent system has to allow for a balance between innovation and yet allowing the public access to have right to those discoveries. In this sense, there will be no patent monopoly and the unrestricted use of products pass to the public. Capitalism at it's finest, (my comment). Moral to The Story: This case has a lot of moving parts and a few things come to mind. First off, how long do patent laws take to expire, because this was 2015, seems like not a long time to earn from royalties and licenses, unless that date can be extended. Second thought, it can't really be said that Marvel would not have ever come up with such a toy idea on their own, but nevertheless they it was Mr. Kimble who won the patent first and my pressing thought is, was the whole litigation matter a publicity stunt to drive up sales and get the marketing for the Web Blaster toy out there. Who knows?

## Chapter 116:

## Justice Neil McGill Gorsuch (born 1967)

Justice Neil Gorsuch was born and lived in Bethesda, Maryland coming up as a young adult. Bethesda being home to the Coast Guard Academy. Upon Justice Neil's family relocating to Maryland as a youth, he attended Georgetown Preparatory School, a specialized Jesuit prep school. After this, it was off to the prestigious Columbia University where he graduated with a Bachelor's of Arts in political Science, he was a High Honor Student and co-founded a student news paper to leave as his legacy before he left entitled, *The Fed.* Next it was off to graduate school, he chose Harvard Law School where he kept his journalist interest and became editor on the *Harvard Journal of Law and Public Policy*. He ultimately graduated with honors in 1991. In addition to obtaining his Juris Doctor Law degree, Justice Gorsuch went on to the University of Oxford in England where he began to research the issue of euthanasia from a legal perspective. After some time, he earned a Doctor of Philosophy in Law. After graduation, he joined a small group and essentially began to practice as a trial lawyer and litigate for various clients. Somewhere along the line, Justice Gorsuch got picked up by the Judicial arm of government and found himself as the Principal Deputy to the Associate Attorney General in the United states Department of Justice. Later he was nominated as justice on the tenth Circuit where he served for 11 years. Justice Neil Goprsuch was nominated to the US Supreme court by President Donald Trump. We will see a bit of Justice Gorsuch judicial philosophy but mostly considered conservative in his rulings and a textualist.

In the first case we will consider, we have a majority opinion written by Justice Gorsuch in a case that was unanimously decided and also Justice Gorsuch's first case on the US Supreme Court. This case was one of financial matters and dealt with the definition of a debt collector and why companies who purchased debts as third party to a primary financial company could not legally be a debt collector according to the FDCPA, that is the Federal Debt Collections Act. In this specific case, we have CitiFinancial who made a number of loans to borrowers who could not, for whatever reason pay back the loans. Over time, instead of waste time, resources, and overhead in attempt to collect the debt from its clients, Citifinancial decided to sell off the debts to a third party. In turn, the "debt collection group" Santander tried their hand at collecting the debt and failed miserably as they wound up getting sued by CitiFinancial's clients, also having a US Supreme court rule in the favor of the borrowers. In so many words, this was the case of *Henson v. Santander Consumer USA Inc.* Moral to the Story: Seems to be the common practice for companies now days to sale off their debt to a third party instead of paying the legal fees to place judgments on their clients to obtain the money they either loaned their clients are are owed from whatever product of purchase. Unfortunately, I've experienced both aspects of this realm, that is, being issued judgement and having letters sent from third party "debt collectors." The silver lining in all this though, according to Justice Gorsuch's majority opinion, that basically, companies have to collect their own debts and their representatives really have no overarching authority if clients were to choose to go to court. Maybe I'm being naive, but hence another break through in the area of credit and finance. There started arising or always has been credit repair companies that would take people's creditors to court and litigate to clean up credit reports. I would think that this is an angle in which they would argue and defend their clients, in that third party debt collecting companies are not the original owners of the debt and therefore can not further harass neither legally take serious action against the primary companies past clients. Seems like a little loop whole that maybe a few would be able to truly take advantage of.

## Chapter 117:

## Justice Brett Michael Kavanaugh (born 1965)

Justice Brett Kavanaugh was raised in Bethesda, Maryland, as Justice Gorsuch; in fact they attended College Prep Academy for High School, Justice Kavanaugh being two years ahead. Justice Kavanaugh, aside from academics. he made captain of the basketball team and also played the position of corner back for football. After graduation, he went on to Yale where he took a Bachelors of Arts in History, graduating with Honors. Next it was Yale Law, where he kept up his leisure participation in sports, and was also active on the *Yale Law Journal.* Justice Kavanaugh graduated again with Honors and his Juris-Doctor degree in 1990. After graduate School at Yale Law, Justice Koavanaugh spent some time serving as a clerk for various Federal Circuit judges, served under the Bush Administration and also did a bit of private practice work. In fact, it was President George W. Bush who nominated Justice Kavanaugh to the U.S. Court of Appeals for the District of Columbia with confidence, as the American Bar Association deemed him "well qualified" (Wikipedia). And it was President Donald Trump who nominated him for the US. Supreme Court.

The first case that we will consider deals with felony convictions and what is considered a violent criminal act; or violent felony. In the case of Stokeling v. the United States (2019), it was determined by the US Supreme court that burglary offenses where the assailant overcomes the victim's resistant, no matter how little the resistance may be is considered a violent felony under the Armed Career Criminal Act of 1984. Due to the just recent court date of two years ago, I will not discuss this case any further but will say, it's a tough haul to be considered a career criminal and danger lurks on either end of being either victimized by street justice, or victimized by the Justice System by facing federal charges for criminal acts of violence that one has committed and in most cases, have repetitively committed without remorse. Of course there are always at least two sides to every story, and most importantly, an idea of multiple perspectives for any given scenario, life choice, experience; notwithstanding, the moral to the story is; Those who choose to victimize the weak, and overcome their victims resistance, if they face their day in court, might find themselves in dire straights with the ramping up of new laws and mandatory sentence requirements. On the flip side of things, I wonder what protections arise for the vigilante career criminal that seeks to fix certain societal discrepancies that regular law enforcement agencies can not legally get to or do; or maybe they can, all the same, just as easily.

## Chapter 118:

## Justice Amy Vivian Coney Barrett (born 1972)

Justice Amy Barret grew up in New Orleans, Louisiana and came from a large family, being the eldest of seven siblings. As a youth, she attended a specialized All Girls Academy; St. Mary's Dominican High School, a Roman Catholic High School. The next step in her educational career was Rhodes College, where she end up graduating Top of her class, majoring in English Literature with a minor in French and awarded or named the "Most Outstanding English Department Graduate." She chose Notre Dame Law School for graduate school, and attended on a full academic scholarship. While in attendance, she held the position of an executive editor of the Notre Dame Law Review and graduated first in her class again, with High Honors. Generally speaking, Justice Barret clerked for approximately two and a half years after graduation for various judges and also did some private practice work, but ultimately found herself teaching and doing research at George Washington University of Law, Notre Dame Law, and University of Virginia School of Law; publishing works in the Columbia, Cornell, Virginia, Notre Dame, and Texas Law Reviews (wikipedia). Topics covered are as follows, but not limited to: federal courts, evidence, constitutional law, statutory interpretation, originalism, stare decisis. She received her first federal nomination to the Seventh Circuit Court of Appeals by President Donald Trump and served well in this position until her nomination to the US Supreme Court by same President Donald Trump in 2020. Although it be difficult to simply categorize one's whole judicial philosophy or put them in a box of conservative or liberal, academic experts have classified Justice Berrett as being mostly conservative in her rulings and a textualist and orientalist in the way she interprets the law. Moral to the Story: Due to the recent appointment of Justice Amy Barrett, I will not discuss any of the cases that she has written majority opinion or dissent upon, but wish her well in her judgeship as well as all US Supreme Court Justices and all those setting in judge-rulership in all the Appellant Circuit, State, and City Courts. May God Truly Bless America and Keep our Land Safe and Free.

## Note from the Author:

**Well, here goes another one for the bookshelves and hopefully will find it's way into the homes of millions across the land. Those attending law school, judges, justice study students, lawyers and para-legals new and old, as well as those who simply have an interest in the Judicial Branch of Government and a minor history of some of those rulings. I claim no expertise nor do I pretend to be an attorney at law, nor Justice having a Jurist Doctorate degree; but these are the words apprehended by me and my own proclivities after given sometimes brief and other times deep thought on what I have read, seen, and experienced in my own time upon the Earth; some forty years now. I hope this work does raise the culture, peek a curiosity for those in all realms for Law school, and heighten our ability to think, discern and understand those things often not considered by ourselves and countrymen about our State and Government; as well as the rules that underpin so many happenings and decisions that go on. Who knows what the future will hold for our nation as International Law's and Councils begin to rise; I cannot speak what I do not know, but we do hope with all gravity, that our nation does remain sovereign in ruling Her Land, Capable of keeping order and safety, and Still able to Grant those innate rights and freedoms consistent with it's denizen's Life, Liberty, and pursuit of Happiness. Irregardless of a changing world, bad actors, other oppressive governments and regimes, May God grant strength to our nation and the world to purposefully grow into our Future Destiny.**

Antonio A. Sweeney MS

August 28, 2021

# References:

1. https://www.britannica.com/
2. https://www.courtlistener.com/
3. https://www.encyclopedia.com/
4. https://infogalactic.com/
5. https://www.law.cornell.edu/
6. https://law.justia.com/
7. http://lawlibrary.wm.edu/wythepedia/index.php/Main_Page
8. https://www.lexisnexis.com/en-us/home.page
9. Library of Congress https://www.loc.gov
10. https://www.supremecourt.gov/about/members_text.aspx
11. https://supremecourthistory.org/history_courthistory.html
12. https://en.wikipedia.org/wiki/List_of_justices_of_the_Supreme_Court_of_the_United_States

Made in the USA
Coppell, TX
05 November 2026

11315639R00135